1991

Understanding War

John McMurtry

Canadian Papers in Peace Studies

1988 Number 2

Science for Peace/ Samuel Stevens
Toronto
1989

Samuel Stevens and Company
University of Toronto Press
5201 Dufferin Street
Downsview, Canada M5H 5T6

Science for Peace
University College
University of Toronto
Toronto, Canada M5S 1A7

Canadian Cataloguing in Publication Data

McMurtry, John, 1939-
  Understanding war

Co-published by Science for Peace.
Includes bibliographical references and index.
ISBN 0-88866-633-0 (bound) ISBN 0-88866-630-6 (pbk.)

1. War — Philosophy. I. Science for Peace
(Association). II Title.

U21.2.M258 1989   355'.02'01   C89-093142-9

Manufactured in Canada by Gagne Printing Ltd.

Contents

Preface

Science for Peace gratefully acknowledges the financial support of the Canadian Institute of International Peace and Security, the Pugwash Park Commission, and several generous personal donations toward the publication of the Canadian Papers in Peace Studies.

Papers submitted to the Publications Committee of Science for Peace for this series are each considered on their merits, having due regard to the purposes of Science for Peace. In addition, the Committee seeks authors for papers on topics that are thought to be of special importance at the time. The Committee has a general policy of submitting papers to independent referees for comment, but is not rigidly bound by this policy, and also seeks to avoid long delays when material of timely relevance is submitted.

Derek Paul, editor
Physics Department
University of Toronto
Toronto, M5S 1A7

Foreword

Anatol Rapoport

Almost everyone is against war or at least says so. Conceptions of war, however, differ widely and generate different ideas about how wars can be prevented. Some of these ideas are complementary, some incompatible. Sorting out these ideas, analysing them, weighing them against each other, and evaluating them in terms of what we know or can learn about the history of humanity and its present condition should constitute a major part of peace education.

Many people deeply devoted to the cause of stable global peace believe that the main difficulty in achieving it lies in human nature. They may not share the defeatist attitude that aggressiveness is an irremovable component of the human psyche and that therefore there will always be wars. But they do place the problem deep within the human individual. Stable peace, in their estimation, can be achieved only if individual human beings become more peaceful.

The present paper does not challenge the idea that pacification of individuals may be a sufficient condition for a stable peace; but it implicitly challenges the idea that it is a necessary condition. The main thrust of the paper is embodied in the idea that stable peace can be achieved by deflecting human aggressiveness (if, indeed, it is an important component of human nature) from human enemies to other enemies. Enemies can be either naturally given or created. The argument here is that there are no naturally given human enemies. Rather, those who are perceived as enemies have become enemies because they **were** perceived as such. On the other hand, naturally given enemies of humanity are easily identifiable. They are pestilence, destitution, degradation of the environment and, of course, war. It is against these enemies that human aggressiveness should be mobilized. Such mobilization would enhance the chances of establishing a lasting peace, because nothing brings people together more than does the perception of a common enemy.

War is an easily identifiable enemy of humanity (along with pestilence, destitution, and degradation of the environment) in view of the obvious threat of literal extinction posed by already existing and soon to be created weapons of total destruction. However, a war against war is incomparably more problematic than a war against the other enemies. To launch a war against pestilence, degradation of the environment, etc. requires a great deal of political will but not a radical restructuring of deeply entrenched beliefs. Much technical knowledge is available that is known to be effective against pestilence or stopping the degradation of the environment, and methods of obtaining more knowledge of this sort are already in use. Waging war against these enemies does not require a demolition of superstitions. When it comes to action making an impact on the physical environment, humans rely on science and think in the problem-solving mode. Such action and such mode of thinking are not paralyzed by encrusted dogmas and rhetorical shibboleths. Launching a war against war, on the other hand, requires not only a formidable political will but also a demolition of pervasive superstitions, which have consistently blocked efforts to mobilize such political will. Among these superstitions are the identification of national security with military potential, the belief in the effectiveness of 'deterrence', the belief that dismantling military institutions must lead to economic slump and unemployment, the belief that military establishments perform a useful social function by 'defending' the societies on which they feed, and so on. All these beliefs qualify as superstitions by the ususal definition of a superstition as a stubbornly held belief for which no evidence exists. If anything, historical evidence tends to support the opposite view, namely, that highly militarized states are rather less secure from the ravages of war, that 'deterrence' has often been a rationalization of aggression, and that a war economy eventually leads to impoverishment rather than to prosperity. Above all, the claim of military establishments that they serve to 'defend' a country is belied by the uses to which these establishments all too often have been put, namely, to intimidate or to perpetrate violence against their own populations. And surely the weapons of total destruction cannot possibly 'defend' anything or anyone. They can only destroy everything and kill everyone.

All of these points, forcefully brought out by John McMurtry, contribute to the enlightenment of all who are willing to give serious thought to these matters.

Another formidable obstacle to be overcome in launching a war against war is the tendency of humans to see other humans as a source of threat. Throughout history, social organization was stimulated not only by the advantages of cooperating in coping with the environment but also, perhaps predominantly, by the necessity of cooperating in protecting one's own against marauders, as well as by the advantages of cooperating in engaging in similar enterprises against vulnerable outsiders, that is, exterminating, plundering, enslaving, or exploiting alien populations. This sort of cooperation reflects the tribal principle of social organization. It has persisted to the present day in the organization and internal cohesion of modern states.

Thus, the basic problem is that of erasing all we-they dichotomies: kin versus non-kin, believers versus non-believers, those who look alike versus those who look different, and so on. The stubborn persistence of such dichotomies, however, suggests that they fulfill some need. Perhaps the need to belong is fully satisfied only if it is made clear who does not belong. In launching a war against war, a natural dichotomy suggests itself. It has been drawn by Freeman Dyson in his book 'Weapons and Hope'. The dichotomy is between warriors and victims. It cuts across all racial, ethnic, economic, and ideological boundaries. As McMurtry most emphatically points out, however, the dichotomy separates **roles**, not persons. In fact, the persons in the role of warriors are also in the role of potential victims, since weapons of total destruction do not differentiate.

The warrior roles are played not only by the uniformed professionals but also by their counterparts in war industries, in think tanks, in research institutes, in lobbies, in short by all having a stake in institutions engaged in the preparation of war and in nurturing the global war machine. A war against war entails an attack on the role of the warrior. It is to this attack that the Clausewitzian principle of 'total war', that is, a war aimed at destroying or incapacitating the opposing force, is most applicable. The object of this war is to destroy the institution of war and thus to instigate the atrophy of the global war machine by cutting off its nourishment.

A war of this sort can be waged by victims with a clear conscience, since it entails no violence perpetrated on human beings. Only the roles of the warrior are to be destroyed, just as the role of the executioner is destroyed when capital punishment is abolished without the erstwhile executioner having to be harmed, not even by employment, since the abolition of capital punishment may well entail finding an alternative employment for the hangman. The abolition of the institution of war may incur an analogous obligation.

Understanding War

John McMurtry

O for a voice like thunder, and a tongue
To drown the throat of war! — When the senses
Are shaken, and the soul is driven to madness,
Who can stand? When the souls of the oppressed
Fight in the troubled air that rages, who can stand?
When the whirlwind of fury comes from the
Throne of God, when the frowns of his countenance
Drive the Nations together, who can stand?
When Sin claps his broad hands over the battle,
And sails rejoicing in the flood of Death;
When souls are torn to everlasting fire,
And fiends of Hell rejoice upon the slain,
O who can stand? O who hath caused this?
O who can answer at the throne of God?
The Kings and Nobles of the Land have done it!
Hear it not, Heaven, thy Ministers have done it!

William Blake

LOVE

Part I

The Problem

The thing is simply this, that out of an average 100 men along the line of fire during the period of an encounter, only 15 men on average would take any part with the weapons. This was true whether the action was spread over a day or 2 days or 3, ... in Europe or in the central Pacific. ... Each man who hadn't fired his rifle thought he had been alone.

Colonel S.A. Armstrong, 1945

Sooner or later, if civilization is to survive ... war must go.

General Douglas MacArthur
in testimony to the US Congress, 1951

The reality is that there is a war to overcome.

Ruben Zamora
FDR/FMLN negotiator, El Salvador, 1984

Underneath the increasing militarization of social life over the past half century has grown a subversive sentiment. Contemporary humanity has learned to abhor the military system of war. There are leading exceptions to be sure, but even amongst men specially conditioned to launch city-destroying attacks from remote foreign sites sunk in mountain-bunkers, the organized killing of people in large numbers has become repugnant to moral intuition.

This marks a revolutionary change from the past when the sacred traditions of all dominant cultures have glorified the mass-kill method as Yahweh's, Krishna's, Jupiter's, Allah's, Isanagi's, or Christ's way of winning great conquests and imposing His will on tribal enemies.

3

Humanity has largely outgrown this genocidal pattern. For ever greater numbers of our species, the mechanized routines of social murder prescribed by the military program are now beyond the pale: the obsolescent last gasp of a megalomaniac tradition increasingly out of touch with the limits of reality [1].

Our established systems of political rule, however, continue to posit the capacity for mass homicide as the ultimate measure and ground of ruling will. Ascendant vested interests by no means confined to the armed forces, derive many empowering advantages from this arrangement, and so refine and escalate national and nation-group buildups with no apparent limit to the number of world-destructions they assert as necessary to threaten each other's populations at public expense. Since democratic representatives or their surrogates are everywhere constrained by these interests, they lag behind their constituencies' increasingly shared skepticism of the armed-force solution to the problem of 'peace and security'. At the same time, scholars in the relevant disciplines tend to presuppose these interests and their imposition as the very framework of the world's construction. Or, if in the critical minority, they presuppose the military form of war, and consider only pacifist non-violence or norms of lawful carnage as alternatives.

The upshot is that while public disquiet with the military and, in particular, nuclear-military method is increasingly widespread, no philosophical or theoretical confrontation of the established military paradigm yet exists to give undertakings of national war any foothold of alternative conception.

4

Part II

Basic Fallacies of the Military Paradigm

1.

What one finds in surveying the vast philosophical and social-scientific literature on war is that a particular and narrow subtype of it is invariably assumed. This presupposed form is so reductively prescriptive that one might be excused for regarding it as a gesture of gallows humour were its intention not so conventionally taken for granted: namely, **war is organized armed engagement that seeks by maximally efficient means to kill or mutilate large numbers of other human beings** [2].

A family of characteristics normally accompany this presupposed principle:

(i) social segregation of a specialist arms-monopolizing group to execute its objective;

(ii) a rank-ordered command structure relying upon motivation by fear to coerce its membership into performing and risking its mass-kill prescription;

(iii) immersive programs of obedience conditioning, indoctrination, and life-uniformity to liquidate individuality and choice;

(iv) an autonomous technological development whose scientific telos is ever more destructive homicidal weapons; and

(v), to provide moral sanction for this overall program, an enshrinement of heroic life-sacrifice for military goals as a supreme ethical good [3].

From this customarily stipulated presupposition of war's necessarily mass-homicidal nature, two main kinds of reflective or theoretical argument have arisen over two millenia of consideration:

(1) arguments which consider those types of occasion

5

when large groups of other humans are to be systematically killed or maimed with good moral reason (i.e. 'just war' theory, 'moral means' arguments, and the like) [4]; (2) arguments which seek by game-theoretical or other 'rational' calculation to prescribe those strategies for systematic human killing or maiming which will by threat or enactment maximize payoffs for one side in the conflict [5].

Further narrowing this assumption base of established war thought is another a priori principle regulating war judgement, namely, the understanding and recommendation of mass-kill methods from the standpoint of a predetermined side's interests and moral assumptions alone, the side upon which one is placed by the circumstance of one's national or allied citizenship (what we may call the *tribal a priori*) [6].

It is difficult to discover a single argument in the immense and varied literature of war that does not conform to these radically reductive and unanalysed premises.

Even where the philosophical or theoretical concern is vitiative and seeks to place moral or legal limits on war's methods or targets, the program of killing and disabling other humans in great numbers remains presumed as an a priori given of war thought.

In sum, an all-or-nothing fallacy — mass-homicide and maiming on the one hand or pacificist rejection of all violence on the other — stands as the ultimate foundation of recognized war choice, while a systematic bias towards one side's moral and material self-interest determines subsequent judgement from this premise.

The depth and consequence of unexamined assumption here are breathtaking, but unnoticed. Our species has, it seems, become so accustomed to its mode of civilizing by military conquest and terror, so locked by its historical practice into homicidal structures of prevailing over perceived hostile groups, that we have become obliv-

6

ious to the most fundamental choices of which 'making war' consists.

2.

Established military and geopolitical thought is typically impaired by these premises into an escalating sequence of inferences. These follow a common pattern.

If T is an extra-territorial or internal group perceived to be in a state of hostility to a position of a state or states, U, then U's national or international command reasons as follows:
therefore,

(1) T is opposed to, and

(2) is an enemy of U. Therefore

(3) T is immoral, and

(4) must be made to yield to U. Therefore,

(5) U must be able to prevail militarily, and

(6) be willing to deploy this ability to prevail over T

(7) to maintain U's national interest. Therefore,

(8) if T continues to flout U's national interest, U must threaten or attack T; and

(9) if effectively resisted, must seek to destroy the enemy, T, by large-scale homicide, disablement and life-means destruction [7].

No step of this thought sequence follows. But all of its non-sequitur moves are conceptualized in customary war thought as steps of 'necessity'. This spurious apodeictic of military logic is affirmed with hypnotic repetition in its standard formulae of justification: strategic necessity, military necessity, necessity of national security, necessity of defence, necessity of the national interest, and so on. One need only lay bare the pattern of inferences here that assert one *petitio principii* after another in an undeviating lock-step towards mass-homicide conclusion, to become aware of the extent of the cognitive disorder.

There is in its sequence a closure of reason and choice that, in the context of individual behaviour, would be judged as systematically and criminally insane [8]. But convention has normalized the pathological. In the matter of intrahuman war, our brains have, so to speak, turned into gears.

What is remarkable is that this monolithic killer-program, so repugnant to ordinary human sensibility (and known as such by the boot-camp and totalitarian methods needed to implement it) has been so long and widely taken for granted as a dictate of rational choice.

What is required here is some opening of the philosophical windows. Unexposed in the military paradigm's inferential sequence is a hidden edifice of metaphysical moves whose every step of construction admits of a spectrum of various and opposed alternatives. What is conventionally advanced as a simple march of national self-interest to the measure of necessity is, in truth, a concealed architectonic of world-ordering choices, on each of which balances the fate of countless human lives.

Part III

Who is the Self of National Self-Defence?

The opposition between self and other admits of as many varieties in the making of war as it does in general, because the basic relationship between self and other can always *be* a war, an annihilative contest in the widest sense. Even in the very restrictive sense of war between human groups with homicidal weapons of engagement, there are many different possibilities of self-other axis at the heart of these oppositions.

At the most primitive level of disjunction, there is the Hobbesian possibility of merely individual selves, organic or national, driven by inborn appetites of power or fear to wage a *bellum omnium contra omnes*, with different concepts of self possible within these parameters: from, at one end, the self posited as a brutish shortness of existence, a mere pawn of chance in the mortal struggle, to, at the other end, vainglorious self-concept whose negation of otherness spans across the state of nature in an infantile structure of omnipotence (as in the assumed self-identities of 'great powers' or would-be world conquerors).

On the other hand, there are countless other, less atavistic possibilities of the national or individual self underlying the life-and-death struggle of war: the self as ultimately seller in a market-place contest of survival and elimination; the self as immaterial soul seeking the annihilative conquest of all attachment to material objects of desire; the self as a vehicle of genetic reproduction in the evolutionary war for continued life; the self as exclusive occupant of a bounded world space drawing lines of death by its very processes of metabolic exchange with the world, and so on.

These various underlying conceptions of self obviously lead in very different directions and, in particular, to rad-

9

ically different sorts of occasion for taking up arms or otherwise warring against one's fellows. What might be the commercial self's opportunity for exchange could be the spiritual self's deadly insult. What could be a provocation of racial impurity to the genetic self, might be a gesture of amity to the spatial self. What might be a provocation to war for any of these selves, might also be for any a stimulus to agreement under a different construction of thought.

There is, in short, a myriad of possibilities of war that may be generated from different concepts and interpretations of who or what we are: hence war's universal invocation of identity in the declaration of its intent, from the self-adoring boasts of ancient Homeric warriors to current nation-states' declared wars against 'communism'.

On the other hand, the self presupposed in war may be a community member at bottom: an ancestral organ of a tribal or kinship body; a loyal vassal of a warrior clan or imperium; a selfless functionary of a party-led state or pact; a patriotic citizen of a national or transnational *demos*, and so on — each type or subtype of self here variously bound by ties of obligation, group paranoia, or other supra-individual program of action towards different kinds and occasions of war. What would be an intolerable insolence to the Japanese *bushido* sword might be a frank exchange among friends in a different community. What might be to the individual self of a capitalist order a simple right of sale could be to the collective self an act of moral enormity. What might be the expendable death of the enemy to one type of collective self, might be a barbarous waste of transfigurable human potential to another.

Then too, the self-other disjunction might be class-structured, and the real self, as Marxians suggest, determined by ownership relations: neither a fully collective nor individual self but rather, confined to an economic class role whose limits of action are set by a given mode of social

10

production — as in wars where the opposing ruling classes support each others' mutual group interests against their own peoples, with the members of all classes remaining throughout 'in their place' [9]. Despite some Marxian disavowals of choice here, this underlying self as well is open to alternative or there would not be unpredictable cases of deviation from class structures and roles.

These are only a few distinctions of alternative to self-other lines of being at the most fundamental level of being-towards-war. Yet each itself, in turn, admits of many further subtypes of possibility. The supra-personal patriotic self, for example, is protean in its varieties. Aside from the many kinds of private self-interest — glory, power, envy of youth — for which patriotic identity may be merely customary pretext, there are different kinds of authentic national identification. One might for example, conceive of one's self and one's nation in terms of its geographical integrity and preservation (as I, a Canadian, do); *or* its current framework of civil and political institutions (as is conventional in the British tradition); *or* its remembered line of the past (as is essential to the Jew); *or* its potential contribution to human well-being (as world citizens aspire to); *or*, as some superpower citizens currently do, in terms of an assumed destiny of world dominion or 'being number one'. These are all general options for the patriotic self facing toward the possibility of war. The underlying portals of choice here are numberless; and each can provide the basis from which judgement leads to *non*-military war — for example, against illiteracy, or flies, or corruption.

Let us suppose, however, that the self sense from which war's project and weapons are chosen is that which is normally only pretended — the self as national being (e.g. American or Soviet patriot) guided by the interest of protecting and advancing some higher human value (e.g. 'freedom').

This self-base obviously opens onto a very different

11

horizon of possibilities than the self-base for which it is, in fact, often merely the disguise: that is, the self as essentially acquisitor of ever more of the world. For example, the believer in national and global freedom could not consistently elect the plan of transferring a maximum of wealth or power from poorer countries to itself, with military arms as the ensurer of conformity to this purpose. For such a project of exploitation would obviously contradict declared patriotic identity. On the other hand, such a program of choice and action would be quite consistent with the underlying self that seeks national accumulation or ascendancy before all else. *Which* self one is here, that is, chooses to be, on either the individual or aggregate levels gives the ontological bearings of what a nation decides to do, to oppose, to conquer, and its mode and means of so doing.

This is what is ultimately meant by the insight that *war reveals a society's inner nature.* That is, war expresses by the lines of life and death it draws what a people will sacrifice to what they will keep, what is ultimately their self and what is not. Almost anything at all is possible here, from nationally distributed self-delusion and the sovereignty of narrow capital or party interests to, at the other end of a nation's accessible range of self-conception, the authentic political will to the world's common well-being. What cannot be ignored is that whatever historically bound horizon of possibility is in practice adopted here, it is not given, as political leaderships and their advocates are wont to assure us, by a priori requirements of national necessity. For nations, as the individuals composing them, self-conception is a radically open question, and with it what they are willing to war against.

Part IV

What is the National Purpose?

From different concepts of Self flow different projects of relating to its Other. The strictly military concept of the self, for example (to which civilian rulers do not subscribe as overtly as they do to its military means) is a primary premise upon which military war's strategies ultimately repose. The self here is presupposed as:

i) malleable in either its individual or group forms;

ii) motivated most effectively by physical fear;

iii) regulatable only by punitive, vertically structured authority; and

iv) achieving its highest expression in the organized armed power of the nation state [10].

From this underlying idea of the national self, higher levels of purpose, such as co-operative autonomy, are necessarily ruled out, and other ranges of more consistently brutal possibility are ruled in. For example, the project of appropriating another country's specific interests as one's own, in ultimate commitment to peaceful mutuality (as in United Nations Charter ideals), is incompatible with the national self of the military metaphysic because these concepts of human nature are oppositely structured in their ideas of effective human motive and capacity. On the other hand, the project of appropriating another country in the sense of subordinating its productive resources, its economic system, its political rule, its diplomatic posture or, at the totalitarian extreme, all of these at once, is quite consistent with the general military idea of national selfhood (as in traditional US 'defense' policy in Latin America, or Soviet 'internationalism' in Eastern Europe). Accordingly, the current norm of great power relations with weaker or less developed countries is accepted by established geopolitical strategy as 'realistic' and 'necessary' to

13

maintain vital interests [11].

There are two points to be made here. First, national projects do not simply follow from underlying national self-concepts, but generally fall within limits of scope that these mark out as consistent or rational parameters of possibility. For example, very different designs of state are compatible with even the national self of military assumption — from, on the one extreme, force-backed appropriation of the entire world as one's sphere of interest, to strictly defensive armed capacity to repel invasion or internal revolution. These are very different and even opposed projects: the former unlimited in its aggressive reach, and the latter simply self-reproductive. Both extremes, and those many alternatives that lie between them, repose on a common basis of national self-concept.

The second point is that these extremes of option within the range of the underlying military concept of the national self, are not standardly distinguished in geopolitical discourse, but are customarily presumed to be the *same*. That is, not only is the alarmist military notion of the national self's nature so taken for granted that its negation is conventionally dismissed as 'naive', but even within this dwarfed baseline of decision, the opposed alternatives of national aggression and national defence are made to look as if there were no choice between them. Thus we have regularly heard the advocates of one superpower or another over recent years characterize its armed-force invasions of smaller countries as 'defensive', as 'necessary to defend its borders', as 'repelling enemy aggression' and so on, even when these attacks on the declared enemy are unilateral, unreciprocated, against impoverished foes, or thousands of miles distant from the invader's national borders (as in Vietnam).

Since various other weaker, stand-by nations typically endorse or reiterate this equation, and call invasions 'defence' and their choice 'necessity', the abolition of funda-

14

mental distinctions and contradictions of terms is normalized, and the myth of national security by mass-homicide aggression is perpetuated.

What usually motivates this systematic liquidation of alternatives is that it provides an acceptable cover for a hidden agenda of ruling group self-interest. For example, it is a well known fact from the distanced vantage point of historical hindsight or cultural opposition, that ruling groups use the goal of national defence or national security as a recurrent pretext for what is, in fact, the increase of their own privileged positions of office or wealth. What is represented as the nation's salvation from external threat is, in truth, this ruling minority's quite private advantage — its continuance in authority in the face of domestic unrest redirected towards an external 'enemy', the extravagant profits of its leading business members from national arms races, or the seizure of foreign lands, markets, resources, strategic sites or labour pools to increase its memberships' state or capital empowerment [12]. Though these concealed projects of appropriation are perfectly obvious underneath claims of the national interest when pursued by rulers made objective to us by time or geopolitical division, they do not normally appear this way to us when pursued by the leaderships of what we suppose to be our own countries. In this way, the many other options available to national self-purpose are kept closed from the view of national citizenries who are in the position to advance and press them. Once conditioned to acquiesce in the military program of thought as a dictate of necessity, civilians are not only restricted to a primitive concept of national selfhood, and then blinded to distinctions of option by an all-justifying imperative of national security, but held from seeing the real interests this train of thinking serves by an imposed identification with it as their *own* freedom. A closed circuit of thought is thus forged — upon which poor men's bodies are piled as on pyres — from which it becomes almost impossible to escape without inviting the charge of disloyalty to national cause as a 'subversive', 'unAmerican', 'counter- revolutionary', 'terrorist' or whatever.

Insofar as there are these hidden agenda of ruling-group advantage underlying and governing what is incanted as national security, an arresting and far-reaching distinction follows. The collective interests of the civilian bodies who continually pay and die for the military program's implementation are, in principle, opposed to the interests of the non-combatant beneficiaries of this program who lead them. If so, and this pattern we know to be widely so where we are sufficiently distanced from its control, then we can understand why the lock-step sequence of the military paradigm is so routinely advanced by those who preside over its prescriptions. Its programmed presupposition conceals this contradiction of interests behind a pretended communality of national defence, and renders anyone who exposes it as a violator of the 'national interest'. The more customary and automatic the military paradigm's acceptance is, the more deeply interiorized its metaphysical premises of national selfhood and purpose become, and the more widely these permeate the overall reproduction of civil life, the more totally closed to change the hidden agenda becomes. Once thus ensconced at the very foundations of the nation's identity and purpose, the military program's further elaborations in defining the national enemy, morally denouncing its opposition, and preparing to annihilate it with maximally destructive means, follow as dictates of national necessity. But these steps of the program's prescription — however habituated and culturally universal — are covert choices whose examination reveals other and deeply variant possibilities.

Part V

Who is the National Enemy?

Who is the national enemy? The answer here is generally presupposed as given by the nature of the world. But it admits of radically various and contradictory options any one of which may decide the fatal course of national or global life. Assuming placement in war-contest, the opposition is perceived as something to annihilate. But even if we thus assume the opposition as a presence to be annihilated, what this opposition is taken to be makes all the difference to the war we wage against it.

Consider. We are not, with good reason, inhibited as national selves from waging war against insect infestations, pestilence, disease or plagues. These are not merely wars in metaphor, but deadly serious wars in the strictest sense of the term. For, as the usage of this concept everywhere confirms:

(1) **war is a deliberately organized campaign to obliterate the existence of perceived enemies** [13].

It follows, therefore, that war need not ever be, as the pre-emptive military version of it misleads us to believe, a menace to humanity. Its target can be only non-human enemies to vital life. Yet with the military form of war, the existence that is obliterated, or planned to be, is very large numbers of other human beings: possibly tens or hundreds of millions, their limbs and organs and other faculties, and their basic means of life-support, along with untold by-product casualties of natural beings and entire ecosystems of fauna and flora. This is a pathological form of war. Although it intends by such devices as hundreds-of-miles-deep safeplaces for its non-combatant leaders to keep some beings still alive, technological development is now at the stage where even its ruling beneficiaries suffer threat of annihilation. It is really a striking feature of the

17

contemporary human condition that the military program of war is still assumed as war's proper form .

What adds to this pathology of fixation upon the military program is that we are perpetually engaged in **other** kinds of war, wars that do not destroy human beings but enable them. Our very historical development and ecological adaptation have, indeed, depended upon our waging these wars — against pathogens, disease-bearing pests, insect and rodent hordes, civil corruption, tyrannies, toxic pollutants ... The list is long. Its pattern underlies both our cultural and evolutionary success as a species. War of the non-military sort is the external immune system of humanity's advance on Earth. But the military format of this species-defensive function is one of destruction that kills at all levels at once, until life itself has become the potential object of its immolation. The military pattern of absolutist command and destruction is now, after epochs of ruling group imposition, out of control and undergirds even industrial devastation itself, whose machine and chemical razings of entire ecosystems find their historical prototype in the military model of conquest.

We can make a generalization about war which puts its evolutionary function in an entirely different light than its military perversion. **The human capacity to make war is, in proportion to its cooperative inclusion, a species-distinctive ability upon which humanity's survival and development depend.**

Much could be said about this. I suspect that an interesting history of human evolution and development could be written from its standpoint — humanity's wars perhaps beginning and certainly playing a primary role in the organizational structures of cooperation characterizing the species' pre-historical and historical advances in collective capacitation. Survival against larger predators, the weeding techniques of the agricultural revolution, the effective coping with vermin and pestilences of all kinds, the conquests of a long succession of plagues and diseases, the recent movement to war on the microbial level, the progress of modern allopathic medicine and hygienic practices to the present day — the theme of war's deliberate annihilation of other beings is very long, and complex. Humanity's pattern of increasing powers is largely explicable in its terms. Today we are waging wars — not in metaphor but, past hypocrisy, with liberative intent, on more levels than ever before: against carcinomatous cells, official lies, industrial wastes, self-pity, criminal conduct, nuclear war itself. The mind dances with the richness of war's profusion of forms, which seem somehow to be all struck from the scroll of possibility once the military form of war engages the conditioned schemas of our thought.

What makes the primary difference between enabling and pathological wars is that the latter by their intention and instrumentation massacre and mutilate large numbers of people, whereas the former do not. War achieves this pathological extreme the more it destroys humans and human capacities. Non-military forms of war do not normally do this, intentionally or unintentionally [14]. When they do, as in inquisitorial wars against perceived satanic influences, it is interesting that they too move into closer and closer family resemblance to that set of characteristics of the military program of war identified in part II. The military form of war, in other words, is a derangement, a deformed variation of an evolutionarily distinctive capacity, and increasingly so with the advance and dominance of its administrative and technical powers.

Because war admits of such hidden polarities of possibility — the very extremes of species health and morbidity — what we elect as the war enemy is decisive in the formation of our life-world. The choice determines whether our wars are humanly liberative or, like Brecht's 'hairy baboon's ass', an abominable tool of the acquisitive and power-addled.

19

As William James has argued, the martial propensities need not be repressed, but can be appropriately and virtuously expressed [15]. Whether they are discharged 'against Nature' in the form of militant youth work crews doing public service (James' rather limited substitute for war), or against human lives in the form of selectively enriching and vainglorious mechanisms of slaughter, makes all the difference. It is what is identified as the enemy in war, not war itself, which is the essential, world-structuring choice.

There is no a priori constraint on what we elect here: not only regarding the opposition's nature, but also its precise lines of presence. We might concur, for example, with the US government's oft-declared projects to eradicate international terrorism, government waste, and violations of human rights by totalitarian regimes, but observe nonetheless that choice remains as to what are identified here as the precise adversaries to be warred against. There is wide room for option. One might choose, for example, to overlook the fact that most murders by death-squad and assassinations of civilian leaders are perpetrated by military regimes trained and financed by the very administration that has declared national war against terrorism [16]. Or one might neglect to consider that the greatest proportion of government waste occurs through global purchase of unproductive weapons whose leading producer and distributor is this same great power [17]. One might choose, in these and other ways, to identify as the enemy to the national project almost anything at all, including forces quite other than those that most evidently qualify.

One might even come to identify as the opposition to every national project a single monolithic Enemy — as devil theories throughout history have done — against which public resources are increasingly mobilized to wage a perpetual and preoccupying war of extermination, whether or not the identified opposition has, in

20

reality, anything to do with the limiting conditions to be overcome, as in witch-hunts in former times [18].

Suppose, for example, that a state leadership's underlying national objectives are:

(1) to secure the collective interests of its ruling political party or ownership group; and

(2) to increase these collective ruling interests by subordinating further areas of domestic or international civil life to military control under the direction of these same interests.

Suppose, further, that such objectives are achieved by:

(i) direct armed aggression and occupation of client states seeking economic or military independence;

(ii) military buildup to secure foreign investments, debtor-nation loan payments, external natural resources, strategic sites or cheap labour pools;

(iii) imposition of state-of-siege law to control internal unrest from below;

(iv) conversion of social expenditures to military-industrial uses that maximize corporate profit opportunities;

(v) investment of national technological leadership in military-related research and development subsidizing private or state industries; and

(vi) transfer to industrialized societies of non-industrial societies' wealth by export of progressively more expensive armaments to these societies' established ruling groups.

What in such circumstances is the national enemy? It is clear that from the standpoint of national citizenries, the enemy is this process of ruling group exploitation and militarization itself.

Yet what will be predictably identified as the nation's enemy will be those persons or groups who *oppose* this very process. That such people or groups will be targeted as

21

the official enemy is an easily testable hypothesis. It is widely confirmable, and nowhere clearly disconfirmed in the world today. The 'enemy' that is in this way identified may be a rival superpower (if there is, in fact, such opposition, as distinguished from, say, tacit imperial collaboration), but may be any group, domestic or external, real or contrived, which is perceived as disturbing the fulfilment of these objectives.

Whatever group is chosen, and however irrelevant to a national people's real life-and-death problems it may be, we can predict that it will be selected in accordance with this pattern as the mortal adversary under some culturally accepted rubric of diabolic qualification, such as 'communists', 'terrorists', 'anti-Soviet agents', 'foreign infidels', or the like [19]. Having been thus identified as the enemy to justify the escalation of militarization, and thereby the increased fulfilment of the objectives, this enemy becomes indispensable to perpetuation of the pattern. Its posited threat, along with claimed vulnerabilities to its attack, are required to sustain the game [20].

In this way a closed loop of ruling thought and action is formed which is generally re-enforced, not weakened, by armed resistance to it: to the present point of multiples of globe-destroying weapons of 'defence', and military expenditures of 1.7 million dollars per minute devoted to the struggle against designated 'national enemies'.

This is the inner program underlying determination of the national enemy where none may, in fact, exist of the kind constructed. But thought is not so easily controlled as to render this underlying pattern the sequence of necessity it is made to appear as. There are other choices open to national populations than acquiescence in a program so fundamentally inimical to their own collective survival and security.

One such choice is to consider the evidence of militarily armed groups in fact posing a danger to the lives and security of national citizen bodies. In most countries of Central and South America, the Far East, the Middle East and sub-Sahara Africa, the greatest and often only armed threat to their inhabitants has for many years demonstrably proceeded from their *own* militaries, who, being inclined to view the civil populations they rule as the national enemy, have established order by such means as mass civilian terror and slaughter, despotic imposition of laws and government, violent looting and extortion, and despoliation of public resources [21].

Even with the superpowers, if we consider the matter from the standpoint of other than counterfactual imagination, the military industrial complexes of the US and the USSR have endangered the security and lives of their own citizens far more palpably than either's aggression against the other: essentially by vast expenditures on arms that have correspondingly derogated from tribute-free citizen time and the safety of social environments, but also by thousands of mutilations and deaths of their own citizens incurred by these superpowers' military invasions of smaller countries [22].

Such a method of defending a nation's people is in the end absurd, because its practice systematically contradicts its declared objective. In countries such as Guatemala, El Salvador, Indonesia, Uganda, Kampuchea, South Africa or Chile, national security establishments have been more destructive of national social life than invasion by a foreign power.

Who is the national enemy, then, is a question whose proper answer is often, perhaps generally, opposite to what the military program would have us believe. If humanity's species-distinctive capacity to make war is to be rationally directed, the primary enemy to target would seem increasingly to be the military system itself.

Part VI

Discovering the Just War

Once the opposition to national well-being is identified, the value ascribed to the chosen adversary remains posed as a problem for judgement. Though unreflective consciousness assumes opposition to itself to be evil, this is an inference that allows of alternative. Rollerball patriots and evangelicals, not to say the invested leaders of their governments, assume a moral justification to destroy opponents to their will. But their judgement is distorted by what Hobbes has called the 'notable multiplying glasses' of self-interest. Such magnifiers not only predispose the outlook of fictional idiocyncratics like Ahab, who judges the great whale he chooses to war against as 'all evil visibly personified', but can govern real heads of state too who may view their chosen opponents as 'the focus of all evil in the modern world'.

Absolute disvaluation of one's opposition is, however, not a necessary consequence of even annihilative intention. It is an option of ethical judgement. It could more diffidently conceptualize its adversary in opposite terms and, like Heraclitus, conceive of the opposition in even military war as just by its very nature, in that it ensures that no part of nature can *overstep its measures*, and thereby orders the world as it ought to be ordered, whether or not one's own self or state is thus restrained by cosmic propriety [23].

Evaluation of the enemy one intends to eradicate may also make an enabling distinction. It may distinguish between the enemy it seeks to destroy by war and what ought not to be destroyed — other human lives. Thus, just as with morally unimpeachable wars against organic diseases and other unambiguously destructive patterns, which are best waged against highly specific and invariant enemies whose elimination entails no loss of human life, the moral war seeks only to expunge the disabling pattern. This pattern is judged to be the enemy (e.g. bubonic plague), not necessarily the being that bears it (e.g. the rodent).

Applying this fundamental but overlooked distinction to human enemies, we can say that such and such a pattern of behaviour (e.g. Nazism) is an utmost evil, and that it obliges us to go to battle to the death against it. But such a value judgement does not necessitate the death of persons bearing the pattern of even Nazism: it is not persons as such who are finally depraved (because they can and may reform), but rather the murderous pattern they choose or are forced to bear.

Analysts of moral choice in war have hitherto failed to consider this fundamental difference between agent and structure of action. Yet it emerges as a foundational option where human enemies are concerned because agency here involves the capacity to choose an alternative to the deadly pattern, whereas non-human disease bearers have apparently no such capacity. They (the diseased ones) traditionally have been killed to get at the pattern (the disease), whereas humans, as such, need not be. Some humans may become 'beasts', and this is the deep meaning of the epithet: they have abandoned their elective capacities and hold incorrigibly to inhuman and viciously destructive programs. In these cases, usually confined to those who derive social command from such programs, the only way to annihilate their pattern may be to annihilate them; or to eliminate by permanent imprisonment their capacity to perform such deeds. But these inalterable cases are far rarer than can warrant the mass-terrorist leap by military thought to projects of killing or threatening to kill thousands or millions, perhaps billions, of people as a 'necessity of self-defence'.

Insofar as the military program itself increasingly endangers the security of unarmed citizens everywhere, its

25

implementation poses the very systematic violence and threat to civilization and peace it purports to defend against. Because it produces and propagates the organized attack on civilian peace and security that its putative value is to prevent, its practice plainly contradicts its goal. More subtly, the evil of the enemy that it upholds in order to justify this practice supposes the very enemy capacity for choice which its homicidal methods overlook. For since moral good or bad presupposes choice, this judgement entails the adversary's option of other course. From the premise of the military position itself, then, it does not follow that the persons of the enemy's general population, as distinct from the disabling pattern they are constrained to bear, require to be killed.

This fundamental distinction between persons and the patterns they bear is deeper than the well-known distinction between civilians and soldiers advocated by more discriminating advocates of military solution like Elizabeth Anscombe [24]. Under our deeper distinction we do not have the right to kill even those who are militarily determined to kill us. Rather, our war is properly to be waged against the pattern they bear, which is typically imposed from above, and by a command which is structured to be untouched by military attack. Entirely different consequences of action follow from this distinction. One doesn't look for ways of blowing up enemy soldiers, but of fighting the economic-military program by which they are bound. This fight can proceed by any number of long-term or short-term strategies of non-military war — from abolishing or deposing professional armies themselves (as in distinctively peaceful Costa Rica or postwar Japan), to national and international activisms of UN peacekeeping, weapon-dismantling, total boycott, coordinated strike, collective disobedience, ideological war, tax-strangling, mass revolt, or political expunction of state terrorist permissions [25].

26

Again, the underlying distinction here is not that advanced by Thomas Nagel in his hallmark article 'War and Massacre' which, like Anscombe's, restricts the proper objects of military killing to enemy combatants. We agree in specifically condemning as moral evils 'the indiscriminate destructiveness of anti-personnel weapons; napalm — cruelty to prisoners; massive relocation of civilians; destruction of crops — piecemeal wiping out of rural civilian populations in airborne anti-guerrilla warfare' [26]. However, Nagel's more judicious and humane alternative of engaging the 'person' of the attacker and no other, and then only in those respects in which this person or persons are a threat (not their families or community or other 'irrelevant aspects' of their being), falls far short of the deeper wedge of distinction proposed here. For it is precisely not the person, who as such is capable of an alternative mode of expression, who warrants destructive targeting. Rather, we argue, it is the disabling program the combatant is now a bearer of, the form of social life coercively governing him, which is the proper object of annihilative attack. Military combatants are, after all, normally forced to be military combatants. They have little or no choice in performing the role for which they may, even according to Nagel, be rightfully killed. The paradox that thus arises — of justly tearing people to pieces for what they did not choose to do — is only resolved if we recognize that it is the coercive pattern, not the people bound by it, against which deadly counter-attack is appropriate.

Recently, Laura Westra has also argued that Nagel's position does not acknowledge the requirement of 'culpable intent' in his distinction between combatants and civilians. She writes:

'Perhaps ignorance, based upon a wilful external effort to present facts, situations and actions in an appropriate rose-coloured light might place drafted enemy armies at the level of partial innocence (something like the le-

27

gal notion of *extenuating circumstances* perhaps). This should still be sufficient to spare them from 'rightful obliteration' at our hands' [27].

While Westra, like her forbears Anscombe and Nagel, continues to advance an important distinction between the guilty and the innocent in military war, she also continues to miss the basic point. Merely personal intentions do not and cannot get to the bottom of the matter. Disclosure of groups within the enemy population whose intentions do not deserve the death or mutilation the military system prescribes for them, does indeed draw the curtain away from the established monolith 'Enemy'. That is all to the good. But as this process of analysis leads from bystanding civilians to conscripted soldiers themselves, it reveals in its wake an underlying form of social coercion and destruction within which the vast majority of those at war on both sides are involuntarily imprisoned — the military form of war itself. It is this imposed program of war and its ruling group interests that are the real enemy against which some new form of war is morally justified, and imperative to the species.

The solution to the problem of whom one can rightfully kill in war will continue to evade us until we move to this deeper ground of the social structures within which both sides of military war are normally constrained to act. Here innocent or guilty intentions must be given their context if we are to understand more than mere appearances and symptoms. The full problem can be plumbed only when the underlying form of social rule within which the majority are largely cogs and victims — specifically, the military program by which this rule is sustained — is brought front and square into the moral picture. Until then, we are without the bearings we require to understand what we judge, floundering about in assessments of guilt and innocence of mostly helpless bit-players in a compulsory killer game. It is this game itself and the

28

various economic, political, and military beneficiaries who preside in safety over its civil imposition, which require moral targeting. That is the step for which recent philosophical exposure of the innocent enemy has prepared us, but which has not yet been taken.

When we do move towards the social-structure framework within which war's massacres occur, and consider in reflection more coherent alternatives of which national security and self-defence admit, much emerges to notice. The enemy which threatens us most directly, we begin to see, is within our own borders, as is theirs, and it is the ruling military-industrial complex itself. This understanding leads to very different and more far-reaching modes of war. It radically reduces the right to kill humans, if any such right remains at all, to those alone who freely persist in murderous actions. At the same time, it systematically widens the enemy to be annihilated to those militarist patterns that prescribe such programs.

Part VII

Modes of War: From Genocide to Liberation

Once we understand the nature of the war-enemy, there arises the question of what mode of annihilation to choose against it. There remain world-defining options here. But for the military form of war, these options are radically determined. With the notable exception of the ancient strategist, Sun Tau, large-scale massacre has been the chosen method, and ever more efficient means of mass homicide the direction of its historical development [28].

When we turn to the normative cornerstone of Western civilization on the issue, we find indeed that total destruction of men, women and children and systems of life support is specifically commanded by the Almighty of the Judaic-Christian tradition. Thus to His voice is attributed the still believed intention to take 'the whole land of Canaan [for Israel] to own in perpetuity' (Genesis: 17:21); and, in explicit prohibition of any 'pact with them', to 'exterminate' all of Palestine's inhabitants, 'Amorites, Hittites, Perizzites, Canaanites, Hivites, and Jebusite' (Exodus: 23:24).

It is instructive to compare this genocidal norm of military war whose prescription remains conventionally reversed as the work of God, with Sun Tzu's more civil but ignored counsel 2300 years ago recommending infliction on the enemy of the fewest possible casualties [29].

The traditional form of military war has nevertheless prevailed. It has been applied by our military allies in recent decades to the cities of Dresden and Hiroshima in the second world war, and since, to various Vietnamese, Indonesian, Chilean, El Salvadorean, Guatemalan, Timorese and Nicaraguan peoples and villages [30].

The more limited intent to kill only the part of the opposition that resists its society's enslavement or domination is a more lenient intent in military history. Its pattern is a connecting thread between imperial systems from ancient Egypt and Greece to the present. It not only occurs, for example, in the Old Testament as another option reportedly entertained by Yahweh, but is celebrated in the Hindu *Rg Veda* and *Arthasastra* as a rightful reward for stronger kings. It is also implied by Plato, Aristotle, and other classical thinkers as a requirement for reducing 'barbarian' peoples. Over two thousand years later, it remains vigorously endorsed by Hegel as the most basic relationship between humans. 'Each aims at the destruction and death of the other', he argues, until one is terrified out of choosing a transcendent attitude to the body and submits in bondage to his adversary. The institutionalization of this process in nation-state wars is then exalted by Hegel as the 'spirit's ultimate instrument' for 'universalizing Right and Law on Earth' [31].

The goal of reducing other societies to servitude by military terror continues to be upheld in the most recent century. 'War', says von Clausewitz in his still axiomatic definition, 'is an act of violence intended to compel our opponent to fulfil our will'. Von Clausewitz also posits as the end of military war the purely annihilative goal of '*destroying* the adversary', but his apparent inconsistency on this point is resolvable if we retain the agent/pattern distinction of the previous section. That is, annihilation of the enemy may proceed by killing people, or by expunging *the pattern they bear*. Von Clausewitz unwittingly employs this distinction, without recognizing it or the general principle it limitedly expresses [32].

Note the bridge between those military modes of war which seek the absolute death of the other, and those which seek merely the liquidation of his autonomy. This transition marks the principal difference between civilization's earlier and later forms of military genocide. The advance that occurs here is that the opponent is no longer to be slaughtered and left as waste, but is to be incorporated alive into the proprietary domain of the conqueror, as in slavery, feudal bondage, and colonialism. As with all advances of conquest stage, the governing principle of ascending value here is *more inclusive enablement*, which follows from the fact that the defeated adversary or victim is not destroyed but preserved, albeit in a form that is reduced to extension of another's will.

In general, intertribal and international contest has remained confined to one or other of these military-genocidal forms of war. Non-homicidal arenas of conquest — by economic competition, by cultural superiority, by the relentless battle for a better life — have been less favoured as modes of international combat than proof of greatness by kill-capacity. We remain with the military paradigm largely stuck at the killer-gang stage of waging war.

On the other hand, the choice exists for non-pathological modes war. Nations, like individuals, might, for example, elect a form of purging, educative war governed by an opposite principle: to abolish the enemy by any means possible that does not prescribe the death or subordination of human life. Consider, for example, Yeshua's attitude to a 'right arm that offendeth thee', or Gandhi's self-declared 'fight to the finish' with the British rule in India [33]. Both propose a war to the death with a chosen adversary judged evil, but each recommends a mode of war that will not destroy, but will more inclusively enable human life by the annihilative victory it seeks. As with the enlightened warrior exemplars of other cultures, from Vedic seer and Tibetan Buddhist to Toltec Indian, war to the death is here a form of contest which repudiates the mass sacrifice of human beings as a method, and wages in its stead a 'fight to the finish' that does not destroy but capacitates [34].

This is not at all to say that non-violent forms of war

32

are the only alternatives to military mass-kill as types of intrahuman war. One need not suppose that to reject military war one must also reject all violence. War can be violent in a myriad of ways not prescribing or threatening mass-homicide: war by total disruption, non-lethal sabotage, weaponless martial art, for example, not to say other imaginable modes of war neither non-violent nor mass-murderous in nature. Here again, the range of understood options opens with the mind's release from absolutist military assumptions.

War by human sacrifice remains, however, a ritual given of the military program. We can discern its compulsive operation in laboratory-test isolation in contemporary military strikes against identified national enemies. Consider, for example, the currently fashionable armed-force raids to 'punish' declared enemies in foreign societies.

The pure pattern is exemplified in 'anti-terrorist' attacks against weaker third-world cities and settlements in the Middle East and southern Africa by Israeli, American and South African militaries, and takes the form of launching homicidal attacks:

(i) that cannot but kill known innocents in large numbers;

(ii) that do not, in fact, kill those alleged to be the wrongdoers against whom the attacks are made;

(iii) that produce no proof before or after that the identified enemy's wrongdoing is or will be deterred by the attacks; and

(iv) that invariably result in further deaths and dangers to innocents of the same nation as those who command the attacks.

The persistent compulsive choice of such a mode of interaction with enemies one would annihilate, in the face of its failure to work, demonstrates the military program's depth of hold. Its prescription of mass homicide in contradiction to evidence, consistency, declared principles of

33

justice, and the security of the defended national body itself, discloses a pattern of ratiocination that if adopted by a non-state intelligence would be judged as irredeemably and criminally insane. But it is nevertheless advocated and justified as if there were 'no choice', as if the 'national will' required such an expression to survive.

What makes the problem a deep structural derangement in the regimen of current civilization is that this military line of thought is transcultural, and more programmatic in state-terrorist 'fights against terrorism' than in the 'terrorist' movements these fight against. It is *a decision-pattern of military commands in general.* Its program is not, however, prescribed by some immutable flaw of the human form. War, organized annihilation of the enemy, admits of as many forms of relationship with its object as life does drawing lines of what will and will not be allowed to exist; and these lines of battle are as open to enabling or disabling choice as are our intentions to fight to the death against plagues, monsters, or self-limits. It is the specific type of war dictated by the military paradigm that afflicts us. Compulsory military service, taxation and command are not expressions of human nature, but impositions by force of war's military mode.

Part VIII

The Political Economy of Militarization

Once the military mode of war has been chosen in ignorance of more rational forms of combat that do not prescribe mass murder as a method, the choice remains as to the weapons to be used to obliterate the declared enemy. It seems only with this final aspect of war intention that the idea of choice has entered seriously into mainstream political thought: the choice of instruments and strategies of group-kill.

Here, if nowhere else, the researched options are detailed, inventive and comprehensive. For efficient means of human slaughter under official command, there is no want of established support. Weapons are, after all, increasingly the world's most lucrative business. The ancient game of contriving means to kill and mutilate great numbers of other human beings is more rewarding than ever to its non-combatant principals. Indeed what is foundationally new in modern warfare is that the interests of military and business commands increasingly *coincide* in military-industrial economies, where once they were opposed. In this new context of expanding partnership between military and business leaderships, funded by escalating state support of armaments purchase, weapons manufacture has almost certainly become the most thoroughly and expensively explored range of choice in humanity's history. From single Trident submarines over two football-fields long and bearing 2040 Hiroshimas' worth of nuclear strike, to *Star Wars* military schemes costing the national income of entire countries to research, the panoply of proposed and realized military commodities and strategies is bizarre in its extremes. No systematic ignorance and evasion of option exists here as on the other levels of war's choice matrix. There are too many pay-offs in revenues, powers, and

35

perquisites to business, military and political leaderships by weapon buildups to choose out of the game.

Were Marx alive today, he would be profoundly interested in the political economy of military production: (1) because of its increasing centrality in the process of production and exchange (which he never anticipated); and (2) because of its now systematic and normalized role in contemporary states' management of economic and political crises.

Let us consider these developments in turn.

(1) Armaments have exceptional and generally unseen advantages as commodities for profitable manufacture and sale. These advantages together operate as a hidden structure of economic determination biasing capital investment towards armaments production:

i) the military product's **uniquely high per-unit price**, whether sold as an overall weapon system or as an individual component, accessory, replacement, or part (e.g. $26,000,000,000 for the first five years of research and development of the US Strategic Defence Initiative system, or $7,417 paid by the U.S. Air Force to General Dynamics for two one-cent pins) [35].

ii) the **specially rapid rate of obsolescence and turnover** of military goods: which follows necessarily from continuous development under established arms-race conditions as well as from destruction by use — a pattern that generates, in turn, a sustained or escalating effective demand for more military commodities;

iii) the **monopoly or semi-monopoly** position of established military manufacturers which follows: (a) from the designation of military production designs and methods as state secrets; (b) from the high capital costs of armaments technology and manufacture; and (c) from the privileged linkages of established military producers with government defence and procurement agencies;

iv) the **large-scale and secure capital financing**

36

of military research, production, and cost-additions: a funding which is ensured by coercive state mechanisms of public taxation, resource allocation, and national-debt imposition, and which is available to no other system of commodity production [36].

These hidden distinguishing features of the military product disclose a *rational self-interest* for the arms race that is generally overlooked. Theories of an unconscious human drive to aggression, a national territorial instinct for expansion, an inborn destructive propensity of the human id, a peculiarly demonic enemy bent on world conquest, an inherent irrationality of nation-state divisions, and other such general ideas to explain the madness of the arms-race are ideological mystifications which conceal its real function. The arms race is a mechanism of economic and political rule. It systematically serves the advance of ruling-group interests in the ways we have identified earlier (part IV) and specifically provides peerless commodity advantages for military-industrial businesses. By its nature the arms race continuously reproduces and expands the demand for its products and opportunities for profit which are unavailable to any other form of commodity production — particularly during times of economic recession or depression.

It is this underlying transnational economic base of the arms race that explains its occurrence in the face of its tendency to contradict the very interests of civilian peace and security for which it is said to be pursued.

(2) On the political level, the use of rapidly developing military means for blocking or destroying political and labour movements that pose a danger to private capital ownership has long played an indispensable *superstructural* role in maintaining post-colonial capitalism as an economic system through social, labour and public debt crises. This is especially true of poverty-ridden third world societies, where military or militarily controlled governments have

been the rule from Latin America to South-East Asia since their decolonization.

This pattern of capital-benefiting militarization has historically impelled and sustained an *anti-capitalist militarization* by aspiring or established state-socialist regimes. That is, the dominant pattern of revolutionary socialist movements and states from the Bolshevik success on has been to militarize their own industrial and political structures under the central command of Communist Party leadership, which has traditionally characterized itself as the 'general staff of the revolution'. This centralized, militarily-secured rule has, then, served the interests of *its* commanding beneficiaries as systematically as militarized commodity production and political rule serve industrial, merchant and finance capital.

Against the military-industrial complexes of capitalism, in historical consequence, now stand the military-industrial complexes of state socialism: both rapidly growing, each generating privileges and protections to their respective ruling groups, and both variously dependent upon resort to armed force in sustaining their systems of mutually reinforcing hegemony. In this manner, an escalating militarization of control of society has been historically engendered across both capitalist and socialist camps alike, with its overall pattern of power and advantage to the ruling blocs of *both* systems remaining unrecognized by Marxian as well as anti-Marxian analysis [37].

Because human societies across the world in this way increasingly reproduce themselves as military bodies and reflex-systems poised for the destruction of discerned group-enemies, non-military options for conquering adversaries have been generally ruled out *a priori*. This mind-set corresponds to the structures of rule that military buildups globally serve and protect. It is, in the language of Marx, a 'form of social consciousness' that reflects ruling-class interests of control and exploitation.

Even if military war is not the God-ordained necessity that religious and patriotic fanaticisms across the world now declare it is, a calmer ruling belief persists that no feasible alternative to the strategy of mass homicide exists to secure us from the threat of foreign enemies.

What this dogma of national security conceals, however, is a novel aspect of our contemporary condition — namely, that the nature of the military program's pursuit has so qualitatively changed in the direction of destructive capacity and ongoing production cost that traditionally accepted arguments for its defensive necessity no longer apply. The historically unprecedented dangers and costs of military buildups can no longer be justified by the external threats of invasion they are held to defend against.

The need for such justification, if not its subversive implication, was obliquely admitted by the recent U.S. Secretary of Defense, Casper Weinberger, who asserted: 'It's the threat that makes the budget' [38].

An alleged proof of proportionality between threat and military budget is now achieved on the basis of three illicit assumptions. Claimed and often invented threats are treated as facts. A causal connection between counter-threat and effective deterrence is supposed without demonstration. And the dangers of provocation by one's own military buildup are simply ruled out of account. Moreover, no justification has ever been given even within these question-begging parameters to demonstrate that a military program is worth its great risks and costs to the national citizenries paying and dying for it. If we insist on logical and scientific method in ascertaining (i) probability of being attacked; (ii) proportionality of defensive counter-measure, and (iii) the effectiveness of poised mass-kill as deterrent, and do not merely presume the truth of official assertions on these matters, we are left without any good reason to suppose that any major military program is still justified [39]. The assumption of a rational *realism* on the part of current military advocacy, then, does not stand up to scrutiny. It is a myth: merely an unverified belief whose propagation corresponds to ruling-group advantage.

What then, if not military buildup, has deterred military war among industrialized nations in recent decades? The answer is discoverable in the technological, economic and civic *contexts* within which the industrialized nations' military mechanisms have been and are now located. These more basic conditions of social and political life have developed in still more profound and far-reaching ways than military means since World War II. Unprecedentedly, *the general populations of the industrialized nations have become domestically secure in the reproduction and development of their means of life* — their food, shelter, employment, health care, and literacy. Corresponding to this historically unparalleled security of social base has grown an ever greater interdependence, interconnectedness and similarity of rational method, production technique, standard-of-life aspiration, and cultural exchange. An overall system of widely distributed life-welfare has thus developed in which actualized military warfare between industrialized nations no longer qualifies as a feasibly self-interested strategy for any dominant population or ruling group. It is this vastly deepened and more inclusive socioeconomic interest in maintaining mutual security which best explains the political refrainment from armed warfare by the nations and peoples involved. Conversely, the *undermining* of this socioeconomic base — by massive unemployment, by increasing ruling-group appropriation of society's wealth, by dismantling of public welfare systems through the militarization process itself — constitutes the most fundamental if unseen danger to this privileged enclave's achievement of military peace.

Very real as well as contrived conflicts of regime interest still persist between the capitalist and state-socialist blocs within the industrialized world. But contest be-

40

tween them is sufficiently intense — and expressive in non-military arenas, and so historically discredited and impractical on the plane of direct military attack on one another, that these blocs' respective military build-ups may be better accounted for as a function of *internal* requirements of rule and profit than as essential to deterring external invasion. The latter option is in neither population's nor ruling bloc's interest, given the continued stability and advance of their respective socioeconomic foundations.

If mutually destructive military capacity *is* the factor by which we are to explain the refusal of industrialized nations over 40 years and countless disputes to engage in actual military war with one another, then this explanation is quite unable to account for the fact that the United States or the USSR, with incomparably greater military force, a well-known priority for national self-interest, and vast resources to win by conquest, have not invaded, say, adjacent Canada or Finland. Nor, more generally, can such a mode of explanation account for the fact that a more powerful NATO did not attack a much weaker Warsaw Pact for over 20 years of declared intense enmity. What has protected the latter countries from such invasion cannot be their development of military programs; for Canada, Finland, or the outlying nations of the Warsaw Pact have not had the weapon parity to prevail militarily against such aggressions. On the other hand, what can account for these countries' relative security from military attack by stronger neighbours is a systematic combination of *non*-military factors: not only the social reproduction bases of the societies concerned, but, as well, political and ideological factors such as the civil memory of the Nazi disaster and customary patterns of international intercourse whose armed-force usurpation would so violate dearly held norms of group life as to make subsequent occupation unviable. *Perestroika* and *glasnost* are outgrowths of this

41

shared civil context of social security and law.

Where military invasion *has* exceptionally occurred between industrialized nations in the post World War II era (e.g. the USSR-led military occupation of Czechoslovakia in 1968), it was to secure an already-established dominion, and was achieved (at irreparable ideological cost) by the systematic co-operation of the invaded nation's own armed forces: a contingency which would seem best preventable not by a national military program which in fact assisted it, but by prepared *systems of society-wide civil disobedience.* Indeed it is precisely these non-military systems of social war that have already prevailed with less developed civilian contexts to work from, against powerful alien militaries in India, Thailand, Iran, the Philippines, Argentina, and perhaps soon in other countries like Burma, Palestine, or Chile. They have arisen, moreover, without any of the enormous resources and support structures of the military system: without public taxation bases, technological infrastructures, long-term training and scientific research, civilian drafts, censored media or traditional patriotic inculcation to establish them as means of collective defence. The pre-emption of these systems of non-military social war from nation-state thinking is not on account of their impossibility as forms of effective national defence, but because of their inherent incompatibility with the military system's advantages to established power élites.

What is finally ignored by the conventional ideology of military 'national security' is the unintended effect of its continued implementation. It is possible that, without anyone's knowledge, the world's current militarization serves some long-term historical purpose other than the safety or security of national peoples, or even ruling-group power and maintenance. The vast tax revenues such militarization increasingly demands in the face of business opposition to government control of capital may fulfil the hidden function of concentrating control of social wealth in the hands of the contemporary state: an unforeseen and rapid conversion of citizens' private money to state ownership that, in the long run, could provide the government-controlled surplus wealth to base a state-socialist economy. Under this view, it would be the ironic consequence of military-industrial capitalism's claimed opposition to Soviet domination of the world that it creates the material conditions and the regulatory impetus for the very statist order it is claimed to prevent.

Certainly, there is a systematic transferral, by government loan financing and present and future tax imposition, of private monies into state control with military and war economies. This unseen pattern of what we might call *universalizing military statism* is not only implicitly present in capitalist economies of substantial military-industrial composition, but calls forth its explicit version in actually existing military statisms, which have become similarly reinforced to compete with and survive against the armed forces of their capitalist adversaries. Whatever the eventual outcome of this process of state militarization may be, it can hardly give comfort to even those whose priority it is to protect the free world of investment capital, let alone to those who still imagine that defence establishments are there to secure civilian lives from military terror and aggression.

Part IX

Conclusion

The bias of our social and political thought towards homicidal weapons systems for self-defence is, in the end, a transcultural prejudice — underwritten by ancient patterns of hostility to extra-tribal groups, and increasingly reinforced by coinciding profitabilility to economic and military leaderships. It has become now the most dangerous prejudice that has ever existed. Its revanchist ascension to state office in recent years under the guise of 'deterrence' has redefined national priorities, multiplied public debts to crisis proportions, and expanded military industry to a normalized race of kill-capacity beyond the limits of planetary life itself [40]. The logic of armed-force resolution has come, indeed, to structure the contents of mass entertainment and national self-definitions, not to say visions of revolutionary alternative themselves. Human culture seems on the verge of default to the military program as the final shared framework of empowerment and meaning.

The established criterion of national legitimacy has long been, it is true, the recognized power of authority to impose its will on a population by demonstrated monopoly of organized armed force. But this underlying measure of national legitimacy and sovereignty operates in accordance with a law of progression: **the more military means are developed in command of social labour and resources, range of deployment and violent effect, and capacity for universal surveillance, the more human existence passes under military control.** Because such a pattern of increasing military capacitation and cost has in fact followed from the arms race and growth of national security establishments, the ascension of military, militarily imposed, or militarily expanding governments to control civilian existence is the now established, if hidden, crystallizing pattern of our global social order.

Its phenomena can be seen everywhere, and are all connected: military threats or interventions to ensure labour supply or intensification; military models of corporate management and marketplace competition; military priorities of public expenditure; military toys, arcade games, fashion designs, and schoolchild chants; armed-force heroes and plots of mass television, film, book, and newsprint media; military organization and contents of leisure contests, spectator sports and spectacles; conceptualization of religious aspiration, political conflict, social development, and organic defence itself in terms of military-bearing battles and attacks; celebration of national collectivity and conscience in the symbology of military displays, anthems, and invocations; and, in increasing closure to alternative means of proving national strength, denigration of non-military options as 'weak', 'soft', or 'unrealistic'... These all manifest a way of life in the world that is unified by a culture of military a priorism that runs increasingly beneath conscious understanding and control [41].

Yet there are, as we have found, other options. The Zen master chooses a sudden slap in the face of the ignorance he would war against. Contemporary populations from the Americas to the Far East have brought down military power-structures by relentlessly systematic non-cooperation. Evolutionary attrition, annihilative ridicule and exposure, society-wide disobedience, economic boycott, technological or cultural displacement — these have all won collective victories far more economically and durably than any modern military machine.

Unlike the military program, their logic is not to destroy persons, but to transform human agency; not to centralize command and weaponry, but to distribute social

45

power and civilian choice.

The most broadly effective deterrent of social aggression from the time of the ancient Chinese to the contemporary global village has been the power of public shame. Indeed, given the new media mechanisms of world opinion to administer public censure, the peculiar sensitivity of even hardened tyrants to its experience [42], and the willingness of most recruits to war to die rather than suffer it, it is an option for behavioral extinction that more readily recommends itself to reason than mass-kill methods which are increasingly known to terrorize and bankrupt the very civil bodies they purport to protect.

Contesting the lines of life and death is a far more open matter than the military paradigm assumes. The nature of the national self and its projects, what is judged the enemy, why, how, and by what means its annihilation is sought — these all admit of profound if unexplored ranges of choice.

Humanity's essential conflictedness cannot, of course, be wished away by a utopian flight into pure peace, beyond contesting and conflict, where communion is won by some final war or renunciation [43]. Men and nations are condemned to the freedom of drawing the lines of the world, of determining what is to live and what is to die, now more than ever by the demands of their technologies and numbers. But even on the most elementary level of reality's definition, war is made not given, a theatre of possibilities reduced to uniformity and the logic of armed terror not by national or natural requirement, but by the military necessity of commanding civilian bodies against their own interests and wills.

The consequence of the military program is, in the end, to reverse the order of war's proper object in ever greater extremes, raising pathogenic command as human life's defence, and destroying the civil, the vitally productive, and the individual by its very nature. The human struggle for survival is, at this juncture of its history, no longer against natural or foreign enemies or even war as such, but against the military program itself.

Notes

[1] Sources of these statements are, in order: S L A Marshall, **Men Against Fire** (New York: Wm Morrow, 1947) pp 56-57; William Manchester, **American Caesar: Douglas MacArthur 1880-1964** (London: Hutchinson, 1979) 622-23; Joseph Frazier *American Press News Service* 3 December 1984. I am indebted to Gwynne Dyer's **War** (Toronto: Stoddart, 1985) p 142 for the first of these quotations.

[2] Ruth Leger Sivard's annual survey **World Military and Social Expenditures** (Washington D.C.: World Priorities, 1974-88) has reported that there are now over 50,000 nuclear weapons in the world (15 to 30 times the megatonnage which would be needed to destroy global life); that military expenditures currently exceed the total income of almost half the world's total population; that more than 1,000,000,000 people live under military-controlled governments (excluding militarily-controlled civilian governments), four-fifths of which regimes use violence against their own citizens; and that almost 20 million people have been killed in wars since 1945, almost entirely in the non-industrialized world, where military expenditures have risen more than tenfold since 1960. Retired US Admiral Eugene Carroll summarizes the growing public intuition in opposition to this state of affairs: 'As Dwight D. Eisenhower has said, people want peace so much that some day governments will have to get out of the way and let the people have peace' (Operation Dismantle Appeal, Ottawa, April 1986).

[3] i) The dean of contemporary disarmament theory, Quincy Wright, presupposes this mass-homicide principle of war throughout the two volumes of his magisterial **A Study of War** (Chicago: University of Chicago Press, 1942) as well as, more tellingly, in his **The Role of Inter-**

national Law in the Elimination of War (Manchester: Manchester University Press, 1961). His presupposition remains shared by subsequent disarmament thinkers. ii) It might be objected by Marxists that a fundamental asymmetry of commitment to mass-murder war distinguishes capitalist and state-socialist regimes. For example, it could be pointed out in support of this position that current NATO regimes hold a commanding lead over Warsaw Pact regimes in relative gross expenditures on lethal armaments, in development of nuclear weapons, in unilateral refusal of nuclear arms-control, in armed-force interventions in other countries, in the overall dollar value of homicidal weapons exported and, historically, in the air-force bombing of civilians and cities: differences which hold for the US and USSR superpowers in particular. For substantiation of these differences, see Fred Halliday, **The Making of the Second Cold War** (London: St. Martin's Press, 1982), Mary Kaldor, **The Disintegrating West** (Harmondsworth: Penguin, 1979), D Smith and M Kidron, **The War Atlas: Armed Conflict, Armed Peace** (London: Pan Books, 1983) and Solly Zuckerman et al., **Apocalypse Now?** (Nottingham: Spokesman Books, 1980) as well as, for ongoing reliable analysis of US and NATO leads in these areas, Sivard, *ibid.* (note [2]) 1985, pp 47-8, the regular publications of *The Defense Monitor*, Centre for Defense Information, Washington D.C., and *The Ploughshares Monitor* (Institute of Peace and Conflict Studies, Conrad Grebel College, Waterloo, Canada). Nevertheless an underlying belief in the necessity of mass murdering 'national enemies' remains endorsed, and even glorified, by state-socialist leaderships. A revealingly symptomatic example of this traditional outlook occurs in a recent statement entitled **Exploit in the Name of Peace** published in 1986 under the auspices of the USSR Academy of Sciences, the Institute of Marxism-Leninism, and the Chief Political Department of the Soviet

49

Army and Navy: 'The Soviet Army proved to be a first-class and the most efficient army in the world. The Soviet Army routed, took prisoner and destroyed 607 divisions, whereas the Anglo-American Allies — only 176 divisions. The losses of the German army in the war against the USSR reached 10 million or 80 per cent of all its losses [killed people].' *Social Sciences: USSR Academy of Sciences* **XVII**, 1 (1986) p 223. The equation of war excellence and mass-kill achievement has been more graphically endorsed by the Latin-American revolutionary leader, Che Guevara, who states: 'Hate is a factor in the struggle, intransigent hate for the enemy which takes one beyond the natural limitations of a human being and converts one into an effective violent, single-minded, cold, killing-machine' (**Che Guevara Speaks** ed. George Lavan (New York: Grove Press, 1967) p 156).

[4] Though questions of war's justification and legitimate means have been prominent in Western philosophical discourse since Saint Augustine's anecdotal reflections in **The City of God** and Thomas Aquinas' Questions 40, 105, and 125 in the **Summa Theologica**, the mass-homicide and maiming model of military war has been invariably presupposed in even these ethico-religious analyses. The system remains unscrutinized in the upsurge of recent secular philosophical articles and books on the subject, most of which are concerned with the ethical propriety of one means of mass-homicide war, the nuclear bomb method, whose catalysing paradox is that it threatens to harm its users. 'To control the military monster, at least to some degree', in the words of Nicholas Fotion and Gerard Elfrom's **Military Ethics** (London: Methuen, 1986), may now be an emergent philosophical concern of increasing vitality, but that this 'military monster' is war's necessary pattern continues to be assumed in even those arguments which seek to restrain it by arms control, spe-

cific targeting, specific weapons abolitions, or world-law armies.

[5] All current decision-theory and strategic analysis of war restricts itself to the issue of self-interest maximization. The prevailing paradigm of military rationality presumes that each side's self-interest can only be won at the expense of the other (the zero-sum game model: see notes [6] and [7]). However, even where there is path-breaking concern to show through such paradoxes as Prisoner's Dilemma that self-interest is best secured by strategies of co-operation (as in the strategic-theory work of Anatol Rapoport and Thomas C. Schelling over the last 20 years), this position itself assumes that war as such requires the use of mass-homicidal weapons.

[6] The premises of this tribal a priori of the military mindset are revealed in value-loaded referring terms the truth of whose descriptive content is simply assumed: for example, characterization of one's own country or ally as 'free and democratic' and the opposing side as a 'totalitarian dictatorship'. These set ascriptions creep into even scholarly discourse, and operate as the premises from which inferences of possible or recommended policies of mass human destruction are 'rationally' drawn. See, for example, **The Use of Force: International Politics and Foreign Policy** ed. Robert J Art and Kenneth N Waltz (Boston: Little Brown and Co., 1971), in particular the articles by John Foster Dulles, Robert S McNamara, Samuel P Huntington, and Henry A Kissinger. For more recent academic example, see Robert W Tucker, **The Purposes of American Power: An Essay on National Security** (New York: Praeger, 1981), Michael Novak, **Moral Clarity in the Nuclear Age** (London: Thomas Nelson, 1983) and, rather more surreptitiously, David Gauthier, **Deterrence, Maximization, and Rationality** *Ethics* **94** (April 1984) pp 474-95. Here Gauthier characterizes

the intended deterrer as 'she' and the intended deterred as 'he', then makes the US 'she' and the 'SU' the assailant: in which positions he then further characterizes the US as in 'fear' of an SU 'nuclear strike' if the US 'refuses some demand' of the SU, or if there is 'US refusal to acquiesce' or 'refusal to submit' to the SU (pp 474, 478, 482, 485, 489, 491, 492, 494). This implied opposition of virtuous maiden (the United States), and violating male (the Soviet Union) is the given position from which a retaliatory nuclear strike by the US that destroys the SU is argued by Gauthier as a 'maximally rational' policy intention, to be implemented even if its declared intention fails to deter. The tribal a priori regulating such mass-homicidal 'rationality' is so entrenched that it can be endorsed by even those who recognize its hold. John Simmons, for example, assumes in his otherwise distinctively critical work, **Moral Principles and Political Obligation** (Princeton, N.J.: Princeton University Press 1979) that 'noone could seriously maintain' that his political obligation was to 'oppose the efforts of his own unjust government at war with another' (p 32). Simmons presupposes this immoral identification as a requirement of political obligation, despite his reasoned repudiation of compulsory military service. His example illuminates our point. Even where the tribal a priori biasing war thought is raised to view and the right of the national military to demand one's life is rejected, still the home-side prejudice of political obligation in all inter-state conflicts is accepted as given and axiomatic.

[7] This is an underlying program of thought and never defended as such in military-strategic rationales, but may be discerned and tested in any such rationale (See, for example, the texts in note [6]). It is a pattern of thought that also governs paramilitary organizations, national secret police, intelligence agencies and the like whose direction or execution of homicidal attacks, torture, imprisonment of

internal and external 'enemies' is often more routine and mass-destructive than those by uniformed armed forces, with which they form by their similar logic of organization and action a common type. The rational essence of the military-mind sequence is encoded in zero-sum game theory which is almost universally presupposed in military and geopolitical strategic thinking (as Anatol Rapaport points out in his **Contributions of Game Theory to Peace Education** in **Nuclear War: The Search for Solutions** ed. Thomas L Perry and Dianne De Mille (Vancouver, B.C.: Physicians for Social Responsibility, 1985) pp 174, 181. In the logic of a zero-sum game, whatever is deprived from one side is necessarily won by the other, and vice-versa. It is 'therefore assumed as reasonable that the opponent will always calculate so as to do his worst to you as he possibly can' (p 175). Operating in terms of this simplistic and maximally hostile framework of rationality, it follows easily that one's opponent in a confrontation of life-and-death stakes is conceived as an enemy, as immoral, as requiring conquest, and — since it is a military confrontation — a conquest by threatened or enacted killing. The program here is incoherent and monolithically presumptive from its base, but is everywhere marked by final certitude in its formalized language of identification and deduction. For exploration of the preemptive finality of military conceptualization as it is applied in national killing operations, see also Thomas Merton, **War and the Crisis of Language** in **The Critique of War** ed. Robert Ginsberg (Chicago: Henry Reguery Co., 1969) pp 99-120.

[8] Richard Wasserstrom has recognized in part this closure to morality and reason in *national institutions* which, he says, have a 'theoretical incapacity' to perceive or to find against even the provable war crimes of their own governments (**The Relevance of Nuremberg** *Philoso-*

phy and Public Affairs **1** No 1 (Fall 1971) pp 42-3).

[9] The joint repression of the Paris Commune by French and Prussian armies in 1871 during the Franco-Prussian War would be such an instance, as Marx points out in his **The Civil War in France** (London: Martin Lawrence, 1933).

[10] See, for example, the empirical study by Bengt Abrahamson, **Military Professionalization and Political Power** (London: Sage, 1972) as well as, from a standpoint of approval, the contributions of Samuel P Huntington and others in Part 1 of **War, Morality and the Military Profession** ed. Malham M Wakin (Boulder, Colorado: Westview Press, 1986).

[11] As US political analyst George F Will has put it: 'Vietnam was positively Athenian next to what we're involved in in El Salvador, but we must recognize we're not there for the interests of El Salvador or anyone else's but ours. Sometimes a great nation has to pursue a policy whatever its cost to others' (John McMurtry, **Fascism and Neo-Conservatism: Is there a Difference?** *Praxis International* **4**, 1 (April 1984) p 90).

[12] Here and elsewhere, we mean to focus by the expression *ruling group* or its synonyms on that group of any society's decision-makers, including foreign owners or officials who, together, direct by occupancy of senior state office, ownership of private capital or ascendant party position that society's production and use of the major means of production and destruction; and who individually derive from these positions of rule a securing or enlargement of their incomes or power to command by military enforcement. Note that this criterion is both broader and narrower in its reference than the Marxian criterion of ruling-class membership: broader by its inclusion of occupants of senior state or party office, and narrower by its exclusion of owners of social means of production whose positions of

rule do not depend for their sustainment on armed force. Though this latter requirement may seem largely verbal, because all members of all ruling classes seem thus secured by the protection of national armed forces, the qualification requires emphasis to reveal the generally overlooked connection between ruling-group ends and national military means. Disclosure of this connection exposes the naive but conventional dogma that national military establishments exist to protect national peoples as a whole.

[13] In his widely reproduced essay **On the Morality of War: A Preliminary Inquiry**, Richard Wasserstrom asserts that 'using a certain amount of deadly force under a claim of right' is the defining characteristic of war (**Moral Problems** ed. James Rachels (New York: Harper and Row, 1972) pp 299, 304). This is an error. A *claim of right* is not necessary to war, even international military war, since it is not a contradiction in terms to say that nation x made war against nation y with no claim of right. Moreover, wars against cancer, destructive falsehood and so on qualify under Wasserstrom's criterion of war, as ordinary language widely recognizes, but by a more consistent understanding of *deadly force* and *right* than Wasserstrom's definition allows. Here again we may see that it is because analysts have failed to consider the primary philosophical issue of the nature and meaning of war that they have illicitly presupposed its narrow military type as its only form, and so have been unable to get to the bottom of its more general sense and value.

[14] Wars against disease and the like may *more inclusively enable human life* by numerically saving lives, or preserving or extending established human capacities. On the other hand, such wars may also and often necessarily disable non-human forms of life by destroying them or depriving them of habitat. This is war's nature: to eradicate certain forms of life. It is in this way inherently

tragic from a point of view in which all forms of life bear value. War can be progressive or regressive in unlimited degrees of possibility, but it is always, by definition, in some respect, deliberately and systematically annihilative. It follows from this criterion, which governs all usages of the concept, that the sacrifice war entails need never be of humans, or even of sentient life. The highest form of war might be, as William Blake conceived it, the non-corporeal war of ideas.

[15] William James, **The Moral Equivalent of War** in **A William James Reader** ed. Gay Wilson Allan (New York: Houghton Mifflin, 1971) pp 211-21.

[16] See, for example, Edward S Herman, **The Real Terror Network** (Boston: South End Press, 1982) particularly pp 8, 127-37, 196-9.

[17] In 1980, the United States government presided through the Foreign Military Sales Act over armaments sales constituting 47% of the world's total, compared to the Soviet Union with 27% and France with 11% (**Canada, The Arms Race and Disarmament** (Ottawa: United Nations Association in Canada, 1981) p 13). Between the fiscal years of 1981-82, US armament exports to the third world under the Reagan administration and the Foreign Military Sales Act doubled from $15.5 billion to $31.2 billion (**One Problem: Underdevelopment and the Arms Race** (Waterloo, Canada: Dumont Press, 1983) p 11). At the same time, annual military expenditures budgeted by the US government under the Reagan administration increased by 69.1% between 1981 and 1986, from $162 billion to $277.5 billion. In comparison, spending by the Warsaw Pact has been calculated as $97 billion less than US Government estimates in the latest year for which Sivard's analysis has been made, 1982, and over $100 billion less than NATO for that same year (Ruth Leger Sivard; **World Military and Social Expendi-**

tures (Washington D.C.: World Priorities, 1985) p 47).

[18] It bears noting, however, that the move whereby the opposition to a society's well-being is identified can be still more irrationally indiscriminate in the selection of victims under contemporary rationales of national security than under past rationales of preserving 'the true faith'. Torture and murder by security forces or their proxies of hundreds of thousands, indeed millions, of internal citizens for the reason alone of their undefined 'subversion' — the contemporary counterpart of demonic possession — has occurred without noticeable global let-up from the Far East to Latin America since the 1930s. In all these cases of state and military sponsored wars against civilians involved in no determinable crime, the choice of who or what is the enemy has been a necessary, if unconsidered, condition of the innumerable murders perpetrated. See, for example, Edward S Herman, *ibid.* — note [16], and R Dallek, **The American Style of Foreign Policy: Cultural Politics and Foreign Affairs** (New York: Alfred A Knopf, 1982). See also note [22].

[19] The extent to which the sense and referent of concepts may be indefinitely expanded by military commands to subsume whoever or whatever is perceived as opposing objectives (1) and (2) is exemplified in the case of Argentina's military war against domestic 'terrorism' between 1976 and 1983. A twelve-member commission established by President Raoul Alfonsin and headed by writer Ernesto Saboto described its pattern in this way: 'Everything was possible. From people who supported a social revolution to sensitive adolescents who went to the shantytowns to help the poor. All were caught in the net: labor leaders who fought for a simple salary increase, teenagers who had been members of a student centre, journalists who were not addicts of dictatorship, psychologists and sociologists who belonged to suspicious professions, and

peaceful youths, nuns and priests who brought the teachings of Christ to the miserable barrios'; reported in *The Globe and Mail* 22 September 1984, p 9.

[20] For example, it is now a widely reported fact that *threat inflation* by successive administrations in the United States has taken the form of invented *missile gaps, bomber gaps, windows of vulnerability, test gaps*, and so on during a prolonged period in which this nation has, in fact, led throughout in the development of intercontinental bombers, submarine-launched missiles, multiple independently targeted warheads, long-range cruise missiles, and nuclear bomb deployment. See, for example, George Kennan, **The Nuclear Delusion** (New York: Pantheon, 1982), **Defended to Death** ed. Gwyn Prinz (Harmondsworth Middlesex: Penguin, 1983), and A Cockburn, **The Threat: Inside the Soviet Military Machine** (New York: Random House, 1983). Though such threat inflation is often thought to be perverse, it systematically serves functions (1) and (2) as a creator of effective demand for military commodities. (See also section VII).

[21] As Gwynne Dyer points out in his study **War** (Toronto: Stoddart, 1985) p 160: 'The vast majority of the estimated 21 million people killed in war since 1945 have died in a quite different and seemingly new kind of struggle: guerilla warfare, revolutionary war, counterinsurgency campaigns, and the like. Mostly they have been killed by their own fellow citizens'. This pattern of military terror against the citizens of one's own nation has been found in almost all cases to have been initiated by state militaries and, in cases of insurgent response, to remain preponderantly committed by *national defence* personnel. See Noam Chomsky and Edward S Herman, **The Political Economy of Human Rights: Third World Fascism and the Washington Connection** (Montreal: Black Rose Books, 1979), a detailed study which relies

mainly on Amnesty International and other non-partisan reports for its data. See also Chomsky's recent **Turning the Tide** (Montreal: Black Rose Books, 1986). A stark illustration of this pattern, currently euphemized as 'low intensity warfare' by geopolitical strategists, is provided by Ricardo Castro, a former company commander in the El Salvadorean national army: 'The thing is, El Salvador has got a long history of killing people who just don't agree with the official line. Also, the rich people — the leading citizens of the community — traditionally have a great deal of input. Whatever bothers them, if they think they've got someone they consider a bad influence, they just send a messenger to the local military commander. Normally, that person would be eliminated' (Reported in Tom Nairn's **Confessions of a Death-Squad Officer** in *The Progressive* (March 1986) pp 26-30). See also **The Military as an Agent of Social Change** ed. Claude Heller, *Proceedings of the 30th International Congress of Human Sciences* (Camino el Ajusco 20, Mexico: El Colegio de Mexico, 1984).

[22] Jerome B Wiesner, president emeritus at the Massachusetts Institute of Technology and science adviser to Presidents Kennedy and Johnson, analysed the situation in this way in a paper entitled **A Perilous Sense of Security** given to the National Academy of Science in Washington in April 1984: 'It is no longer a question of controlling a military-industrial complex but rather of how to keep the United States from becoming a totally military culture — a society in which military ideas and goals are accepted unthinkingly, and every domestic and international problem is subjugated to the demands of the military system'. The same stricture would seem to apply to the USSR, whose relative ratio of national expenditure spent on the military, percentage of citizens in armed-force uniform, military-command structure, and armed-

59

force personnel in other countries is greater still, though on different account (see notes [3] and [27]).

[23] Fragments LXXXI, LXXXII and LXXXIII, **Art and Thought of Heraclitus**, translation and commentary by Charles H Cahn (New York: Cambridge University Press, 1970) pp 204-15.

[24] Elizabeth Anscombe, **War and Murder** originally published in **Nuclear Weapons: A Catholic Response** ed. Walter Stein (New York: Merlin Press, 1961) pp 45-62.

[25] Here and elsewhere, we mean by terrorism: the support or action of killing or maiming people that is indifferent to the legal innocence of its victims. By this definition, the preponderance of terrorist activity in the world today can be seen to proceed from state-military establishments, whose declared objective is to prevent it.

[26] Thomas Nagel, **War and Massacre** in *Philosophy and Public Affairs* **1**, 22 (1972) pp 123-42.

[27] Laura Westra, **On War and Innocence**, *Dialogue* **XXV**, 4 (Winter 1986) pp 735-40.

[28] The difference here can be noted in the conceptualizations of national defence policy of the United States and the USSR. Princeton physicist and former consultant to the US Defense Department and the Arms Control and Disarmament Agency, Freeman Dyson, reports the difference as follows: 'The nuclear strategy of the United States was based for many years upon a concept which was definitively stated by Secretary of Defense McNamara in 1967 "...Offensive capability or what I will call the capability for assuring the destruction of the Soviet Union is far and away the most important requirement we have to meet ...". The counterpart to McNamara's statement of assured destruction is the statement made in 1971 by the Soviet minister of defence "...The Strategic Rocket Forces, which

constitute the basis of the military might of our armed forces, are designed to annihilate the means of the enemy's nuclear attack, large groupings of his armies and his military bases; to destroy his military industries; and to disorganize the political and military administration of the aggressor as well as his rear and transport" ' (Freeman Dyson, **Weapons and Hope** (New York: Harper and Row, 1984) pp 226, 231).

[29] Sun Tzu, **The Art of War** trans. and ed. Samuel B Griffith (Oxford University Press, 1977) p 39.

[30] See, for example, Chomsky and Herman, *ibid.* — note [21], William Gibson, **The Perfect War: Technowar in Vietnam** (New York: Atlantic Press, 1986), Reed Brody, **Contra Terror in Nicaragua** (Boston: South End Press, 1985), Edwardo Galeano, **Open Veins of Latin America** (New York: Monthly Review Press, 1975).

[31] G W F Hegel, **The Phenomenology of Spirit** trans. A V Miller and commentary by J N Findlay (Oxford: Clarendon Press, 1977) pp 111-9. **Introduction to the Philosophy of History** Hegel Selections, trans. J Sibree, ed. Jacob Lowenberg (New York: Scribner's and Sons, 1957) particularly pp 362-380, 410, 416, 434-436, 464-468; and Hegel's **Philosophy of Right** trans. T M Knox (Oxford: Clarendon Press, 1977) pp 111-9.

[32] Karl von Clausewitz, **On War** ed. Anatol Rapoport (Harmondsworth Middlesex: Penguin, 1982) pp 101, 103.

[33] Louis Fischer, **Gandhi** (New York: Mentor Books, 1960) p 72.

[34] Consider the war to the death against self-attachment that is allegorized as military war in the Hindu classic **The Bhagavad Gita**, or Buddha's counsel to his disciples in the **Dhammapada** prescribing an internal war against the enemy of the self in place of conquest of others: 'If a

man were to conquer in battle a thousand times a thousand men and another to conquer one, himself, he indeed is the greatest conqueror' (chapter VIII, verse 4). Overt condemnation of the military mode of war is seldom risked, but the first known advocate of weaponless war, Lao Tzu, says: 'Fine weapons are instruments of evil/ — Therefore those who possess Tao turn away from them/ — Even when he is victorious he does not regard it as praiseworthy/ For to praise victory is to delight in the slaughter of men/ — For a victory let us observe the occasion with funeral ceremonies' (**Tao-te Ching** trans. Wing Tsit Chan (Princeton University Press, 1978) chapter 31 p 155).

[35] 'The General Dynamics Corporation proposed to sell the [US] Air Force two 1-cent pins for $7,417 ... General Dynamics also proposed to charge the Air Force $302,106 for a maintenance stand on wheels, consisting of a heater and an oscilloscope', *United Press International*, 2 November 1983. 'No knowledgeable person could have faith in the Star Wars system. I don't think that even the people involved think that they can build this invisible shield' said David Parnas, then University of Victoria Lansdowne Professor of Computer Science, after resigning from a $1,000 a day consultancy on a 'key advisory panel to the Strategic Defence Initiatives Organization'; (*The Globe and Mail* 10 July 1985).

[36] Specific examples of the operation of principles i), ii), iii) and iv) may be found in Richard J Barnet, **The Economy of Death** (New York: Atheneum, 1967); George Thayer, **The War Business** (New York: Simon and Shuster, 1969); Seymour Melman, **Pentagon Capitalism** (New York: McGraw-Hill, 1970) and **The Permanent War Economy** (New York: Simon and Shuster, 1974); Anthony Sampson, **The Arms Bazaar: From Lebanon to Lockheed** (New York: Viking Press, 1977); **War, Business and the World Military-Industrial**

Complexes ed. Benjamin Franklin Cooling (Ft. Washington, N.Y.: Kennicat Publications, 1981); Charles Higham, **Trading with the Enemy** (New York: Dell, 1983).

[37] Marx and Engels, especially Engels, have much to say about military affairs in their writings, but nowhere criticize the military program as such, as distinguished from its alleged strategic misuses by various regimes and movements. Both remark frequently, rather, on the contributions of military organization to historical productive-force development, and on the importance of sound military reasoning in the determination of historical conflicts. Marx himself implied that proletarian revolution would probably, though not necessarily, be constrained to follow the military program, albeit generalized to 'the people in arms', in order to wrest state power from a capitalist class unwilling to relinquish its rule. (See, for example, **Capital** Volume I trans. Samuel Moore and Edward Aveling (Moscow: Progress Publishers, 1967) p 235; and **On Britain** (London: Laurence and Wishart, 1962) p 499). Most Marxists have followed in his general presupposition of the military paradigm of war, with little or no theoretical recognition of the systematic militarization of socialist organization which has occurred everywhere that revolutionary state ownership of the means of production has been achieved. That the armed overthrow of the bourgeois state has invariably ended in a civil order bearing the military birthmarks of centralized structures of absolute command, armed-force priorities, social regimentation, uniformed youth training, and so on, has more or less eluded Marxist theoretical attention. In consequence, the overall historical sequence of armed repression ⟶ armed revolution ⟶ military socialism ⟶ intensified military capitalism ⟶ universalizing militarism — has been lost on both Marxist and anti-Marxist analy-

sis. Each side of the ideological battle has been disposed to see only one half of the pattern. In this way, social theory in general has remained incognizant of the underlying structure of occurrence which serves, in turn, the narrow interests of both capitalist and Party ruling classes through their militarized opposition. (Works which provide useful supporting evidence for comprehension of this pattern are David Holloway, **The Soviet Union and the Arms Race** (New Haven: Yale University Press, 1983) and Alva Myrdal, **The Game of Disarmament: How the United States and Russia Run the Arms Race** (New York: Pantheon, 1976).

[38] Theodor White, **Weinberger on the Ramparts** *New York Times Magazine* 6 February 1983, p 19. This proportionality principle is to be distinguished from the quite different idea of due proportionality between harm inflicted on the enemy in a war and the end sought by it, a traditional norm of *just war* that is criticized for its excessive latitude by Donald Wells in his landmark article **The 'Just War' Justifies too Much** *The Journal of Philosophy* LXVI, 23 (1969).

[39] No argument in all military-strategic literature, despite its meticulous detail, proves (i), (ii) or (iii) for any modern national defence establishment. 'Defence' buildup usually follows a less scientific pattern of justification, illuminatingly summarized by Lord Solly Zuckerman, former chief scientific adviser to the British government: 'First came the weapons; then they had to be fitted into a presumed tactical doctrine, which in turn had to be fitted into an illusory strategy, usually elaborated by armchair warriors' (**Nuclear Fantasies** *New York Review of Books* **XXXI**, 10 (June 1984) p 8).

[40] A simple preliminary test for claims of deterrence as a rationale for military buildups is to ask whether the putative deterrent is a move up to, or beyond, the threat

capacity of the identified adversary. Most strategic analysis of deterrence does not consider this asymmetry test in discussion of international conflict, but rather assumes a priori its own side as always the threatened party — even when its perceived adversary has significantly less capacity of violence with which to impose its will. In this way, the language of deterrence can become a mask for the quest of dominion. It is interesting to note in this connection that the Strategic Defense Initiative through the United States Department of Defense, which has been justified as a response to USSR missile power, occurs in a context where a study by the same Department of Defense reports that 'in the 13 technologies required for advanced ABM [anti-ballistic missile] development, the US is ahead in 12 and the two sides are on the same level on the thirteenth, directed energy devices ...'; John Polanyi in his presentation to the External Affairs Review Committee of the Joint Parliament of Canada, Toronto, July 1985. US Rear Admiral Eugene Carroll (ret.) has analysed the general situation here as follows: 'Even if the Soviet Union agreed completely with all US terms today, not one of the 17,000 new weapons that we plan to build [intercontinental MX missile, Pershing II missile, Trident II missile, Cruise missile and battlefield tactical missile] would be prohibited! It is clear that the Administration's proposals are not intended to reduce nuclear weapons. They are in fact a facade behind which we are going to proceed with the modernization and expansion of US nuclear capabilities ...' (**The Prevention of Nuclear War** ed. Thomas L Perry Jr. (Altona, Manitoba: Friesen, 1983) p 224). The strategic reason for this nuclear build-up has been analysed by Randall Forsberg and colleagues in these general terms: 'The nuclear arms race has nothing to do with defense, little to do with deterrence and much to do with a monopoly of US intervention in other countries while blocking Soviet intervention' (**The Deadly Connection:**

Nuclear War and US Intervention *Proceedings of the American Friends Conference, Massachusetts Institute of Technology, December 1982* p 3). This identified rationale has been conceptualized and endorsed as *extended deterrence* by a strategic policy adviser of the Reagan administration itself, Robert W Tucker, in his **The Purposes of American Power: An Essay in National Security** (New York: Praeger, 1981) pp 118-87.

[41] A typical example of the imperialization of the military model and its conceptual framework is to be found in an article entitled **Our Immune System: The Wars Within** *The National Geographic* **169**, 6 (June 1986) pp 702-37. Here, body cells which perforate membranes of foreign cells are portrayed as 'killer T-cells' with guns mounted on them; the production of anti-bodies by 'B-cells' is conceptualized as a 'biologic arms factory'; the anti-bodies themselves, whose action is to bind onto, engulf, and absorb dysfunctional cells, are referred to as 'potent chemical weapons'; the organism's lymph nodes are re-christened 'munitions factories', and artificially produced monoclonal anti-bodies are conceptualized as 'production lines for guided missiles'.

[42] It might be objected that public opinion may sway a democratic leadership, but not a genuinely tyrannical one which can only be broken by the force of military defeat. It is interesting to note in this connection that in an interview published by the *London Observer Service* in December 1979 between the distinguished Reich historian, Alan Bullock, and Hitler's armaments minister and confidante, Albert Speer, Speer reveals that the turning-point in Hitler's 'decline' occurred when his 'ability to make daring decisions was lost': a failure of internal power that Speer attributes to the 'shattering effect' upon Hitler and his close entourage of unattended military shows which caused them to believe that 'this war was not popular

with the Germans'.

[43] Consider, for example, the stirring invocation of Emmanuel Levinas in his **Totality and Infinity: An Essay on Exteriority** trans. Alphonso Lingis (Pittsburgh, Pa.: Duquesne University Press, 1969) p 22: 'Morality will oppose politics in history and will have gone beyond the functions of prudence or the canons of the beautiful to proclaim itself unconditional and universal when the eschatology of messianic peace will have come to superimpose itself on the ontology of war'.

Author Index

CONFIDENTIAL

From the desk of Barbara

Stony Man Farm

In this file you'll find the necessary information to bring you up to speed on Stony Man Farm's latest mission. International terrorist Kapoch Egorov continues to elude the world's grasp. It is now up to us to find him and bring him to justice before he unleashes his deadly weapon across the globe. Our three top agents—our Femmes Fatale—are already on the case.

First you'll observe Bethany Riggs in South Africa. Her mission, code name "Shaken and Stirred," is to escort a key witness to safety. But be alert. We've reason to believe that British Intelligence has sent their own agent, Jason Chandler, to capture the witness for their own purposes. If he and Bethany cross paths, the results could be explosive.

Next you'll find agent Kylee Swain operating under the call sign "The Get-Away Girl." Her career as a movie stuntwoman has always been the perfect cover to place her anywhere—except near ex-CIA agent Mick Stone.

Finally, for an assignment we've dubbed "End Game," we've enlisted Victoria Grayson, the brilliant computer hacker who can outsmart any criminal. Her only known weakness: DEA Agent Bishop Tyler.

These three women are beautiful, intelligent...and deadly. And Egorov will stop at nothing to defeat them. There's no way to predict which remote regions of the world this mission will take us to, or what lengths we'll be forced to go to in order to complete it. But rest assured, no matter what it costs, these women will *always* get their man.

B. Price

DORANNA DURGIN

obtained a degree in wildlife illustration and environmental education, then spent a number of years deep in the Appalachian Mountains, riding the trails and writing science fiction and fantasy books. This award-winning author eventually moved to the Northern Arizona Mountains, where she still rides and writes, focusing on classical dressage with her Lipizzan. There's a mountain looming outside her office window, a pack of dogs running around the house and a laptop sitting on her desk—and that's just the way she likes it. You can contact her at dmd@doranna.net or P.O. Box 31123, Flagstaff, AZ 86003-1123 (SASE please) or visit http://www.doranna.net/.

MEREDITH FLETCHER

doesn't really call any place home. She blames her wanderlust on her navy father, who moved the family several times around the United States and other countries. The one constant she had was her books. The battered trunk of favorite novels followed her around the world when she was growing up and shared dorm space with her in college. These days, the trunk is stored, but sometimes comes with Meredith to visit A-frame houses high in the Colorado mountains, cottages in Maine, where she likes to visit lighthouses and work with fishing crews, and rental flats where she takes moments of "early retirement" for months at a stretch. Meredith has a number of books planned involving women much like Kylee Swain in "The Get-Away Girl." Interested readers can reach her at MFletcher1216@aol.com.

VIRGINIA KANTRA

credits her enthusiasm for strong heroes and courageous heroines to a childhood spend devouring fairy tales. A three-time Romance Writers of America RITA® Award finalist, she has won numerous writing awards, including the Golden Heart, Maggie Award, Holt Medallion and *Romantic Times* W.I.S.H. Hero Award. She loves to hear from readers. You can reach her at VirginiaKantra@aol.com or c/o Silhouette Books, 233 Broadway, Suite 1001, New York, NY 10279.

DORANNA DURGIN
VIRGINIA KANTRA
MEREDITH FLETCHER

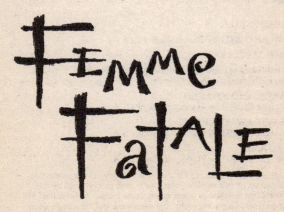

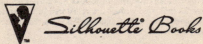

Silhouette Books

Published by Silhouette Books

America's Publisher of Contemporary Romance

Special thanks and acknowledgment are given to
Doranna Durgin, Meredith Fletcher and Virginia Kantra
for their contributions to the FEMME FATALE collection.

SILHOUETTE BOOKS

FEMME FATALE

Copyright © 2003 by Harlequin Books S.A.

ISBN 0-373-21850-8

The publisher acknowledges the copyright holders
of the individual works as follows:

SHAKEN AND STIRRED
Copyright © 2003 by Harlequin Books S.A.

THE GET-AWAY GIRL
Copyright © 2003 by Harlequin Books S.A.

END GAME
Copyright © 2003 by Harlequin Books S.A.

This edition published by arrangement with Harlequin Books S.A.

Visit Silhouette at www.eHarlequin.com

Printed in U.S.A.

CONTENTS

SHAKEN AND STIRRED
Doranna Durgin

* * *

This is for Pat and Kathy, and in memory of Carol—
for passing along the love and skills of this genre.

Dear Reader,

Greetings from the Northern High Country in Arizona. This is one of those great days to put the final touches on a project—there's snow on the San Francisco Peaks, intensely blue sky all around and the crisp air of a high-altitude, early-winter day. But much as I love it here, I also had a great time with Beth and Jason exploring South Africa. Not only did I learn about a fascinating locale, but Beth and Jason were a hoot.

In planning a story, one creates characters with a certain intent, but it's like casting actors—until you put them together and let them loose, you never quite know how the chemistry will turn out. These two grabbed the story and went romping off, leaving me writing as fast as I could just to keep up. Who knows what they would have gotten up to if I'd taken a day off!

The other unique part of this project was the chance to write as part of a continuing story arc—with two writers I very much admire, in a genre I've long enjoyed and, as a science fiction and fantasy writer, hoped to join. Variety—and love!—is the spice of life. The experience has been a pleasure, and I'm grateful to have been invited.

I hope you enjoy Beth and Jason's exploration of how two very different people can mesh as partners, as well as the stories that follow—and ultimately, the larger story arc that encompasses them all.

Doranna

Chapter 1

S*omehow it's* always *a warehouse.* Bethany Riggs ran
through the mental checklist of the weapons at her dis-
posal, checked again that her Sig-Sauer P226 was an easy
reach in the square cargo pocket of her deceptively casual
squall parka, and eased out into the predawn gloom surrounding the entire dock area. *Not always a warehouse in
Cape Town, South Africa...but a warehouse nonetheless.*

Tonight...she'd bring a spy in from the cold.

Making a mild face at the drama of the thought, Beth
hunched her shoulders into her medium-weight parka,
chilled by hours of lurking in the fifty-degree night. She'd
arrived early to scope out the site after Lyeta Denisov
made contact late the evening before, leaving Beth no
opportunity to examine the southern arm of the Table Bay
docks in the daylight. A long jetty filled with warehouses,
cargo docks and the mixed atmosphere of diesel fuel and
sea foam, it was the perfect location for a late-night meet.

If only she'd had the chance to vet it more thoroughly.

Then again, neither had anyone else, which was no doubt Lyeta's intent. There were plenty of people who wanted Lyeta Denisov…wanted her back, wanted her stopped…wanted her dead.

But Beth was the one who would get her—albeit on Lyeta's terms. The Russian woman, betrayed by her lover and hunting both safety and revenge, offered information on the man's internationally notorious, terrorist-friendly spy organization in return for protection. Beth's handler from Stony Man Farm was only too glad to give it to her. Stony Man, MI6, the CIA…they all wanted spymaster Kapoch Egorov. But after a botched rendezvous with the CIA, Lyeta had turned to Stony Man. As black as black ops got.

Yeah, I'd be careful, too. Beth crouched briefly at the end of the long series of warehouses and cargo cranes, comfortable in the black leg warmers she'd pulled up over low-riding jeans. Her flexible high-top dance sneaks weren't the warmest footwear, but left her confident she could move exactly when and how she wanted. Soon enough Lyeta Denisov would arrive, just before the docks began the slow warm-up steps that led to the daily rhythms of activity. For now, only one ship floated beside the long, straight dock; the cargo containers were neatly stacked inside the warehouses, leaving the dock itself empty and desolate. The heavy scent of the nighttime sea lay over the area, and the constant rhythm of the waves lapped against Beth's ears.

One might even call it peaceful.

Beth didn't. The underlying tension of the night kept her alert and ultra-aware of the open nature of this area, and of its vulnerability. Too many exit scenarios called for diving into the cold, cold water of Table Bay; too many possibilities led to entrapment at the end of the jetty.

The looming skeletons of the stationary cargo cranes offered so much visual clutter in their foreshortened lineup that she found it nearly impossible to decipher the structure of one from another. Still, she pulled a Phantom night vision scope from one of the parka's roomy pockets, sweeping its monocular view across the docks, across the ship deck, up and down the line of cranes. The man she'd previously spotted on the ship hadn't moved. He remained slumped over the far rail, the thick glowing dot of his cigar marking his position. There was no one else in evidence.

Which didn't mean they weren't here. Lurking, as she was. Hidden.

She glanced down at her sturdy field watch. Not much longer. Then she'd have to come out from hiding and so would Lyeta Denisov. They'd meet, assess each other... and then Lyeta would come with Beth.

Or she wouldn't.

Well, she wouldn't actually have a choice, not once things progressed that far. Barbara Price of Stony Man Farm had made it quite clear that Stony Man wanted this woman. *Wanted.* And without a safe haven, Lyeta Denisov's days were numbered.

Beth swept the area again, glanced at her watch, and tucked the Phantom scope away. She stood, shook out her legs, and bounced up and down in place a few times. No dancer went out onto the stage without warming up, and this performance would be pure improv. Maybe a casual stroll, maybe some nice modern aerobic work...

She started off with the casual stroll, breaking cover from the warehouse to walk the long dock without apparent concern. Her hands, tucked into her pockets for warmth, curled around the Sig's custom Nill-Grips on her left and a collapsible baton on her right.

Since 1652 this port had earned its nickname for the warm welcome and supplies it offered weary travelers. *Tavern of the Seas.* Time to see just how warm a welcome Lyeta Denisov would receive.

Or if she'd show up at all.

Beth walked the length of the dock, hesitated at the far end to check the area with her nightscope—cigar man had finished his smoke and gone below, but she saw evidence of no one else. Except...except there was a rounded shadow by the warehouse, and it caught Beth's eye. Closer examination revealed nothing specific, but she'd learned long ago to heed her eye. The skin up the back of her legs tightened, all the way up the back of her thighs and higher.

Here we go.

She walked back out on the dock, dawdling conveniently near the shadow she'd seen.

The shadow did not disappoint her. Hard soles scuffed the pavement, just enough of a clue so Beth whirled to face the shadow spot, abandoning subtleties.

"Not a good place for a walk," said the man who emerged from those shadows, a burly fellow with all the bulky muscle of a dock laborer readily evident under his thin jacket. He spoke with the thickest of South African accents, words clipped and difficult—although Beth had no difficulty following his meaning, no difficulty at all. "I was getting cold, till I saw you."

"Go away," she said shortly. "I'm busy."

"American," he said, not sounding surprised so much as pleased. "I've never had an American."

"Yeah, yeah." She made a shooing motion. "Busy, I said. Go away."

"Americans are nice," he said, moving closer. He had a billed cap pulled down over lank hair, enough stubble to count up a week or so, and the definite odor of old beer. "But so ignorant of other places, other cultures. They make stupid mistakes all the time."

Annoyed, Beth said, "Possibly I'm stupid, but I'm *not* nice." A glance at her watch inspired an inward curse at the oaf's timing. She walked away, brisker now, wanting to put distance between them before things escalated into an exchange that might distract her.

He made no attempt at stealth; two long strides and he was upon her, his hand—the one she'd been waiting for—landing heavily on her shoulder and clenching the fabric of her parka. He spun her back around, but the anticipation on his face turned to surprise as she offered no resistance, moving easily under his hand—adding her own spin to his pull so she came around quicker than he'd ever considered. She saw that, too, on his face—just before she gave the baton an expert flick to extend it, whipping it across the big muscle of his thigh.

He gave a supremely startled *"Uh!"* bending over the pain to come face-to-face with the barrel of her Sig. She tucked the muzzle under his chin and lifted his face to look up at her. "His name is Wyatt," Beth cooed, lifting the muzzle just enough to let the end sight dig into stubbled skin. "Steadier than any boyfriend I ever had, but prone to premature...ejaculation, if you get my drift. Now...did I hear you say something about going away? Perhaps about walking in the opposite direction, really fast? Because as I think I've already mentioned...I'm busy."

Through clenched teeth he said, "Wouldn't... want...to...keep...you."

"Funny, that's what most of my men say," Beth told him, stepping back just far enough to indicate she would give him the chance to leave.

He took it. Hobbling, cursing—''You befok, stuk-kie!''—he headed up the dock and went beyond, toward the dawn-quiet Victoria and Albert Waterfront. Where American tourists *belonged*.

Unfortunate for him that Beth was far from a tourist. She spared him not a second thought, replacing Wyatt in her pocket and collapsing the baton against her hand.

''Pig.'' The words came from a deeper darkness beside the building, laced with disdain and a cultured Russian accent. ''You should have hurt him.''

''I did,'' Beth said mildly. *Now here's a woman packing a grudge.* ''He deserved more, but he wasn't worth jeopardizing my contact with…you.''

''Yes. With me.'' Lyeta stepped away from the stack of pallets leaning up against the building. The scant moonlight painted her hair dark and her eyes impenetrable, but there was no mistaking her lean elegance, or the costly cut of the long, muted coat she wore. ''You have come with proof that you are who I expect? You are Flash?''

''Sure,'' Beth said. Flash for *Flashdance.* Too cute, but all hers. ''If I'd been anyone else, I'd have screwed up just then. I didn't. Let's go.''

''So simple.'' Lyeta said the words with amusement. ''You don't even ask for the information I promised?''

''I say we get away from these docks before we run into any more of its friendly inhabitants. We can be a nice cozy hotel room before the dockworkers show up. You don't come up with the goods there, I can still walk away and leave you to everyone else.''

''You could have someone waiting at that cozy hotel room.''

''You choose it, then. Though you're going to have to trust me at some point—or else stay behind.'' Not that

Beth would let it happen. But for now, Lyeta could think as much.

Lyeta tipped her head back to eye Beth, her shoulder-length hair swinging slightly with the movement but not as freely as it might have. Dirty, Beth thought. Wherever Lyeta had spent the night, it hadn't been a cozy hotel room. At least, not one with running water. Then the woman gave a sudden sigh. "It does not do to stand out in the open."

"Your choice," Beth reminded her, keeping the woman in her peripheral vision as she gave the dock an-other once-over. Mr. Friendly could come back. He could even bring Mr. Friendly II, or a whole gang of Mr. Friend-lies.

"I did not know when I chose this place…" Lyeta hesitated. "There have been attempts," she said. "Your CIA, I am certain—the debacle at my attempted meet with them was no coincidence. They are not secure."

"Not *my* CIA," Beth said with a little snort. "Come on, then. Plenty of hotels right here on the waterfront. We'll give each other narrow-eyed looks for a while, you can hand over your little token of good faith, and we'll call for room service." Not exactly standard room ser-vice…Lyeta might need food, but she wouldn't get it until she was packed up in a nice anonymous car headed for the airport and Stony Man's waiting jet.

"My *little token of good faith*," Lyeta said, offended. "Only the innermost workings of Egorov's organization, laid out for your pleasure."

More than offended. There was pain behind that af-fected haughtiness.

"It's true," Beth said, recalling her briefing. That they were lovers…and that Egorov, dying or not, had begun jockeying his fortune around, making plans to shut Lyeta out. "You *do* love him."

"He betrayed me." Lyeta's voice turned chipped-ice cold. She tightened the belt on her already sleek coat and stepped out beside Beth, setting a stiff pace.

"So you betray him," Beth said. "Natch. That's the way it works, isn't it?"

"I buy my own safety, first and foremost." Lyeta's boot heels clipped against the pavement, masking Beth's nearly silent progress. Then her pace faltered, and a softer, saddened tone made a brief appearance in her voice. "It is of no matter. He dies soon anyway. Nothing I do here today will truly reach him."

For Kapoch Egorov was dying. Lyeta's information would give Stony Man the ability to strike his organization during its most vulnerable time...the leadership transition after Egorov's death.

"He'll know you did it," Beth pointed out as they approached the last of the cranes. "That would sure as hell annoy me, if I were in his shoes. It would *reach* me."

Lyeta stopped, whirling to face her with a cold ferocity that spoke of her formidable nature...and told Beth just exactly how this woman had survived and flourished within Egorov's cutthroat organization. She reached inside her camel-hair coat and only the coolly aristocratic arch of her fine brow kept Beth's finger from tightening on the trigger of the gun that, as quickly as that, filled her hand. Still within its pocket, but Lyeta had no doubt of its presence, and Beth made no pretense of hiding it.

They locked gazes for a long moment, and then Lyeta brought out a minidisc, dangling it between her first and second fingers in a graceful gesture. Beth took it without removing her gaze from Lyeta's, her own fingers brushing against gloves of the finest, supple kid leather. Lyeta said,

"There. That is the information I have for you. In exchange for this early gift, you will not burden me with your opinions."

Beth shrugged, opening her parka just enough to tuck the mini CD into the flat zippered pouch velcroed inside her jeans behind her hip. Snug fit. "Okay," she said. "But let's not dawdle, huh? Did you know that an average four-foot, ten-second wave puts out more energy than 35,000 horsepower per mile of coast? And these waves are *cold*, besides. I don't want to have to find out just exactly how cold and energetic." *In other words, we've been out in the open long enough already—*

Too long.

The crack of the rifle hit Beth's ears the same moment Lyeta jerked backward, her expression stunned. Even as Lyeta crumpled, Beth grabbed her by the shoulder of her expensive coat and yanked her toward cover, scrambling to get them both behind the massive steel leg of the crane.

"Told you," Lyeta gasped in a breathy whisper. "CIA—"

"Why would *they* kill you?" Beth said fiercely, yanking Lyeta's coat open to assess the damage. "They might *want* you, yes, but kill you?" Seeing the dark stain across Lyeta's chest, she didn't bother reaching for her miniflashlight. Dawn's faintest light told her everything she needed to know, and she patted the coat back into place with resignation. Damn it, this woman was her charge, in *her* hands. She looked up along the line of cranes. Perfect sniper nest even with the scrutiny she'd given it, and the very reason Beth wouldn't have chosen this location…but Beth had not been consulted about location.

Lyeta touched her chest, lifting her fingers to see the stain on her glove. "Not the CIA…someone within it. On

Egorov's payroll. I'm certain of it. He knows I have the key…."

Beth kept one hand on the dying woman and swept her nightscope across the docks, searching for movement. She spotted the sniper up in the middle crane, the one next to them, and then ducked more completely behind the steel pillar as she recognized the characteristic, entirely familiar motion of a male silhouette bringing a rifle to shoulder. An instant later, a bullet pinged sharply off steel, a foot higher than her head.

He's not very good. His shooting habits told her so; that Lyeta still breathed told her so. He hadn't kept his stance or his target; he hadn't fully reacquired before shooting again. But he had them pinned all the same.

Calculating escape, calculating how much longer Lyeta might live and already patting the woman down for anything that Stony Man might find valuable, Beth nonetheless gave Lyeta a sharp look as the woman drew a painful breath. Already Lyeta's eyes were losing focus; she looked at her bloody fingertips with a baffled expression…a woman who had escaped death for so long and now couldn't quite understand what was happening. "I have it," Lyeta told Beth. "The key to his entire computer system. Not just to get in…the master key. Scherba's key. *I have it.* I hid it. You…you get it. Take it."

"Where is it?" Beth said, digging a small pistol from Lyeta's coat pocket, and taking the neat wad of cash she found in a pouch tucked inside the woman's short tailored vest. A computer keycard…it would be flat, small, perhaps half the size of a playing card, albeit thicker. If Lyeta had it hidden against a thigh or along her bra strap, there'd be no quick way to get it. Beth pulled out her knife, reluctantly prepared to cut through Lyeta's clothing. Reluctant…but ruthless. Doing what it took. She gave the neighboring crane a quick glance, discovering there was now enough gloomy light to see it without the scope. *Then he can see me*... "Lyeta, I don't have time—where is it?"

"*He* did this." Lyeta's breath came shallow and fast. She didn't seem to notice Beth frisking her, and her hand sank slowly down to rest on her stomach in spite of her efforts to hold those bloody fingers up where she could see them. "Make sure he pays *before* he dies, you understand? Make sure he knows this came from me...."

"Done, *done*," Beth said, unable to hide her impatience. An arriving vehicle announced itself with the unhappy chug of its engine and the quick slam of doors. Dockworkers? Or more trouble? "But unless you tell me where it *is*—"

"The Blue Crane," Lyeta said, sounding almost dreamy. Her chest gave a strange jerk, her body unable to continue but not quite ready to give up. Her eyes rolled back; her head tilted.

Oh, no, not yet— Beth grabbed Lyeta's bloody shirt and pulled her away from the steel pillar against which she leaned. "*Where?*"

"Blue...table. Bottom. Tell him...from me." And Lyeta's head lolled. The blood welling on her white shirt and deep blue vest, fully visible under the lightening sky, seeped away without being replaced.

Beth made a noise of disgusted frustration and eased the dead woman to the ground. "Great timing, just great. You'll have to excuse me if I check for myself, just in case those last words of wisdom refer to your favorite childhood playground." But her hands were gentler and more respectful than her words as she ran her hands over Lyeta's long legs and womanly body, checking pockets, checking places where women over the centuries had learned to hide valuables. Finally Beth sat back on her heels in frustration, closing the woman's coat over her bloodied body.

The new arrivals were nowhere to be seen; nor was the sniper. Not a persistent sort...probably, as Lyeta said, Egorov's man playing more than one role and with much to lose. Too much, with the dock coming to life around them.

She could say the same for herself. The still isolation of the night had already lost itself to puttering boat motors and an increased road noise; soon the waterfront would be alive with tourists, and this dock thick with workers...and police. Not to mention the lurking CIA, MI6, and whoever else had come out to play.

Beth jammed the few items she'd gleaned from Lyeta into one of her many parka pockets, wiped her bloodstained hands against the dew on the dock pavement, and got to her feet in one swift motion meant to turn into a brisk escape.

But she turned away from Lyeta and froze.

Leaning against the steel pylon closest to the warehouses, a man regarded her with deceptively casual intent. One hand hung loosely by his side; the other disappeared into his open jacket at belt level. Not reassuring. "Find what you were looking for?" he asked, his words shaped by a clipped British accent.

"No," Beth told him, keeping all thoughts of the minidisc from reaching her face. For this sardonic creature was not of the Cape Town docks. She knew MI6 when she saw it, from the green oilcloth jacket encasing broad shoulders to the black jump boots that betrayed his readiness to move at the slightest provocation. She gave him a quick assessment—just over six feet, balanced in build and, she was willing to bet, hard tuned under that dark olive oilcloth. It was his haircut that gave away his nature, too short to be casual, just shy of being high and tight. And his eyes—gray and hard. Add in that educated accent...the casual observer wouldn't look twice, but Beth's expert examination easily classified him: *Stuffy MI6*. The soldier type, not the deep cover spy.

Too bad he was so easy to look at. Damned waste.

"Shame you killed her for nothing," he said, nodding at Lyeta's body.

Beth didn't turn back. She knew what it looked like. "Not that it matters," she said, easing her hand toward her pocket, "but I didn't."

"No, of course not." But his gaze went glacier cold, along with those clipped British words. "My hand's already on my gun, in case you're wondering."

"It crossed my mind." She eased her hand away from the pocket, reconsidering more subtle measures. She'd have to let him get close. Not necessarily a hardship. A pleasure yacht glided across the mouth of the bay in her peripheral vision, its deep engines thrumming beneath the sound of the smaller boats at the waterfront. "I don't suppose *walk away* is in your little rule book of options."

The corner of his mouth twitched...annoyance, not amusement. "Not the last time I looked. And I wanted this woman *alive*. We're going to have to talk about that."

Ah, great. Hotel room interrogation, quick and dirty...there *were* no rules for such things. It didn't matter that they might be on the same side—they'd question her until they were sure and then while they were at it they'd wrest all they could from her. Not officially, of course. Officially she would remain the suspected sniper. Beth contemplated the edge of the dock behind her, and the drop to the water below. Maybe it wasn't that cold after all.

"I can destroy your knee before you reach the water," he said. "Although unless I free my gun up, it might take a couple of shots to find target."

She glared at him in extreme annoyance.

To her surprise, it made him grin. "There," he said. "At least you're not simpering your way out of it all. Can't bloody stand that." He removed one hand from his jacket pocket. A pair of handcuffs dangled from his index finger. "Put these on."

High-security cuffs with a specialized lock cylinder. Pick-proof. Great. She gave him another glare, and the corner of his mouth twitched again. Definitely amusement this time. He gave the cuffs a little jiggle. "It's the easy way," he said, taking no heed of the dock coming to life around them. "It's going to happen regardless."

That's what you think.

He might hesitate to fire his weapon with so many witnesses…he might hesitate to hurt her and take the chance she couldn't respond under questioning. *Might.*

It was worth the gamble. She had the mini CD tucked away in her jeans; she had to get it to Barbara Price, not lose it to this stiff-necked MI6 agent. They were allies, yes—assuming she'd guessed right about his affiliation— but each agency handled things its own way. Beth put her trust in Stony Man.

She gave him defiant resignation and held out a hand; he tossed her the cuffs. She snatched them out of the air and whipped them right back at him, directly at his face. Then she whipped herself around, lunging for the side of the dock and thinking *watercoldcoldcold—*

Oof!

She slammed to the pavement, losing her breath with a grunt. Solid, all right. Hard, heavy muscle. She let herself go limp—let him feel her do it. Waited for that instant of reaction, his slight recoil. It gave her just enough room to throw her elbow out to the side and jam it back into his ribs. Instantly, he captured the arm again, seeking to pull it behind her back and lever it up. *Damn, he's actually good.* But where he had strength and weight, Beth had lithe agility…not to mention a loose parka. She drew herself together underneath him, squirming within the parka, the slick skintight material of her leotard slipping easily against the parka lining. She pulled her energy into a tight ball and then exploded beneath him.

If she'd been a comic superhero, her MI6 opponent would have tumbled away—but she was just a spy on dark ops, so all she did was gain herself a little maneuvering space. An opportunity.

She took it.

She scrambled out from beneath him, darting for the safety of the warehouse—the people, the machinery roaring to life, the maze of stacked shipping containers—and jerked to a stop as he snatched the back of her parka. In an instant she ripped the zipper open, slipping free to the sound of his curse. Her surge of triumph lasted only a moment. As she reached the crane pylon he slammed into her again, pinning her against the cold steel. "Good God," she gasped, panting heavily; his chest moved against her back as he, too, sucked in air. "Is that the only move you know? Slam and squash?"

His breath gusted against her ear in what could only be a laugh; it ignited her temper. Trapped against the pylon, her arms caught beneath her chest, she still wasn't nearly as incapacitated as he thought. Her fingers fumbled with the scoop edge of her leotard, pulling it down, scraping at the skin-toned patch there. *Careful.* She peeled off the protective adhesive layer against her skin and, in spite of his hold on her, flipped around in his grip to face him.

"Aren't you wiggly," he observed. All confidence, no longer worried about restraining her. He thought he had her. He even had reason for that confidence—as she'd turned, he'd skillfully jammed his knees inside of her own. There'd be no sneaky attempts at kneeing his groin.

It was an excruciatingly vulnerable position, one that triggered instinctive fear and awareness.

In spite of Beth's anger—her annoyance at this man's interference, her annoyance at the sniper, her annoyance at Lyeta herself simply for dying in the first place—something of that vulnerability must have shown on her face. This close to his gray eyes, she could see them widen, darkening with the sudden awareness that their scuffle had grown unexpectedly intimate. Hip to hip, thigh to thigh, nothing between their upper bodies but her thin black leotard and the formfitting waffle-weave shirt he wore under his open jacket.

Mistake, mister. Yours. She lowered her eyes; he pressed so close that her lashes grazed his chin. "I'm not the only thing that's wiggly," she said, and then glanced up in time to see hunger lurking in his eyes.

But he didn't do as she expected. He didn't shutter those feelings, didn't move back from her. Pressed up against her, he dipped his head to murmur into her ear. "That happens."

Second mistake. Her hand eased up into the space between them, almost close enough to strike. Mr. MI6 had warmth burning beneath that cold gaze. His eyes were on her face, on her lips, and if he heard a dockworker's shout of question, he ignored it. His face, clean shaven—*even at this time of day?*—brushed against hers, the clean lines of it made harder by his tight haircut. And suddenly, beyond all expectation, she felt her own hunger stir, a warm pooling in her chest and sinking downward. *Not the plan...* But she let him see it, nothing so obvious as moving against him, just her lips parting as though they might receive his, close enough to feel his breath wash over them, close enough...to...touch.

She snaked her hand up to slap him lightly on the neck, placing the patch directly over his carotid artery. He had just enough time to give her a puzzled look...and as it changed to understanding, not quite enough time to say the unpleasant word that formed on his lips. "Fuuhh—" he managed, and crumpled to the ground not far from Lyeta, doped with the latest version of a knockout drop.

"You wish," she informed him, much more primly than her body felt. She stepped over him, assessing the dock on the way, instantly spotting all the heads turned their way. Damn, they'd drawn attention. How could they *not?* And as soon as someone saw the pool of blood around Lyeta, they'd get attention, all right. She hoped Mr. MI6 was up to it. She bent to snag her parka on the way by and nearly stumbled when it didn't come with her. "Oh, just *let go*," she said under her breath, but the parka was caught beneath him and even as she knelt to roll him over, someone by the warehouse shouted, pointing at her. "Oh, *fuuhh*," she said, in complete accord with the drugged agent. She managed to move him aside with a hard shove on his nice tight ass, putting her parka's gun pocket within reach. She grabbed for it. The pocket ripped but the gun was hers again, and in the background the shouting had turned to running feet. Beth didn't even look at them as she sprinted away, leaving Lyeta, Mr. Drugged MI6, and her very favorite parka on the pavement beside the crane.

But she had Lyeta's mini CD, containing enough information to bare Egorov's organization. She had her clues, so cryptic as to be worthy of a Saturday morning cartoon show. *Blue Crane. Table. Bottom.* She had Lyeta's death, already pinned on her by Mr. MI6 in spite of the poor performance of the sniper.

And she had her work cut out for her.

Chapter 2

Jason Chandler opened his eyes to the blurry sight of men leaning over him, a circle enclosing him with curiosity and suspicion. His head pounded, his mouth tasted altogether wrong, and his stomach—

With a spastic lurch of motion, he rolled over just in time to lose his midnight snack in the pool of congealing blood beside him. The men leaped back out of range but did not abandon him entirely. Even as his stomach considered giving another heave, one of them said, "The police are on their way, fella."

Fine. Good. Whatever. Jason spat, scrubbed his mouth against his rough sleeve, and stumbled across a vague memory of the moments before he'd passed out.

Passed out? Not bloody likely.

He got an unsteady foot beneath him, pushed up off the ground to stand swaying within the still suspicious—and now wary—group of dockworkers. There was something on his neck...? He scrabbled fingers across his neck and found it, a small patch stuck right where it would do the most good. He peeled it off and flicked it to the ground, staggering away from Lyeta Denisov's body and ignoring the protests of the self-appointed posse around him. She'd be thoroughly searched—and so would the scene—but he was not the man to do it. MI6 might sneak an operative in, or they might pay off a local for information. He himself was too dirtied by this scene to play any of those roles.

But not too dazed to forget his opponent's parka. He scooped it up with a lurch and moved off.

The small group of men moved with him, unwilling to let him go and unwilling to take him on, although they all seemed to realize they'd made a mistake by retreating at his illness. Now he had room to move, and time to grab the gun exposed by his rucked-up jacket.

One of them got bold anyway, stepping directly in front of him. Jason barely had the wherewithal to stop in time, a fact that only further emboldened the man. He had reason to be confident—he was the biggest of them, brawnier than Jason himself and marked with the scars of a dozen bar brawls.

Jason dragged his hands down his face and considered the Browning Hi-Power. Not yet. Especially not with the nasal Cape Town police sirens battering through the sounds of the early-morning waterfront. Damn it, how had he let that woman reach Lyeta before he did, killing her only moments before Jason could snag her? How had he let his subsequent confrontation with her drag on so long? And most of all, how had he let her blindside him?

He knew the answer to that last, and he didn't like it.

Any moment now the sun would break over the mountains circling behind Cape Town, and he had the unpleasant feeling that the instant its sharp rays hit his eyes, he was going to heave whatever remained in his stomach. He gave the tough guy a bleary look and said, "Leaving now, mate."

The man opened his mouth to offer up some threat, some demand that Jason stay here, but Jason turned on him, pulling himself together long enough for one of his coldest, hardest looks. The kind his former fiancée had claimed sent small children shrieking for their mums and small dogs yipping to hide under the couch.

Jason had never had much use for small dogs. But children...

That, he had discovered the hard way, was another thing altogether.

The thought put him over the top, adding enough ferocity to his expression that the man glanced at his colleagues and fell back uncertainly.

"Good," Jason growled, easing his hand toward the automatic on his hip. "Because if I have to use my pistol, I'm going to get really cranky."

"Don't know as you could hit your own foot, with that *babbelas*," the man pointed out "For all that you killed *her*."

Babbelas, babbelas...slang for hangover. *Close enough*. "You already let *the killer* get away," Jason said. Impatience colored his voice, seeding doubt in some of the bravado surrounding him. "And my sorries, fellas, but you're in my way."

"*Ag,* let 'im go—not worth the *bliksem*," someone said, sneering to cover his uncertainty. "We've all seen him. The cops'll have his picture plastered around the city before we go on lunch break."

"Do your best," Jason muttered, knowing his section would clean up after him. They'd give him grief for it, but they'd do it like the champs they were. And...

He'd deserve whatever grief they heaped upon him, anyway.

He left the uncertain mob behind him, grateful to the dock foreman as the man bellowed, "Back to work, boy-kies!" and in retrospect grateful to the boykies themselves, who'd tromped the scene so thoroughly that even without intervention from MI6, the locals would have a hard go of solving this one. But as the sirens closed in, he felt the dockworkers take heart, their reluctance to let him leave beginning to overcome both their wariness and their boss's bellowing. Jason picked up his pace to an uncoordinated jog, making it around the end of the building to the little nook where he'd stashed his rented BMW motorbike. The helmet matched the yellow paint on the bike; between the two he felt like a large banana. *Sad bastard, I am.* On the other hand, as he puttered a sedate pace down South Arm Road, politely pulling to the side for the two police cars rushing toward the end of the jetty, he thought perhaps it was the best secret spy outfit he'd ever had. The Sad Bastard outfit.

Once the cars were past, Jason throttled up the bike and left at a good clip, but he didn't go far. Circling around on Dock Road to the parking area at the far corner of the waterfront area, he pulled into the vast lot and found himself virtually alone. Chilly it might be—making the sun a welcome sight to most people—but Jason found a tree-shaded spot and pulled in, toeing the kickstand out and dragging his helmet off.

As he hung the helmet on the handlebar, he took a deep breath, flexing his shoulders, straightening his back, and hunting for the reserves that would help him overcome the hangover from whatever nasty little drug the woman had used on him. The deep breath turned out to be a bad idea; the movement turned into a dash for the landscaping, where he lost the rest of his already much-regretted snack.

He returned to the bike and resolutely snagged a water bottle from the pannier, rinsing his mouth and spitting the results on the pavement. Then he found a tree in the landscaping and put his back to it, sliding down to sit with his elbows on his knees and his head tipped back.

Think. Think!

This assignment had gone pear-shaped so fast as to deny comprehension. One hour, he had been following Lyeta Denisov, waiting for the right moment, the right place, to bring her in for questioning by MI6. Not a friendly questioning—no one in MI6 truly believed Denisov had turned on her lover Egorov so completely—but not a fatal one, either. The next hour, after taking a taxi to an inexplicable encounter at the dock, Denisov was dead. Jason groaned. What a total cock-up. With so few vehicles on the road he'd had to hang back a considerable distance, and he'd lost the taxi as it neared the waterfront. Only an educated guess had gotten him to the right place...just in time to see the woman bending over Denisov's body.

Just like that. A few moments of fumbling on his part, and Denisov and her information—possibly the real reason for her flight from Egorov's influence—were gone. And his only clue had departed with that woman. She knew *something*. She had to. She'd killed Denisov for a reason.

Odd, though, the way the two of them had been in conversation even as Denisov died. Denisov had no reason to talk at that point...*unless she wanted to.*

Whatever the woman's motive, whoever she worked for, she was Jason's only chance to turn this assignment around. With a deep breath—a deep, *careful* breath—he returned to the bike long enough to retrieve his only booty from the encounter: the parka. It turned out to be a good one, ripped pocket notwithstanding—he recognized the Land's End brand as an upscale American product. It didn't mean she was American, but given her accent he thought it likely. He sat back down to search the garment, coming up with an impressive array of toys. A Phantom nightscope, a collapsible baton, several small knives balanced for throwing...but not one scrap of paper. Not one easy clue. The parka told him what he already knew—that the woman was accomplished. She was good.

Jason smothered a spark of anger at how she'd taken him down...how she'd exploited the sudden flare of connection between them. He supposed he was lucky she hadn't killed him.

He didn't feel lucky.

He felt just the same as he had on the dock, no less intense for the passage of time. The moment when she'd turned in his arms, when she'd looked up at him—and he could have sworn she'd been taken aback at the way he'd physically overpowered her, but the next moment proved him as wrong as a man could get. That moment when they'd looked at each other with the surprised awareness of man and woman, when she'd all but invited him to move that fraction of an inch closer...

And then she'd taken him down. Neat as you please.

He cursed his stupid body. It still wanted that kiss. It wanted *more*.

Think, he reminded himself. Assess her, don't obsess about her. He had a report to give, should be giving it right now. *Think.*

Short hair, pulled back and barely long enough to stay that way—dark in the predawn light, looking abrupt enough in its short little ponytail to translate to a blunt cut. Her eyes were dark, hard to assess in existing light. Her build slender but strong, beyond toned and into serious workouts. Her movement…he closed his eyes, trying to analyze that movement. A lithe, balanced movement, as though every step put her exactly where she wanted to be…as though at any given moment, she knew just where her body was in space.

Not everyone had that sense, that ability. Most people didn't know where their own two feet were at any given time. But this woman…she knew. She knew and she used it like a tool.

Dancer.

As the notion struck him, he thought immediately of the other clues: the slight toe-out posture, as natural as breathing to a professional dancer with ballet in her background. The strange, flexible sneakers. The skintight leotard, a comfortable second skin that had made her hard to get a grip on once she shed her parka. The leg warmers that only accented her length of leg.

And maybe even the theater in her background to make that look of *want* in her eyes believable enough to put him off guard. A split second of off guard…

Remember what happened next, bloke. Don't let it happen again.

Besides, he'd had enough of the fiery creative types in his life. The impulsive types and their impulsive decisions, living so far outside the rules that they forgot rules were made for a reason. They took their own paths…and they'd rip a bloke's heart out along the way.

Jason's eyes snapped open, his priorities in line, his goals reassessed. Find this woman and get whatever information had come from Lyeta Denisov. Then Egorov would go down, and Jason would put this encounter behind.

* * *

"You look knackered, Stellar." Bear, Jason's home contact and technical wizard, made the observation with annoying good cheer.

Jason gave his laptop—currently in video-phone mode—a wry look. "A gentleman wouldn't mention it," he said in his starchiest tone, and only got a grin for his troubles. He'd made several unplanned stops on the way back to his hotel in Cape Town proper, a fact that had not improved his mood a whit even though he'd taken the chance to wash up and brew himself a quick cuppa before sitting down at the hotel room desk. "Just let me know if you have an ID on her."

"She's a big zed," Bear offered, in the least technical of terms. He poked the pointed end of a pencil into his bushy head of grizzled hair—the reason, beyond his given name of Theodore, that his call-name was Bear. Within the view screen behind him, the wall was absolutely blank, although personal observation told Jason that the other three walls were entirely covered with notes and printouts. Bear stuck the pencil behind his ear. "Care to explain exactly what happened down there? Aside from the fact that you went arse over elbow?"

From Bear's point of view, *down there* was a literal term. He'd snagged satellite access of Cape Town, and although it had its limits, at times it could be a godsend.

"Figure it out for yourself," Jason said shortly. He'd already reported the crucial bits, merely confirming and elucidating upon what Bear had witnessed for himself. He leaned against the straight wooden back of the hotel desk chair, angling the laptop to suit. "What have you heard on your end?"

"Our Mystery Lady left a goody behind, up in a little nest."

The crane. He'd seen the woman glance up at the crane as she bent over Denisov's dying form. He'd even meant to check it out once he had the situation contained.

So much for intentions.

"A nice M24 SWS," Bear said. He groped to his right without looking and his hand returned laden with a cup of tea. "A tad close in for that weapon, but I guess if you want to be sure you get the job done…"

"It had to be close," Jason mused. "It wasn't just a takedown, it was a retrieval." Or else the woman would simply have disappeared without risking exposure next to the body. Jason never would have seen her at all. "The locals have that?"

Bear glanced at another computer screen and shook his head. "Doubt it even occurred to them to look," he said. "All of their witnesses saw you and our Mystery Lady tussling and little else. Looks like you're the victim of reverse discrimination, mate. They're assuming it was you, and that the women were together. Soon enough they'll realize that bullet in Denisov didn't come from a handgun, but that's only if we don't manage to make her body disappear in time."

Jason waved a vague hand of dismissal. They'd take care of the body, just as they'd managed to get a cleanup team in behind him to find the sniper rifle—normally a job he'd have handled, if he hadn't already been compromised.

Though he couldn't help but wonder why she'd left the weapon in the first place.

He scrubbed his hands over his face and looked up in time to see Bear watching him with sympathy that instantly vanished. "Right, then," Bear said brusquely. "Here's some good news. Your Mystery Lady didn't run far. Don't know how she got there, but she left the docks on foot and headed for the quaint cultural experiences of the waterfront. As far as we know, she's still noodling about the shops, though we don't currently have an exact location on her. It strikes me, Stellar, that the gentleman's thing to do would be to return her coat.''

"You must have a mind-reading program installed into that OS of yours,'' Jason said, pulling the parka from the end of the bed. This room was not so large that he couldn't sit at its desk and reach just about anything he needed. He'd give the parka another examination before returning it to its owner, just in case it held any other little hidden thing to make his day miserable. With the cool fall nights, she might well be glad to see the thing again—though no doubt she'd have little welcome for him.

"Look after yourself on this one,'' Bear said, and frowned. "And keep in touch. I've got dead air coming up for a while. That's the hell of stealing sat feeds…can't control the maintenance.''

Jason bunched the parka in his hand. The movement released a clean, crisp scent…something citrusy. He had to stop himself from bringing it closer to his face. "I always look after myself.''

"Yeah?'' Bear said dryly. "Then quit grinning like a fool.''

"Get off.'' Jason kept his voice mild. "I'll be in touch.'' He stabbed the quit key for the communications program and flipped the laptop closed.

He looked at the parka another long moment. It was a deep teal thing, or perhaps dark turquoise. The tan lining looked like it probably held secrets, things he needed to find before he returned it to her. He'd give it a good search, change his own clothes, and head right back to the waterfront. But for starters…

For starters he lifted the coat closer to his face and inhaled the scent of it.

Blue Crane. As Beth fled for the refuge of the commercial waterfront, she considered Lyeta's last words... and her own options. *Follow up on finding that computer keycard.* Okay, that was a given. *Check in with Barbara Price.* Also a given. Barbara might have some insight on Lyeta's words...or she might know more about the MI6 agent now involved.

For Beth had no reason to consider him out of the game. He'd lick his wounds—not for very long, either— and then he'd be back after her. He thought she'd killed Lyeta; he suspected, rightly, that she had information of value. And he had a grudge.

She needed to stay ahead of him.

Returning to her hotel didn't appeal to her. If Mr. MI6 had gotten a good look at her face, they might well have an ID on her by now, at least enough to know she was CIA-trained. They might well have broken her cover... they might be *at* her hotel. She could handle it if they were, but she didn't want the delay the encounter would cause.

Best bet...get lost in a crowd. Find a corner to contact Barbara, courtesy of the highly enhanced PDA she had stashed in her sling pack, which she'd hidden near the warehouse and nabbed again on the way out. She couldn't do much to disguise her basic look, but as she hesitated in the quiet shadows of the drawbridge on West Quay Road she pulled the band from her hair and bent over to give it a quick upside-down brushing. When she stood, flipping the blunt cut to fall into place around her shoulders, she had a different upper silhouette...and she could obscure her face simply by tipping her head.

The sling pack also held a sheer silk-knit gray twinset sweater; she pulled it on over her leotard, hiding her lean curves. Her backup pistol went in an ankle holster, and Wyatt into his discreet custom fanny pack. A light application of lipstick—just a shade more intense than her natural color—a little foundation to conceal her faint smatter of freckles and give her that fresh-faced morning tourist look, and she was ready to venture into the waterfront proper, an area with such intensity of charming character that it almost hurt. Shopping opportunities, African crafts and handmade items—all imported, since Cape Town itself had no booming cultural arts community—food for the hungry, quaint benches with a perfect view of Table Mountain and its end caps of Devil's Peak and Lion's Head—*3563 feet high,* she recited to herself—boat rentals, an IMAX theater and, out by the road to Cape Town proper, an aquarium.

Caffeine, Beth decided. Caffeine was the way to start this day, and by then the Victoria Wharf Shopping Center would be open. If she could find a tourist-oriented bookstore or even a computer store with demo systems hooked up to the Internet, she might be able to make something of *Blue Crane,* at least as it related to South Africa. With luck, *under the table* would make more sense in the context of that information. Or Barbara would be able to help, and contacting her from a computer store was not likely to gather any attention at all. Testing a toy, that's all.

She found a coffee shop and ordered herself something with foamy chocolate, choosing a powdered sugar doughnut. She considered contacting Barbara here and now, but it was too quiet here. Too obvious. She pulled the PDA from her sling pack, but powered it up only to consider Lyeta Denisov and her former lover, Kapoch Egorov. There was Lyeta, a stunning digital image that could well have been used as a cover photo for any upscale women's magazine—if it hadn't been for the cold, cold stare of her light blue eyes. Not a warm, inviting presence…very much a *beware of me* lady. In person, Beth had only seen her in blue Phantom night light or in the gloom of predawn; the photo jumped with the vivid color of Lyeta's long red hair, the gentle waves of which did nothing to soften the sternness of her classic beauty. The photo proclaimed what she was: a woman of power, with intensity of life and ultimate self-confidence.

Beth found herself scowling and pressed her lips together, a fleeting self-admonishment. She took a deliberate sip of her cooling coffee. Lyeta was dead, and she'd chosen the path that ended her own life so prematurely. Now it was up to Beth to make sure Lyeta's death—and her life—counted for something.

Beth returned to the PDA menu and picked the photo of Egorov. Another time, another world, he would have been called a crime kingpin. Now he was just a rich man of influence to most people, a charismatic man in his fifties with piercing blue eyes and a rakish scar on his cheek. But behind the scenes, Egorov played cultures against one another with terrorism as his tool and money and power as his reward. Now he was discovering what most people knew…that all the power in the world couldn't cure what mankind had not learned to cure.

So he would die, and if Beth had her way, before he went he would know that his CIA mole had failed to kill Lyeta in time to protect his legacy.

Although the mole still had the chance to stop Beth. And the mole had far too many advantages for comfort—unlike Beth, he was not on the run. Mr. B.S., for Bad Sniper, although it amused her that the initials were multipurpose. And unlike Beth, Mr. B.S. likely had a local team behind him, legitimately on the hunt for Lyeta and now the woman who'd supposedly killed her. Whereas Beth could not hunt for the mole, but simply do her best to evade him—and MI6—while she tried to understand Lyeta's nonsensical death whispers.

Not undoable. But it would take some concentration...and just the right moves.

Not to mention doing without sleep for a while. She closed Egorov's photo and did some quick surfing on the PDA, blessing its many enhancements as she hunted for anything "Blue Crane."

The little screen quickly filled with results, and she nibbled the doughnut, pondering and scrolling. Details on the bird itself, which didn't seem like a useful thing to pursue. Various sports teams, mostly high school, didn't strike her as particularly promising.

But ah...the fact that the Blue Crane was South Africa's national bird...

That seemed like something. Just what, she wasn't sure. But it was worth tucking away in the corner of her mind while she finished her coffee, blew doughnut crumbs off the PDA and slipped it back into her sling pack. As she slid out from behind the little round glass table at which she'd been seated, she caught the eye of the bored teen behind the service counter. He came right to attention, blushing a little behind his poor complexion, obviously considering those moments in which he'd been not so surreptitiously eyeing her. She asked him, "Know where I can find the Blue Crane?"

"Which one?" he blurted. He hastened to add, "There are so many of them right here on the waterfront...that's not even counting the ones in town."

Beth contrived to look confounded. "I don't know," she said. "I'm supposed to meet someone there."

He shook his head. "You better ask 'em, or you'll go bossies trying to track it down. Or try the shopping center, I suppose. There are a couple to choose from there. It doesn't open for another hour, though."

"*Dankie,*" she said, and he grinned at her. Not necessarily a good thing; she didn't want to be remembered. But then again, as the only customer who'd done anything more than rush in and out, she'd already gotten her share of attention.

But she'd learned something here, and that was worth something. Not only was her hunch right—there were local establishments with *Blue Crane* in the name—but she had her work cut out for her in sorting them out. It was a start…and Barbara Price could help her prioritize her search. She might even have the right tidbit of information to send her to the right place the first time.

Beth thought of the Breakwater Hotel, and decided against it. Even if it weren't compromised, she couldn't walk there and back before the shopping center opened. At the same time, the area had grown populated enough— mostly fishermen at this hour, but the occasional early- morning walker and overeager tourist—that she didn't want to stay put. So she wandered, relaxed but her eyes surprisingly alert for a tall, hardened form in a dark olive oilcloth jacket. She strode past Market Square and over by the amphitheater, until she could make her way back to the shopping center and ease into the charm-laden building—a unique structure of indoor malls that from the outside looked like parallel buildings lined up against one another in stepping-stone fashion. The Blue Crane flower shop caught her eye right away; she didn't stop. Unless she saw something that tugged at her, she'd simply "acquire" the shop locations to start with. Until then…

Quit looking for him, she scolded herself as she noted

a pair of broad shoulders in drab olive. When the man turned he had a smartly trimmed beard and impressively hooked nose. Her MI6 man had had a straight blade of a nose with an interesting broad spot that spoke of a mild break. *It's scary that you remember that, Flash.* By a Local Artists Only storefront, she caught sight of someone with a lean silhouette and light step, and instantly turned…

To find no one.

Good going, I Spy. Clearly she'd been too long without a date. She'd have to do something about that when she got back to the States. Until then…

Blue Crane Sport and Surf. Blue Crane Books. Blue Crane Body Naturals. Beth stopped in, intrigued by the basket-held displays. Easy to leave something in this place. She made a point to run her hands along the bottom of every readily accessible basket, not really expecting to find anything. While she was there she bought new toothpaste and brush and found her favorite citrus body soap. *The four main classes of surfactants: Anionic, cationic, nonionic and zwitterionic.* Zwitterionic—as words went, who could beat that?

And upon leaving, she found herself facing an electronics and entertainment store. "I knew you'd be here somewhere," she murmured at it. Better yet, it was one of the more populated stores in the center, full of kids playing with the games and adults admiring the big-screen entertainment system on display. The music was too loud to suit her purposes, but she found a spot near the entrance behind a stack of quiescent boom boxes and pulled out her personal digital assistant. A few quick shortcut commands with the stylus and the screen showed her the little dancer icon that Stony Man's tech master, Aaron Kurtzman, had installed on her PDA OS with much sly pleasure.

The dancer had blunt-cut hair and a unitard outfit, but was far too highly endowed to have made it as a professional; she danced across the small screen until Barbara Price's image replaced her. It didn't matter that it was late evening in Stony Man's time zone; Barbara was somehow always there, always looking like Beth's call was the most important thing in the world to her. Today Barbara didn't bother with small talk. She said, "Things went badly."

"They went badly," Beth agreed, adjusting the ear bud that made Barbara's end of the scrambled conversation private. "But not as badly as they could have. I have what she was carrying."

Barbara frowned, with the faint drawing of her brow the only real manifestation of the expression. "Then why the delay? I expected to hear from you hours ago."

Beth quickly sketched the events on the dock, and said, "I think I should stay. If Lyeta was right about Egorov's involvement, then the Bad Sniper mole might be after the keycard. It'll be a race to see who finds it first, and we have no idea what the mole already knows. You'll lose too much time bringing in someone else. I'm already in place."

"You're compromised," Barbara pointed out.

"You should be able to mitigate some of that from your end." Beth kept her voice mild as two young teens hesitated by the boom boxes, swapping technical turns in Afrikaans accents thick enough to baffle her.

"Possibly." Barbara gave her a thoughtful look. "But this isn't the situation we sent you in to handle; you're not prepared for it. You shouldn't be alone, for one thing."

"You never know," Beth said, and she switched to

Russian for a few blunt words she didn't want overheard.
"Maybe Mr. MI6 will come along and I can convince
him to play nice. I can use him, ditch him, and come home
with the goods." She added a quick description of the
man, embellishing with a wicked grin.

With the ear bud in place, Barbara could speak freely.
"That's not a bad idea." She tapped a few keys on the
keyboard that was just out of sight on the PDA screen
and said, "Of the MI6 agents known to be anywhere near
that area, the description you gave me identifies your man
as Jason Chandler. Very old-school, but he's had SAS
training. He can handle himself. He'd be a good backup,
if you can convince him you didn't shoot Lyeta. She
scrolled through a few screens of text, her eyes flickering
as she took them in. She nodded with approval. "He's a
good one, Flash. If you get the opportunity, take it." Then
she gave a little frown, staring at the off-screen monitor
more closely. "I don't see anything here about 'really
great ass,' however."

"He's SAS-trained," Beth said airily. "And what is
SAS but ass spelled sideways?"

Barbara smiled briefly, a genuine amusement that Beth
rarely saw in her. "The truth is, I should pull you and
send in another team. But...you're also right. We don't
have the time. If we can get our hands on a copy of
Scherba's master keycard, we can take Egorov's organization apart from the inside out—not to mention get a
handle on Krystof Scherba. He's been a problem for a
long, long time."

Beth snorted. "Wasn't he notorious on an international
level about the time he was thirteen? And what's with all
those tattoos, anyway?"

"Yes to the first...and as to the second, if this works
out, perhaps we'll get a chance to ask him. Our profiler

believes them to be merely an expression of his anar-
chist's makeup.''

''I think he just wanted to make his mother mad,'' Beth
muttered, thinking of the discreet tattoo on her own ankle,
acquired when her own age still hung in the teens. Lucky
for her the little rattlesnake was small enough to cover
with a flesh patch for those times she couldn't afford any
visible distinguishing characteristics. She tucked her hair
behind her ear and gave her nose a thoughtful rub. ''If
I'm staying, I could use a little help sorting through the
Blue Crane establishments. Unless we come up with
something else, it's still the best bet. Though I sure would
like to know where she stayed last night. Picking through
her belongings would be a luxury right now.''

''She was off everyone's radar as far as I know, but if
I hear anything on that, I'll send it along. The Blue Crane
information will come your way shortly.'' Barbara gave
a slight shake of her head, not entirely happy about the
conversation. ''Be careful, Flash,'' she said. ''I mean it.
If we didn't need this so badly...and get Chandler on your
side. I mean that, too.''

Beth sighed. She'd intended to forget that part of their
conversation. ''I hear you,'' she said, glancing around the
store to see she'd caught the attention of the boom box
boys. ''I'm going to stash the first package at my backup
location. So if anything happens—''

''Noted.'' Barbara cut her off with a brusk tone. ''I
want you to stay in touch, Flash. We enjoy your unconventional ways, but this is one time I want you playing
by the rules. *Call in.*''

''My unconventional, *successful* ways,'' Beth said, but
it wasn't an argument and they both knew it. ''I'll call.''

She closed the connection just as the boys got close

enough to look over her shoulder. One of them asked, "Is that a new game?"

"Yes," Beth said. "A prototype interactive spy game. It's still in alpha testing, so don't look for it on the market anytime soon."

"Then why do you have it in here?" the other boy asked, cleaning up his thick accent so she could understand. No doubt her own words had given her States origin away, although she could have affected any accent she wanted.

Beth gave an airy wave at the electronics that surrounded her. "We're trying out a new signal security system to assure proper function even in an environment thick with electromagnetics and radio waves," she said, amusing herself. "Next I'll be going to try it beneath the SABC tower."

"Duidelik," the kid said in approval. His friend nodded wisely and they let Beth wander away, but not without further discussion between them. "Ag, china, you see her takkies?"

Teens in any culture had their own language, it seemed. Beth knew they'd been looking at her dance sneakers, and she had to agree they didn't blend in. While she was at the shopping center, she needed to pull out the old Stony Man credit card and grab up some clothes meant for something other than a deep night contact on the docks.

On the other hand, if she could get to her backup location, she'd have everything she needed. Perhaps that was the next step...

Her PDA beeped as she headed for the store exit; she hesitated at a spiffy little flat-screen HD television, caught by the familiar, homey look of a CNN broadcast. She flipped open the leather PDA wallet to confirm receipt of a file named bluecrane.txt, smiling to herself. Barbara

Price, superwoman. There was no one else Beth would rather have picking up her field calls.

"Shane Dellamer," the display television murmured at her, and she glanced up to see a cookie-cutter announcer with ticker-tape announcements scrolling across the bottom of the screen and a small, clear image of Shane Dellamer himself. He looked every bit as cold as his reputation, an impression not helped by his flat gray eyes. "Mr. Dellamer, challenged by his political opponents to answer charges that the many facets of Dellamer Enterprises will pose no conflict of interest should he be elected, declined to respond with anything other than a reference to his campaign platforms. Dellamer Enterprises is involved in successful ventures spanning munitions to entertainment; Dellmore Pharmaceuticals just posted a significant profit increase from last year."

Shane Dellamer. Multinational, multicorporation...the man had his fingers in everything. Beth wouldn't be surprised if one day she ended up in the field dealing with the dirty underside of all that success.

First things first. She tucked the PDA away in her sling pack, her mind on the taxi she intended to catch and the bolt-hole she was about to dig into. Maybe she'd grab some takeout on the way. *Brain food*. With one of Barbara's lists to sort through, brain food was definitely in order.

If only she hadn't looked out into the mall to see Mr. MI6.

Jason Chandler.

And he was looking right back at her.

Chapter 3

Jason almost missed her. He'd been through the shopping center once, cruising the sunlit, mall-like interior and shifting from one parallel set of stores to another. He thought perhaps he'd never need to see another African mask or stylized walking stick again, and he'd set his mind to filter out everything but the silhouette he remembered from that morning. Slender, straight, stiff little ponytail at the back of her head.

Almost... but not quite. Not anymore. Now her athlete's curves were nearly hidden in a finely knit sweater buttoned at the top, her hair framing her face and changing it from fresh and sporty to strikingly aesthetic. At first he looked right past her.

And then she moved, easing absently toward the store exit, and his gaze snapped back to her.

There was no mistaking the quality of that movement.

She saw him an instant later. Annoyance flickered across her features, and then resignation. At first he thought she might bolt, but then she walked toward the seating arrangement in the center of the walkway, a sunken area bordered by tall, exotic and leafy plants—and deliberately passed by him so closely they almost brushed against each other.

Bloody well looks like an invitation to me.

She stepped down into the seating area, sat on one of the contoured wooden benches placed along the back of each planter in the triangular space, and crossed those long legs of hers. She had a sling pack now. No telling how well armed she was even without the goodies that had been in her parka but Jason imagined...

Well enough.

They stared at each other a moment, and then her gaze went quite deliberately to the squall parka nestled on the seat beside him. He nodded at it, giving no indication that he'd used it to cover his Browning. "Yours, I believe."

"Mine," she said, composed. "Though I don't suppose you left me any of the fun stuff."

"Depends on what I missed."

"Everything," she muttered, and scowled as if she were arguing with someone who wasn't even there; she certainly wasn't looking at him. "You missed everything."

The next step, he supposed, was to convince her she might as well come with him.

Right, because that worked so well last time.

He eyed her as she struggled with her internal conundrum, and wondered just how she managed as a field agent. Nothing was hidden on that face with its spare but expressive features; like her body, it was not a face of excessives. Audrey Hepburn as an athlete, with eyes that were wiser and lines of jaw and cheek that came lean instead of square...not to mention that incredible neck.

And just as her internal struggle was plain to him now, so had been her anger on the dock, and that single moment of vulnerability when he'd crushed her against the crane pylon.

On the other hand, boyo, she got you with that sultry act. Pure and simple. It had stirred something within him that very much stayed stirred.

Creative types. Couldn't trust 'em. Never knew when they'd go haring off on some impulse, or get carried away by all the emotion that fueled them. Never knew when—

That's enough, Chandler. Jason stopped himself cold, slamming the door on the over-lurking wellsprings of painful loss that lay in wait for such careless openings of thought. *Another time, another place. Keep your head* here.

He discovered she was staring at him, one eyebrow arched. And well she might, to witness him with such a loss of concentration within striking distance of a woman he'd attacked—who'd responded in kind and prevailed— earlier in the day. She plunked her sling pack in her lap and crossed her arms over it. Defensive gesture, indeed. "How'd you find me?"

"No bloody thanks to whatever it was you slipped on me," Jason said, not how he'd meant to respond at all. "Have mercy next time and just bean me one."

She blinked in surprise. "You had a reaction to it? It's only supposed to leave you a little confused."

"You can find evidence of my *reaction* to it all along the dock." Even to his own ears he sounded churlish.

In her place he supposed he might have smiled, too. Just a small smile, quickly hidden. "Gosh," she said, about as American as she could get. "I'm so, uh, sorry to hear it. Really."

"I'll just bet," he said. He slid his hand under the

parka, neatly snagged his Browning, and scooped up the bundle so he could slide over to her bench, settling close enough to look intimate to anyone who happened to glance at them. She smelled of the same fresh scent as the parka. "Now, you want to talk to me about what went down this morning?"

She managed to look amused. "And why would I want to do that, Jason Chandler? Because you think I killed the woman I was trying to protect? Or because you tried to take me away in cuffs? You're not going to do that part again, are you?"

"Not planning to," Jason managed, thrown entirely off balance by her casual revelations. *She knows who I am. She was trying to protect—?*

No, he wasn't sure he believed that. His hand certainly didn't believe it, curled reactively around the Browning grip the way it was.

Or maybe it was just smarter than he was, and knew he was too off balance around this woman to play the game.

She said, "I don't know what weapon he used, but he was a fool. He was way too close to target, and even so, didn't manage an instant kill. Worse yet, he didn't follow through. We were wide-open while I dragged Lyeta behind that crane leg. Sloppy, sloppy. If you think you can pin work that bad on me, then you don't have any idea who you're dealing with, do you?"

Jason gave a one-shouldered shrug. "Everyone has a bad day. Bad enough to leave the rifle behind. And maybe some prints?"

She snorted. "As if."

After a moment he said, "Ah. One of those American nonsense phrases that's supposed to mean something."

"It means I'm leaving." She stared off at one of the

plants, defiant in a way that made no sense to him. In sudden insight, he recognized it—she was in some way challenging her orders. Not surprising. "I'm not desperate enough to work with you."

"To work *with*—" Caught flat-footed, he stole her American nonsense phrase. "As if!"

She slanted a shadowed gaze at him. "That really doesn't work coming from a manly MI6 guy like you."

Creative types. They followed a logic that meant nothing to anyone else. They switched directions so fast you were always hanging with one foot over the edge of a hairpin curve, a helpless little cartoon character trying to catch up.

And yet still, there was something stirring in such intensity. Such a self-directed approach to life.

Not stirring enough. "You want manly MI6?" he asked. "How's this? My nice macho nine-millimeter Browning is only centimeters from your bum. It's a lovely bum, and I'd hate to make holes in it, but I've got a ten-round magazine and it's full." As an afterthought he added, "It's got black epoxy finish. Very sexy."

"My bum?" she said faintly, although not from any obvious fear. More like disbelief of what she'd just heard.

"The pistol," he said. "Black epoxy. All the blokes want one." Good Lord, she had him talking nonsense just like she did.

"Yeah?" She actually seemed offended that he'd been talking about the pistol and not her sweet rounded body parts. "*Mine* is a Sig-Sauer P226. Nine millimeter, sixteen-round magazine, European proof marks, custom Nillgrips. Name of Wyatt." She raised an eyebrow at him, proclaiming her trump. "That's not counting my rifle, of course. Which you *haven't* got. You've got some fool's weapon instead."

"But I've got my pistol," he reminded her. "Centimeters from your bum, remember? And unless you're hiding a third arm somewhere, your *Wyatt* is not in hand. So when I suggest we quietly leave this little shopping mecca and head for a place where we can discuss why you killed Lyeta and what you found on her body—as well as what she told you—I hope you pay serious attention. And while you're at it, you can hand over that nice fanny pack. Looks like it's carrying a bit of weight. Wouldn't want you to tire."

"SAS spelled sideways," she growled. "And what if I don't? This is such a nice place to make a scene, don't you think?"

"Only one of us is wanted by the local Boer for murder," he said complacently, not bothering to mention it wasn't her. "You go ahead. Make your scene. I'll be the manly MI6 agent who tracked you down." He nodded in thoughtful satisfaction. "I like the sound of that. Then we'll *still* talk—only you'll be behind bars."

She glared at him. It was an amazing glare, coming from blue-green eyes the same color as the parka. Deepest turquoise. Those eyes should have been illegal all in of themselves, never mind what else she was up to. The shopping center visitors walked happily by the sunken conversation area, chattering kids in tow, laden with touristy totes and smelling of suntan lotion. Jason had an unhappy awareness that the population of the center had nearly doubled within the past hour; it was well and away time to be out of here. Cape Town's beautifully moderate weather would bring tourists out in droves as the day wore on.

And she still glared at him. "You know," she said, "I've got things to do, and you're wasting my time. Has it ever occurred to you that we're on the same side? That

I didn't kill Lyeta? That you're just getting in my way, stopping me from accomplishing something that will benefit us both—not to mention just about anyone else on this little global village we call a planet?''

"No," he said automatically. "Or why resist coming along with me in the first place?''

She made an inarticulate noise of frustration. "Because you're *in my way*. I don't have the time to waste!''

"I'm afraid you're going to have to convince me with something more along the order of details," he said. "Lots of details." But he hesitated, aware of the doubt sitting rather heavily in the center of his chest. The genuine frustration, the way it showed on her face along with everything else—

That doesn't mean it's real—she already proved that.

"Six billion, two hundred million people on this planet waiting for me to get in gear. One million, six thousand right here in Cape Town alone," she grumbled. "And I'm sitting here waiting for you to make up your mind."

Ow. "As it happens, my mind's made up." It wasn't. But if he followed procedure, if he brought her in, then it didn't *have* to be made up. The decisions would be made for him. "Give over the fanny pack and let's go."

"Stiff-necked stuffed shirt," she muttered, renewing her glare as she unclipped the fanny pack. "You *deserve* that haircut."

As the BMW motorbike idled in front of a red light, Chandler turned his head just enough to shout at Beth. "Keep still," he snapped at her.

She rested her chin on his shoulder, heedless of the way the helmet clipped him on the head. "I'm bored," she said. "And you made me wear this helmet. I feel like a banana." At least she had her parka. The sweater had been fine in calm sixty-degree air at the waterfront, but even though the sun had continued to warm the day, the wind from their passage drew goose bumps on Beth's arms.

He gritted his teeth as the light changed, resolutely turning his attention back to the traffic as they headed into Cape Town proper. She could see the muscle of his jaw twitch, squaring it even more. He took them through areas with incredible Victorian architecture with iron lace railings and exacting paint jobs and into the more modern part of the city until buildings rose high above them, ultramodern architecture gleaming of glass and steel.

Beth, her hands handcuffed around his waist, felt it the better part of valor *not* to pitch an escape attempt right here on the moving motorbike, leaving potential smears of herself all over the road. Work with him, Barbara had said. It didn't look like she'd have a choice.

Or rather, the choices were such that allowing him to take her to a quiet place for a chat was the least of all the evils. And if she could break away somewhere along the way, so be it. Meanwhile, she snuggled up against his back and let her hands rest on his belt buckle, tapping restlessly...and quite clearly getting to him. Good. The more she annoyed him with the little things, the less seriously he'd take her, the more distracted he'd become—and maybe that moment to break away would be hers for the taking.

They turned onto Strand Street and after a short jaunt through the traffic-filled lanes, swooped down a ramp into the cavernous parking garage below the towering Holiday Inn Cape Town. When he flipped the kickstand down and cut the motor, the resulting silence held the peculiar quality of underground garage acoustics everywhere.

"'We are the Pilgrims, master, we shall go...'" Beth murmured.

He jerked around to look at her—or tried to, for he was still enclosed in her arms. He frowned at her, those glacial eyes searching hers. They were close enough for Beth to see how the edges of his irises were darker than the rest, as though someone had applied watercolor in a circle and the color slowly, dramatically seeped inward. In this lighting, his pupils had gone huge; it made him look more vulnerable...not so much of that chipped ice British exterior. "How'd you—"

"It's on the clock, right?" she said. "The SAS memorial at Credenhill."

"Hell bloody yes," he said. "What are you doing with it?"

"Trivia. Just one of my many endearing qualities," she murmured modestly. Not to mention it had the effect she wanted, which was to throw him off stride again. She really didn't want him to start thinking efficiently. It might occur to him to search her, in which event he'd surely find her little S&W in the ankle holster.

He looked at her another moment and then gave a sudden little snort, turning away to abruptly lift her hands over his head.

She fumbled with the helmet, finally removing it, and when he took it, used her cuffed hands to first muss her hair slightly and then smooth it back. Then she held them out expectantly, palms up.

"Not a chance," he said, hooking the helmet over a handlebar and bringing a leg over the front of the bike seat.

"You don't think it'll be a little obvious if you take me in there in cuffs? You don't think I can find a way to make it obvious?"

"I think I can find a way to make you regret it if you do," he said.

"Oh, I'm trembling. Big bad SAS. At least take one of the cuffs yourself. It'll be more comfortable for me and, gosh, we can hold hands and no one will ever know it's because there are handcuffs involved. It's not like I can run off and leave you again. At least, not without killing you and rifling your body for the key. That'll be hard to do in the lobby, even for me."

He shook his head; she couldn't decide if he was incredulous or just hiding a smile. She sat quietly and with quick, efficient moves he freed her left hand and snapped the cuff closed around his own. Taking her hand, he said, "What's your name?"

"Excuse me?"

"Your name," he repeated. "If I'm going to walk into the hotel holding hands with you, I need to know your name."

"Ah. An old-fashioned kind of guy." She hesitated, considering pseudonyms and considering the warm, gentle pressure of his fingers over hers. Finally she said, "You can call me Beth," with all the implication that it wasn't truly her name.

"All right, Beth," he said evenly. "Here's how it goes. We'll walk through the public areas of the hotel quietly, and we'll stay quiet all the way up to my room. Keep in mind that you're wanted for murder; being with me isn't the worst situation you face. If you make it hard on me, that could change."

"I believe I've already made it hard on you," Beth said, and widened her eyes in affected innocence.

Goodness, he blushed. Mr. Manly MI6 *blushed*. But he wasn't going to admit it. He said shortly, "Let's go."

She dismounted the bike, walking alongside him with

casual ease. They took a short flight of stairs, automatically adjusting for the tight space and the rhythm of each other's movement. When he pushed open the glass-fronted door to the lobby, Beth had to stop and gape a moment. The lavishly appointed lobby sparkled at them, worthy of any gala. In the center, a slab fountain rippled discreetly into a small pool filled with tossed coins, creating only enough water noise to be soothing without being disruptive. Brass shone and plush, spotless carpets led the way to a bank of elevators. At the far end of the lobby, a glass-sided staircase curved up to the balcony of the second floor, from which a murmur of conversation trickled. Conference and meeting rooms...no doubt a ballroom. No doubt all as posh and glittery as the lobby.

Between the door from which they'd just entered and the far staircase, the lobby offered overstuffed chairs and couches. It was to these that Beth marched, taking the initiative abruptly enough so Chandler followed along, his reluctance stiffening his grip on her hand.

"Relax," she said, automatically spotting the main exits and the smaller bellboy exit off to the side; other exit signs beckoned beyond the elevators. She marked the interior management doors—the places from which people might unexpectedly appear—and she headed for a small couch that kept their backs to a large square pillar. Before the couch sat a low table, laden with brochures. *Blue Crane Winery.* Just off the N2 in Faure. Weekly evening reception...tonight. Bet there'll be plenty of tables, she thought. And under one of those tables she might find Lyeta's computer keycard. She turned her attention back to Chandler, not certain if he'd seen her distraction, and said, "I'm not causing any trouble. I'm giving you the opportunity to talk. Right here, right now."

His fingers tightened painfully around hers. "Not what I had in mind."

"Not in your rule book?" she said, letting scorn lace her words. "I learned long ago that everyone else's notion of a rule book isn't necessarily what's best for me. There are only a few people in this world who can lay down rules for me, and you're not one of them."

"Good Lord," he said, sitting next to her on the couch more bemused than anything. His gaze flicked to the brochures before them, then away. "I'll bet you don't get along with your mum."

"My mum," she said, and smiled tightly. "No. But let's talk about you and your mum instead."

He shook his head, more to himself than at her. "Let's talk about why you were with Lyeta."

Beth hesitated. *Work with him.* There'd be no *working with him* if she couldn't convince him they were at least nominally on the same side. And...for all she'd played him, kept her options open and done her best to keep him off guard, she could see the benefits of teaming up. If he ran his ops by the damn rule book, at least she'd know what to expect of him.

So she said, "Let's talk about why I *wasn't.*"

He regarded her steadily, looking relaxed in the short, comfortable couch. Beth knew otherwise. She could feel the tension in his thigh next to hers; the heat of being against him warmed her.

"You mind?" she asked, reaching for the zipper of the parka. With the handcuffs in play she couldn't take it off, but when he gave a short nod she was glad enough to unzip and open it. She said, "The average sniper is eighteen hundred percent more effective than the average soldier. That goes up, of course, when you put an M24 SWS in the hands of that average soldier as opposed to his M16. But there's still no comparison.''

He gave the smallest of smiles; she had the feeling he was beginning to catch on to her non sequitur way of thought. ''I'm sure you'll somehow make this fascinating bit of trivia relevant.''

''You betcha. Because I'm far more than your average sniper. And as I said at the shopping center…the person who shot Lyeta…*that* was your average soldier. Your people should have been able to tell you that much.''

''You still want me to believe you didn't kill her.''

''Yes,'' she said. ''I want you to believe that.''

''Why?''

She bit her lip and decided she really had nothing to lose. Not while she had his attention here in the lobby, and wasn't yet actually in formal questioning…or not so formal questioning, for which even stuffed-shirt MI6 guys didn't follow the rules. ''I think we can work together,'' she said. ''Things went bad at the dock. Lyeta wasn't supposed to die. That leaves me with unfinished business. You're no better off, or you wouldn't be trying to squeeze me for information. If we work together, we both win.''

''That's assuming we're on the same side,'' he said, although how he did it with that slight humor in his eye, Beth didn't know. It gave her a window into an entirely new facet of him, one she hadn't considered. One that made her more aware than ever of just how warm she was, bundled in her squall parka and sitting hip to hip, knee to knee, on the small couch. One that made her remember his eyes as they faced each other in the parking garage, and give her a foolish little hiccup of yearning. It had been so long since any man had tempted her beyond the purely physical…

Not this man. Not this time, this place.

She gave herself a mental throat clearing and responded, "We've got to start on the same side before we can go anywhere else. We're at a dead stop until then."

He gave her hand a little squeeze. "And I suppose this is the first step. Unlocking these."

"That would be my guess." She watched him; he didn't turn away from her gaze. In fact, he returned it, considering her words...considering *her*.

She saw the decision in his eyes the moment they shuttered; something in him went distant from her. He unconsciously squared his shoulders. Disappointment clogged her throat...something more than purely professional. Her foolish little hiccup of yearning, squashed.

But before either of them could say anything, a perfectly nondescript man swept in through the front entrance at just about the same time another came from the bellboy's door, and a third from beyond the elevators. Ooh, nice. Coordination. Beth and Chandler hadn't been spotted yet, but it was only a matter of seconds.

"Damn," Beth said. "You couldn't have chosen some little out-of-the-way hotel? Some place inconspicuous?"

"We'd be safe enough in my room if you'd come with me," he said, matter-of-factly enough so she had to admit to herself that he was right. "Anyway, this place has tea makers. And a trouser press in each room."

"Mustn't be without those," Beth murmured, and was a little surprised to see that twitch of amusement at his mouth. Not such a stuffed shirt as he liked to seem, after all. Momentary regret squeezed her along with a surprised realization that they might have worked well together.

But here came her chance to escape and continue work on her own, and it looked like she'd better grab it. She wouldn't do Stony Man any good at all, sequestered somewhere in thirty-two stories of Holiday Inn with loose-lips drugs in her system and a thorough search turning up the mini CD she still carried.

Chandler leaned close, murmuring, "I don't think they'll start anything so publicly. They'll try to bluff us out of here first."

With real apology in her voice, Beth said, "I'm sorry."

He gave her a startled look, a big question mark of an expression.

Still apologetic, Beth said, "*I'm* going to start something."

And she did. She bent to grab the little S&W at her ankle, thoroughly alarming the perfectly nondescript trio. As they hastened to reach the lobby, Beth flung her cuffed hand up against the square pillar behind them, bringing Chandler's hand with it. She jammed the gun up against the links connecting the bracelets and fired, blasting the cuffs apart while the bullet buried itself in the pillar. The blast of sound sent people screaming and diving. Chandler snatched at her as she flipped over the back of the couch, catching only a brief handful of her parka before she ripped free and sprinted for the curving staircase at the back of the lobby.

They weren't after Chandler. They probably didn't even know about him. They'd followed her, and therefore him…and now, as she pounded up the stairs, she'd given him a choice. He could chase her down, or he could delay the men who'd come for her.

As she gained the second floor and raced across the open space for the exit sign she thought would spill her out into the street behind the hotel, she heard the sounds of fighting. Fists meeting flesh, bodies hitting the floor, furniture breaking. She glanced over the edge of the second floor balcony and saw two nondescript men reeling while a third hit the floor. She smiled, the smallest curve of her lips, and sprinted away. Two men from the disrupted meetings along the row of balcony conference rooms tried to stop her, blocking her way in the officious way of men who don't have authority but take it anyway. They thought better of it at the last moment, simultaneously spotting her revolver and throwing themselves aside. She hit the stairwell, bounded down the stairs three and four at a time, and landed at the bottom to come up still running.

And all the while, she kept that little smile on her face.

Chapter 4

Once on the street, Beth raced around the nearest corner, took the first opportunity to double back, and spent long moments watching the hotel's main entrance and garage ramp. She saw nothing of Chandler or his silly yellow motorbike, but after ten minutes, a dark, tinted-window sedan drove up the ramp at carelessly high speed and made a fast and equally careless turn onto Strand Street. Beth secured her revolver in its ankle holster, rued the loss of Wyatt and her fanny pack, and turned away from the hotel, jogging along the side street at a decent clip.

He'd chosen to protect her from the nondescripts. From the CIA mole's people, who might even have been bona fide CIA, misled by the mole. Chandler could have chanced it, gone after her himself...and hadn't.

No doubt there was something in the rule book about keeping alive those you want to question.

Not far from here, she'd auditioned for a dance troupe production, establishing her cover. She always auditioned upon arrival when she was using her dancer cover, thanks to Barbara's uncanny knack of locating productions suited to Beth's strengths. Sometimes Beth won a role in her cover audition and had to feign injury to avoid the commitment. Sometimes on long-term jobs, she auditioned with intent, got the part, and carried the cover throughout her assignment. In this particular instance, she was still waiting to hear about callbacks…but it didn't matter one way or the other. Because whenever, wherever she auditioned, she cased the theater for her own use.

They were all the same in the ways that were most important. They all held rooms and warrens and corners of old props, new props, costuming, dressing rooms, makeup….

They gave her a place to hide. A place to baffle the unfamiliar, and one that often provided her with the tools she needed to improvise her way out of trouble. Wigs, clothes, makeup, a first-aid kit. Sometimes a place to clean up, even if it meant a sink bath and hand soap in her hair. This particular theater had turned out to be an ancient thing, with basement hallways to rival the underground lair of the *Phantom of the Opera* and a rich assortment of wardrobe offerings. She'd almost ditched her hotel and stayed there in the first place, but opted to keep it back in case of trouble.

Well, she had trouble, all right. But she also had a wine tasting to make, and—she glanced at her watch as she ran—just enough time to manage it, assuming the wine country bus line was running to schedule today.

Blue Crane. And lots and lots of tables.

Jason stared at Bear in perplexed disbelief. ''She's CIA?'' She hadn't acted like CIA. No reason not to reveal herself as such when he'd caught her, and to pull interagency politics to handle their conflict. And besides, according to Bear, the men at the hotel had been CIA, and they didn't have that comradely air about them.

"Quit looking narked and pay attention," Bear said, a lack of patience in his voice that caught Jason's attention. He straightened in the desk chair and looked properly alert. "She *was* CIA. Sniper-trained, too—not something she often took advantage of in those days, but when she did…she's good, Stellar. Cracking good."

"She said…"

She'd said a lot of things. That she hadn't killed Lyeta. That she was far more than your average sniper. Ohh, yes.

She'd said she wanted to work together.

"Stupid," he muttered out loud. There'd been no mistaking that instant of disappointment on her face—or that she'd known the instant he'd decided to stick to the mission profile. How long had it been since someone read him so well? They would have meshed well, if he hadn't been so reluctant.

Rules are rules for a reason. Never mind meshing well; he knew better than to trust the judgment of someone who acted on impulse. Shooting apart handcuffs in the middle of a crowded lobby, for instance. Not giving him the chance to talk to her on terms that allowed him to trust her—even to help her.

Bear ignored his grumbling and went on. "We don't know what she's up to now. But I can tell you she isn't known to use an M24, which is what our Lyeta-killer used."

"Basic U.S. Army issue," Jason said, pulling himself out of his internal thoughts to speculate out loud. "Recently available to the public, if I recall correctly. You know, if she didn't kill Lyeta, if she was somehow working *with* Lyeta... But you don't have her in any of your current agency databases. Sounds like dark ops to me.''

"Welcome back to the conversation,'' Bear said, heavily sardonic. "The point being, the murder weapon isn't her weapon of choice, and others could have obtained it. The point being...I don't think she did this. On the other hand, I'm not sure it's relevant. You need to bring her in. She's still the last one who spoke with Lyeta. She still has information we don't.''

And she's still in danger.

"We need to bring her in,'' Bear repeated. "If she's after something we don't know about, we need to learn about it—and get it ourselves. I don't suppose somewhere between honking up breakfast at various Cape Town locations, apprehending her, having a nice snuggly bike ride, and scuffling with the CIA, you picked up any idea where she ran off to?''

Jason thought of the brochure that had caught her attention in the lobby. *Blue Crane Winery.* He thought of the home entertainment store where he'd found her. *Blue Crane Nest Entertainment.* A perfect pattern of two. He said, "As a matter of fact...'' and let the sentence trail away a moment. Then he looked in Bear's craggy features via the jerky image interface of the video phone and smiled. "I believe I have a date at a wine tasting.''

With any luck, I'll get there before the CIA. She might have been one of them once, but he had the distinct feeling she was better off with the British side of the force. The question was...were they after her because they thought she'd killed Lyeta...or because they knew she hadn't?

Beth slipped into the theater, avoided the loud discussion in front of the stage—producer and choreographer, if she interpreted the various levels of indignation correctly—and eased down the backstage stairs to the storage rooms below. She had a room all picked out. It was one in which several mattresses were stored, and was just across the hall from contemporary costume storage. If she recalled her briefing materials correctly, this theater had recently staged an avant garde play populated by The Beautiful People; one of the reviews had specifically commented on the quality of the designer knock-off clothing.

With luck, she'd find just the thing for a wine tasting.

She squeezed into the room she'd chosen, past the massive disassembled bed frame that blocked most of the door. A selection of mattresses leaned against one wall of the small room; the bed frames leaned against the other. A few other pieces of bedroom furniture filled in the corners, with chairs upturned on top and dusty mirrors behind them. A rope-and-pulley arrangement above the mattresses held several old-fashioned bicycles.

Beth threw her sling pack over the handlebars of one of those head-level bikes and pulled the mattress from the outside of the stack to land on the old brown patterned linoleum with a *whump*.

Then she flopped down on it herself, covering her nose and mouth with one hand when she saw the dust she'd raised. She let her body go limp, every single muscle. She ran a mental inventory, checking bruises and sore spots, making sure she hadn't missed anything that might fail her under stress later in the evening.

This day had started in the middle of the night, but she still had most of it to go.

She allowed herself a fifteen-minute doze—precious time, but the respite would make all the difference in the world—possibly in her life. Upon rousing, she forced herself to lie there another few moments, reconnecting with the details of the mission.

What few details she knew.

The mole was on her tail, all right, and appeared to be taking advantage of company resources. Either that or he'd gone completely rogue and was using Egorov's people; she hadn't let them get close enough to find out.

Jason Chandler had been close enough. She felt a moment's guilt in leaving him to take care of the trio at the hotel, but then again…he seemed quite capable of taking care of himself. A slow smile crossed her face as she reconsidered the quick glimpse she'd gotten of him in the lobby, the nondescripts arranged in various attitudes of physical defeat in a circle around him. They'd made their exit quickly enough after that.

But no doubt the nondescripts were still after her. And if they weren't after her, they were certainly after the computer keycard Lyeta had hidden. In fact, they could be nothing but desperate for it.

I'm going to get there first.

Chasing down Blue Crane establishments was a fool's errand and she knew it. She needed to know where Lyeta had spent her time. For all Beth knew, Lyeta had come straight to the dock upon entering Cape Town; the last traces of her existence might be in another country altogether. So for now, until she had more information, Beth would dress the part, avoid pursuit and capture, and continue to mull the cryptic meaning of Lyeta's last words.

But Lyeta didn't mean for them to be cryptic. She'd been dying, and trying to communicate. She had used shorthand, but why tell Beth anything at all unless she meant for it to be helpful? Without Lyeta's dying confession about the keycard, Beth would have walked away regretful, but she would have walked away. And Lyeta had no incentive to send Beth on a wild-goose chase. The words, as vague as they were, had to mean something simple and obvious. Something that, in context, provided no puzzle at all.

Beth just had to get them in context.

But first she had to get to this wine tasting. She'd seen enough of the brochure to know it was an informal affair, more of a weekly publicity open house than a bona fide wine tasting, and she very much hoped they'd have food available. She felt positively hollow...nothing in her system since the early-morning doughnut, and all that running, leaping and evading in the meantime.

"Beth's rule of spy survival," she said to the grimy, yellowed acoustic tile ceiling above her open eyes. "A growly stomach messes with stealth mode." Another rule, left unsaid: A grimy spy messes with a cool, elegant cover.

She found a maintenance closet and took the best sink-bath she could manage with a roll of harsh brown paper towels. Her hair, flattened by the yellow helmet and speckled with plaster flakes, suffered under a hand-soap shampoo. She washed her leotard out and hung it up to dry, snagging a baby-doll shirt from the wardrobe rack and easing back upstairs to find the toolbox that every stage manager kept on hand. The argument up on stage had given way to silence; a peek into the seating area showed only one man, deeply involved in making notes all over a script. She crept to the back of the stage, well out of his earshot.

She dulled the hacksaw blade and dealt herself several nasty cuts, but eventually the hardened metal of the security cuff gave way. She carefully buried it under the rest of the garbage in the bin by the back door. Then it was back downstairs to hunt out a dress and makeup.

When she emerged, the only thing still *Beth* about her was the sling pack and squall parka—and those, she planned to stash before she entered the visitor's building at the winery. She wanted them close. Otherwise, with her hair pulled back into a clip with a style that was at once casual and classy, and her dancer's body poured into a slinky black dress with a plethora of top strapping and plenty of skin showing along her back and shoulders, she was ready to slip into the Cape Town nightlife. Silver evening shoes with more heel than she preferred adorned her feet, and she had a lined, black velvet shawl to cut out the chill of the night. Neither were ideal; they didn't give her the flexibility to take action—or to retreat into the night—that she might need.

Then again, she had danced in higher heels than these. She could certainly fight in them if she had to.

But she wouldn't plan on it. In, search, and out again. She didn't know how the nondescripts had found her at Chandler's hotel and she couldn't assume they wouldn't find her at the winery.

She breezed out of the theater as though she owned it, checked the banker's clock next to the theater front, and headed for the wine country bus stop with a firm, confident step.

Even with the six-thirty sunset making for a dark bus ride, Beth could still see the country change around her. The trees grew from scrubby to tall and sparse to lush; the land grew rugged. Thirty minutes along the N2 and they were just outside Faure and the Hottentots Nature Preserve. The Blue Crane Winery took five more minutes of patience. As they pulled up outside the main gate, the bus driver wished Beth a pleasant evening and smoothly accepted the ten-rand tip she offered. He made sure she'd disembarked safely before carefully pulling the door closed.

She smiled at the man who opened the visitor center door for her and walked into the main room of the small center. Cozy and brimming with character, charm...and money. Several tables were set up against one wall; conversational seating units occupied most of the other, and the open space in between already boasted a handful of socializers. The beautifully presented wines were offered for both serious tasters and casual explorers, with prefilled wineglasses grouped by wine and demarked by small crystal bowls of unsweetened bread cubes. Young red, mature red, white wines... But these functions clearly attracted more than the swish-and-spit crowd; on the middle table was a lovely, mouthwatering, drool-worthy display of finger sandwiches, meats and cheeses, not to mention the hors d'oeuvres that Beth made no attempt to identify. *Mmmm. Dinner.*

But first, the tables. She didn't have time to waste here, not when she couldn't be sure what the mole knew.

Casually, lingering here and there along the way, Beth did a cursory check of the table edges, pushing the cloth back and up to feel for anything other than screws, corner blocks, and other structures that came along with the table. It would be too easy if she found anything that way, of course, but it was the first step nonetheless.

Second step...a pause for some of those delicate goodies. Beth allowed herself a small glass of a full, sweet red wine, drinking slowly and trying to eat slowly as well. Hard when her stomach was so empty. Polite conversation murmured around her, and the winery rep circulated through the crowd passing out the same classy brochures available on the tables. He came up on her just as she popped a tiny sandwich in her mouth. She managed a quick, surreptitious chew-and-swallow, expressed her delight at the winery and the wine, and inquired about their shipping policies. He handed her a second brochure with a little less gloss and a little more content. Pleased with his conquest, he moved along to the couple beside her, who had been sipping with such careful concentration and serious effort that Beth pegged this for their first wine event. Good. They would keep the winery rep busy for a nice long time, during which she could choose her moment, hitch her skirt up, and...

Crawl under the tables.

Jason's eyebrows climbed a notch as he saw his Mystery Lady spy ease to the edge of the room; her head disappeared, sinking from sight. He left the antechamber and coatroom to enter the tasting room for the first time, ducking through the other visitors just in time to see Beth's leg withdraw out of sight beneath the table.

A quick check reassured him that no one else had seen her. If he hadn't been watching her and her specifically, he wouldn't have noticed, either. As it was he'd gotten a grand sight of a grand leg, and could be pretty sure of one thing: she was looking for something.

Something of Lyeta's.

With care, he followed her progress down the line of tables, watching as the long, elegant tablecloths gave a delicate shiver here, wafted in a nonexistent wind there. It occurred to him...

They still had to talk. And he wanted to talk to her without fighting her, chasing her or drawing the attention of the nondescripts. He eyed the last table, eyed the crowd and waited for the moment—inevitable, really—that someone, somewhere in the room, dropped a wineglass.

He was under the table, sitting cross-legged and casual, by the time she paused in her examination of the above her and spotted him, her tiny flashlight wavering. Ahh, an expression to treasure. The way her deep turquoise eyes, shadowed to darkness by the cavelike circumstances, widened with startled surprise. The way her mouth, sleek and quirky and darkened with some kissable shade of lipstick, dropped open just long enough to betray the depth of that surprise. And even the twinge of annoyance that flared across her face and dropped away, replaced by a distinct refusal to be impressed. And the way he was in the perfect position to look right down her—

"Lovely dress," he said, keeping his voice low although he wasn't terribly concerned about being heard over the general conversation level in the room. "Shame to use it as a dust mop."

"I'm testing the material for durability," she said, not missing a beat now that she'd gotten her initial astonishment under control. She flicked her flashlight back up at the underside of the table. "It's a private test. Go away. You're disturbing my dust."

Even as she spoke, another look crossed her face, one that had nothing to do with him at all. She turned the flashlight on the floor between them, then on the space she'd already traversed. "Damn!"

He passed a fingertip over the floor directly in front of him; it came up dusty. "I don't know why you're here," he said, "and I don't know why you're *here,* under-the-table here, but...it doesn't look like anyone else has been arranging assignations under the wine lately."

She gave him a grumpy look, aiming the flashlight back up at the table. "Neither have we. This is a one-woman show. I believe I told you to go away."

"I don't believe I ever said I would."

She scowled fiercely at him. "You're in my way. You're quadrupling my chances of being caught under here. Go—"

"No." He really regretted it that time; he'd heard an edge of desperation in her words.

"Don't be zwitterionic!"

He raised an eyebrow at her. "Very nice," he said in approval. "I shall have to go home and look that one up."

"Don't bother," she grumbled. She tugged at the shawl she'd flung over one shoulder as it started to slip, and shoved it back into place. "It's not right. It just sounded good."

"Look," he said. "This isn't a good time or place—I know that. But I had a good time and place, and you ran off."

"It was your time," she said. "*Your* place. And your conversation. You were the one who ended that conversation, if you recall. I made you an offer and you refused."

He shrugged. "Circumstances change."

"They do, don't they?" she said. "If you think I can't change *these* particular circumstances, think again. That was a one-time offer. You don't get close enough to pull out your favorite toy handcuffs. Not again."

"You blew my favorite toy handcuffs apart," he said crossly. "And...I may have been wrong to turn you

down, damn it.'' Damn it, because he was on the verge
of closing the rule book and leaving it behind. Bear had
said to bring her in...that was as good as orders.

But Bear wasn't here now. Bear hadn't seen this
woman in action. Bear hadn't seen her fiery spirit chan-
neled into a sizzling glare and aimed his way. Even if
Jason somehow dragged Beth all the way back to the hotel
room, the delay between asking the questions and getting
answers would be...significant.

Now she eyed him warily, waiting to see where he was
going with the conversation—but only for a moment.
Then she turned her attention back to the table, running
the flashlight along the inside edges of the area over his
head...and sighing, turning the flashlight off.

''Not there?'' he asked, and then, at her warning look,
added, ''Never mind. Let's just get out of here, and then
we'll talk about...talking.''

''Wishful thinking,'' she said, but tucked the flashlight
away in her small handbag and gathered up her skirt so
she could move.

Leaving the little refuge was trickier than sneaking into
it; peeking out from beneath offered only a limited view
of what transpired in the room at large. With two of them,
it was perhaps inevitable that someone noticed them
emerging. Noticed Jason, and as Beth unfolded those
long, limber legs of hers, he bent over her in a solicitous
motion that allowed him to snag her earring right out of
her ear. She opened her mouth for instant protest, but it
only took the faintest hiss through his teeth to shush her.
As she stood, he gallantly handed her the earring—though
not before displaying it to the several people who had
turned to stare at them in surprise. ''Here it is,'' he said,

as would a triumphant hero. "Hard to believe it bounced all the way back there."

"Yes," Beth said through slightly gritted teeth. "It is, isn't it?" She plucked it out of his hand and expertly replaced it in an absent way that made Jason wish he'd been the one to brush her hair aside, to gently touch her ear.

Maybe that was the reason for what happened next...or maybe Beth was just very, very good at playing a crowd. She turned to him and said, "Thank you, sweetheart," and if she was still gritting her teeth when their lips met, Jason found no sign of it. Instead he found lips that were warm and pliant, a reality of sensation and emotion. The light, public kiss instantly turned deep and hungry, full of motion and then the light caress of tongue against lip, and then she *nibbled*—

Almost desperately, Jason broke away from her. Another move like that and he would have pulled her in close and tight, never mind the crowd and the circumstances and the fact that this woman was more than likely to use his reaction for her own purposes.

Bear would never let him live this down.

Bear will never know.

He became aware of a light smattering of polite applause; he looked away from Beth's dazed but wary expression and found they had indeed gathered an audience. Rather than deny the moment, he took it with rakish aplomb, offering the room at large a little bow of acknowledgment. When he glanced back at Beth, he saw she'd carefully arranged her shawl to cover both breasts. He stopped his instant impulse to reach for her, to pull her against him and feel the reaction she so casually concealed, and let her feel what she'd raised in him.

That's not what this is about.

It was a tiny voice, a sane little thing, but it hit him like a splash of cold water. *Thank goodness.* As Beth took a deep breath, she touched a chagrined finger to her lips and said, "Perhaps I'd better go reapply my lipstick." Playing to the crowd, just as he'd done, and getting a light ripple of laughter for her troubles.

Something inside him tightened with disappointment. Her creative self, coming through. Dancer...*performer*.

Then again, it was just as well. One of them needed to be able to think, and it didn't look like it was going to be him.

Chapter 5

Beth couldn't believe it. Couldn't *believe* it. "Was that necessary?" she snapped at Chandler as she wrapped her borrowed shawl more tightly around herself. Smiling at each other, playing their suddenly assigned roles, they'd made it to the antechamber and now had some privacy. *Not enough.* With a jerk of her head, she indicated that they should go outside. Chandler grabbed up his jacket from the row of coats, a heavier thing than the oilcloth and more appropriate for a motorbike in the chilly evening, and followed her out.

The door had barely closed behind them when he said with indignation, "*You* did it."

She turned on him just long enough to fling a glare his way, then took a quick detour into the landscaping to rescue her sling pack and jacket. "What're you *talking* about? I—"

I did. At least, every bit as much as he had. It had just seemed so natural. Damn it. She emerged from the bushes with her glare intact, and jerked her squall parka on right over the shawl. She hadn't expected to see that stuffed-shirt expression of his traded in for something more like chagrin and resignation.

"Look," he said. "I've made a real dog's dinner of this. I lost Lyeta Denisov for a matter of moments, and I'll be damned if she didn't get killed on me. And you were there…"

"Don't remind me," Beth said, feeling as sour as she sounded. "I *was* there, and she got killed anyway. I watched that spot for hours…they must have been in place before I got there. I don't know how…maybe they had a bug on her. They seem to find me easily enough."

A broad path covered with chipped wood footing led away from the building; Beth discovered they had headed for it in silent accord, neither having given it much thought. Neat rows of grapevines stretched out before them, rustling slightly in the breeze.

After a moment of silence, Chandler said abruptly, "I don't believe it was you anymore. Who killed her, I mean."

"Well, thank you so much for that. I presume it wasn't my offended protests that convinced you."

"No," he said, a matter-of-fact honesty she could appreciate. With the entry light of the visitors' center behind them, the moon provided their only light. It softened the hard lines of his face, and revealed his thoughtfulness as he glanced at her. "Your old CIA records. And what I've seen of you so far. You're right…you wouldn't have done such a sloppy job."

"Nice to have gotten that out of the way," Beth said, but the moonlight had softened something in her, too. "But you're still after me."

"After you?" he said. "No. Wanting a conversation with you, yes."

"Whether or not *I* want the conversation," she said, and stuck to her original definition. *"After me."*

"Better me than your friends from the hotel." He stopped walking, putting a hand on her arm so she turned to look at him. "What're they after? If they wanted to take you out, they'd have done it by now."

She raised an eyebrow at him, counting on the moonlight to show him her entire *excuse me?* expression.

He gave her a sudden grin, a damned charming, cocky grin. "They'd have tried harder, at least. No, they want—"

"What you want, probably," Beth interrupted, preferring it to the speculation. Charming and cocky. Just what she needed.

He took a step closer to her, and the cockiness faded into something more serious. "Talk to me. This morning you said we were on the same side—"

"I said we *might* be."

"And I think we are. Whatever you're looking for, whatever *they're* looking for…I'd rather they don't get there first. How about you?"

Beth put her fingertips against her closed eyelids, rubbing gently. To trust, not to trust… Barbara had said to work with him. But that didn't mean at the expense of losing the keycard to MI6. Beth had to get the card to Barbara, and then Stony Man could decide what to share with its allies. Finally she said, "I'm not sure what they want. I'm guessing it's just to confirm what I know, and what I've passed along *before* they kill me. They don't *need* me—they seem to have their own information sources." Egorov, no doubt. The advantage of being in place before Beth got here, maybe even before Lyeta got here.

"Do you know who they are?" Chandler said, pushing just a little too hard.

She opened her eyes to give him a steady look. "No." And she didn't. Until she heard from Barbara, she had nothing but guesses.

And for all she knew, she had a message waiting. Too much time had passed—getting here, fruitlessly searching the tables, wasting time in the most romantic setting known to man with the least romantic conversation she could think of. She gave a little shake of her head, knowing it would mean nothing to him. It was time to return to her snug little theater storage room and reassess where this mission stood.

Standing there in this most romantic of places, a handsome man beside her, dressed as she was for an evening of wine tasting and classy social flirting, and she was about to make her escape to the dark, eccentrically crowded warren of a theater. I must be crazy, she thought. Except she didn't know if it was because she wanted to *go,* or because she wanted to *stay*—to stay with this man who kept trying to reel her into his MI6 lair.

Her stomach, fed only with a few dainty morsels and half a glass of wine, had no such waverings; it knew exactly what it wanted. More. More food, more drink, time to digest. It growled. Loudly. The breeze in the grapevines was no match for it.

Somehow, Chandler did not laugh—though Beth saw it lurking in the way his eyes crinkled at the corners, and in that little twitch at the corner of his mouth. He said, "Come with me. Along with the trouser press, the hotel offers room service. Not only that, it has running water."

"The three stooges found me there once already," Beth

said without thinking, and then realized how much she'd revealed with the comment. That she was considering it. That she wanted it. Food, a chance to contact Barbara, maybe even a real shower instead of a paper-towel sink-bath in a maintenance closet. That Jason Chandler came along with the room...something to deal with later.

"They didn't find the room...and they won't. Not even if they identified me in the lobby."

"I doubt they did that," Beth said, turning to head back for the visitor center. Still undecided, but moving forward with the faith that she'd make the right choice when the time came. "I think their heads were spinning too hard."

"A possibility," he said, sounding cheerful about it. They walked in silence for a few moments, until they reached the visitor center and went right on past it, into the parking lot and up to the yellow motorbike. Chandler asked, "Anything else stashed in those bushes you want to grab?"

"I've got it all," she said, surprised at how tired she sounded.

So was he. There was no mistaking it under the single parking lot light that replaced the moon. Surprised, and...concerned. "Beth," he said, "I know we're on different teams. Our goals might not be the same. I know there are things you're not telling me, and you can be damned sure there are things I'm not telling you...but what I *am* telling you is the truth."

"Mmm," she murmured, thinking about the bus schedule and thinking she probably wouldn't have to wait too long to grab a ride back into town, and then looking up to find that those gray eyes of his weren't cold at all and suddenly wondering how she'd ever thought they were.

Reason enough to turn around and walk the other way.

As if he read her mind, Chandler slowly reached for

the small pannier on the motorbike, not taking his eyes off her as he unlocked and opened it...to pull out her fanny pack.

He offered it to her.

"You searched it," she said.

"Yes." He hefted it slightly. "But left it as it was."

Wyatt. With as much restrained dignity as possible, she accepted the fanny pack and knew instantly from its heft that the Sig was still in place.

"Nill-Grips, all right," he said, with some admiration, smart enough not to get pushy on top of the gesture of trust he'd just offered her. "You weren't having me on about the sixteen-round clip? Given that they only come in ten or fifteen."

She gave him her own version of a cocky smile. "If you use a follower from a ten-round clip, you can get sixteen snug little bullets in the fifteen-round clip." And boy did it come in handy if you were up against someone who counted up to fifteen and then thought they had that instant of safety it takes to reload.

He caught the implications immediately and grinned back at her. And then, after just the right pause, he sat on the bike and said, "Come back with me. No handcuffs this time."

After the slightest of hesitations, she said, "Oh, darn," and swung her leg over the bike.

Bliss.

Nice warm hotel room, nice soft bed...

But not yet.

Beth dropped parka, shawl, and sling pack onto the bed. She prowled around the room, noting the closed laptop on the desk, the closed suitcase in the corner, the absence of personal items that might normally be scattered around the room. A glance in the bathroom showed her a tidy, zippered shaving kit. Everything ready to go on a moment's notice...nothing to reveal any smidgen of a clue about the room's occupant.

The room itself was as advertised, down to the tea maker and trouser press. Not to mention the hair dryer, the thick, luxurious bathrobe hanging in the closet, and shampoo and soap enough to wash off even this day. The king-size bed was covered with a puffy quilt, the drapes came in a three-tiered layer of sheers, liners and gorgeous brocade, and the wall hangings weren't even bolted down in an obvious manner.

Don't let it suck you in, Beth told herself quite sternly. She looked again at the closed laptop, noting the lock and the empty PCMCIA slot that quite probably held a security keycard of its own in order to function. Just like the one she was looking for, only Lyeta's copy was of Krystof Scherba's master card. It was a keycard that would allow any laptop to function not only in Scherba's network, but would give the operator the ability to manipulate and invade other systems in the network.

Ah yes, that did it. Brought her mind right back to the business at hand...and the fact that she was no longer in on it alone. She finished her circuit of the room, pulled all three tiers of drapes closed, and flicked on the main room light to find Chandler regarding her with a mixture of amusement and understanding. And...waiting. Waiting to see what she'd do next or, more specifically, just how difficult she'd be to work with.

"You know," he said, "This could have gone much easier if you'd told me you were working an allied mission to start with."

"I haven't even said as much at all," Beth told him smoothly, dropping to the bed to dig in her sling pack for her PDA. She dug out the minuscule charger and plug adapter; might as well take advantage of the reliable source of electricity while she was here. "You're assuming, because you know I was CIA. Well, look at your data again, wherever it is. *Was* means *was*. It doesn't say a thing about what *is*."

"Very well, then," he said, sounding particularly annoyed and British. "Whatever you're doing, at least nominally we're working toward the same goals. And you had me pegged as MI6 right from the start."

"That I did," she murmured, dropping over the side of the bed to hunt for the outlet between the bed and the bedside table. Why hotels across the world had to hide their outlets behind furniture, she would never understand. She righted herself to find him looking a little taken aback at the view with which she'd presented him.

"It's just..." he said, recapturing his thought. "If you'd *told* me..."

"Then what? You'd have done just the same. You play by the rules, Chandler. Every move you make confirms it. And the rules meant bringing me in to *talk*—SOP and you've confirmed it since. You only got off that kick once you'd learned enough to decide for yourself that I hadn't killed Lyeta, and I'm betting you *still* have a yen to follow orders and let someone, somewhere, know I'm here with you. If you haven't already."

He looked stung. "I haven't," he said. "Blimey, I don't know why you fiery creative types think it's within your prerogative to assume you can predict other people's decisions and then act on them."

"What?" Beth said, entirely taken off guard—fiery creative types?—but not so much she couldn't feel a flare of anger. "I'll make the decisions I feel are in the best interests of accomplishing this...what I want to accomplish, thank you! In *my* best interests. And who told you I was a dancer?''

That was stupid. Whatever files he'd gotten his hands on, of course. The CIA had not taken advantage of her talents as Stony Man had, but certainly it had been in her records.

But he gave a short shake of his head. "No one," he said. "It's the way...you move."

Ah. She had to think about that.

She liked it.

She sighed. There was no denying her easy response to this man. He was handsome and self-confident—with good reason, as she'd seen—and by golly he had some charming moments. But by golly, just like every other handsome self-confident man who'd ever touched her life, he was rule-bound. And the thing about rule-bound men...they seemed to feel a duty to impose their rules on everyone, especially the free and easy souls who thought so differently than they did. Even, as she discovered when she'd been young and naive and not yet so superbly trained in the art of self-defense, when that impulse extended to smacking you around to make a point.

The CIA had gotten her after that, and the CIA had given her the tools to make it through this world on her own terms, tools honed by Stony Man and Barbara Price. Stony Man had given her the room to use all of her skills...and they valued that fiery creative streak in her. The same one that had gotten her out of more tight situations than she cared to count.

"Did you know," she said, "that oysters can change sex at will?"

She'd flabbergasted him, as much as he tried to hide it. "What does that have to do with any bloody thing?"

"Nothing," Beth said, suddenly tired. Or at least, sud-

denly realizing again how tired she was. "And everything." It was the way her mind worked...the trivia, the
non sequiturs, the way she could change directions in mid-
stride without stumbling—both physically and mentally.
And it had to do with choices. Her choices, his choices,
how differently they handled those moments.

It made perfect sense to her, but she didn't think he'd
ever understand it. His very reaction to her free-form
thinking—the resistance instead of any willingness to follow—pretty much proved the point. Except...she looked
over at him, discovering the frown she expected...and
something else. A struggle, beneath the surface, reflected
in the shadow of his eyes and the faint working along his
jaw. *He's trying.* Not quite able to follow what she was
trying to express but not dismissing it. *Trying.* When was
the last time a man had done that?

Never, that's when. And *never* had led her expect short,
widely spaced affairs that never quite touched her heart.
Not even so much as watching this man *try* touched her
now.

"It's okay," she said, gently enough to be unexpected
by both of them. "Maybe one day I'll dance for you."

She hadn't meant it the way it sounded—and the way
it sounded created an instant tension between them, one
Beth could not help but enjoy and respond to. He stood
near the desk, looking as though he might make it to the
bed in one decisive step, and Beth almost willed him to
do it.

But.

But she had work to do, and so did he. Distractions
couldn't be tolerated, not with the kind of pressure she
was under, and a casual fling definitely fit in the distraction category.

That's not right, protested a little voice in her mind as

she turned on the PDA, entered the password, and checked her messages. *There's nothing casual about what just happened.* And nothing simple, either. Great. Not only distracting, but complex. And getting close to irresistible.

Thank goodness she had other things to think about. She found a short message from Barbara—short and to the point. No one had found any trace of Lyeta's recent presence in public accommodations, but she'd used a deep cover credit card to purchase a sleeping bag the day before she'd met Beth. The day before she'd died.

Sleeping bag? Had she spent the night on a park bench somewhere, playing the homeless person?

"What's up?" Jason pulled the desk chair into the room, flipped it around, and straddled it, resting his arms along the back. He seemed to have decided to put aside the past few moments, as inexplicable as they were, and go forward. That, too, tugged at Beth as an appealing surprise. "That's a mighty frown."

"Is it?" she said, putting a hand to her face. "I guess so. Just…missing pieces."

"Nothing quite fits yet," he agreed.

He watched, unobtrusive, while she called up the new data file Barbara had sent—the same list of Blue Crane establishments, this time prioritized. She gave them a quick glance, recognizing that along with type of establishment—restaurant, spa, hotel—Barbara had made geographic priorities. Those within a certain distance of the dockside meeting, and along the line of probable travel into the country. She sent a quick thought of gratitude Barbara's way. The way things stood, with the nondescripts on her tail, the real CIA agents who believed her guilty of the shooting, and MI6 no doubt pressuring Chandler, she'd need a lot more time than she had to check out even the top-rated places on the list.

After waiting longer than she herself might have allowed in his circumstances, Chandler said quietly, "You haven't really told me anything yet. I know you're looking for something, and I very much imagine it's something Lyeta put you onto before she died. But..." He trailed off, shrugging at her and leaving *but you owe me more* unspoken.

On the one hand, she did. She owed him for this safe place, for the shower she was about to take, for the chance to catch her breath. On the other hand...

She owed him nothing. They were both doing their jobs, and the only reason she was here was because he hoped to learn something from her. That didn't mean he *would*. With a decisive poke of the PDA stylus, she shut down the invaluable little tool, tossing it onto the bed to finish recharging. It was safe enough. He might try, but he'd never get through Stony Man's security protocols. She rubbed her fingertips over her tired eyelids and said abruptly, finally responding to his last comments, "I'm still thinking."

"Weighing options," he said, interpreting her words fairly accurately this time. "Desperately searching for a choice you consider to be better than actually telling me anything." He'd definitely got her that time.

She didn't deny it. "Yes," she said ruefully. "And I'm tired and I'm not thinking clearly. So I'm going to take a shower and hope that helps." She stood, stretched in a way that was meant to test her bruises more than loosen muscles, and then snagged the bathrobe off the closet hanger on the way to the bathroom.

"I'm going to order dinner," he said, so conversationally that she got the definite impression he was lying low, studying her…trying to figure her out. That when the time was right, he'd pounce. "Would you like something?"

"God, yes," she said. "Something that comes from a cow. Or a water buffalo, or whatever passes for red meat on their menu."

"You're a carnivore," he said. "Got it."

She looked back at him as she entered the bathroom, robe bundled in her arms. "For tonight I am," she said, as much to herself as to him. "I'm an oyster…adventurous."

Chapter 6

The water hit Beth between the shoulder blades just the way she liked it...hard and pulsing. But she didn't allow herself the luxury of a long shower; she hit the soap and shampoo in quick succession, cranked the water off with a decisive twist of wrist, and stepped out to reach for one of the hotel's thick, cream-colored towels.

She almost missed it. Jason's voice, stiff and formal and quite clearly in mid-conversation. "—tomorrow morning," he said. "I'll see you then."

Ahh, so he couldn't help playing by the rules after all.

Beth tried to ignore the bitter disappointment biting at her throat. It had been stupid to trust him this far, and if she hadn't been so intent on finding the keycard that she was willing to compromise her work-alone habits...

Or face it, if she hadn't been in over her head, with so little in the way of leads and meanwhile Egorov's men all over her...

Whatever. It was time to go. She gave her wet hair a

brusque toweling, the kind that made it dry with a bed-head look instead of a sleek, shiny bob, and cinched the bathrobe tightly around her waist. It was too big, of course—one-size-fits-all rarely *did*. She'd give her pack a quick check, throw the dress back on, and make her way back to the theater.

But she paused, looking at herself in the mirror as she rubbed lotion into her face and hands. Beth of the wet hair, flushed cheeks, and lotion-smeared face stared back at her. "Dinner first," she said to that Beth. On MI6's nickel. That suited her just fine.

"Did you say something?" Chandler asked her, muffled enough that he must have been across the room. Playing with his laptop while he had the chance, she figured.

"Talking to myself," she called back, cheered by the thought of a nice juicy steak. The restaurant here was like the rest of the hotel—it thought much of itself, and purported to have fine dining. She hoped Chandler had ordered dessert, too. She'd eat...and then she'd run. And early tomorrow she'd start in on her prioritized list, hoping for more intel from Barbara and keeping her eye out for Egorov's mole and his buddies. Or his subordinates—they might well be honest CIA, manipulated by an expert. She'd have to update Barbara, let her know the Chandler thing wasn't working out and the CIA had been infiltrated thoroughly enough to keep Beth on the run. Hmm. Might as well do it right under Chandler's nose.

But when she breezed out of the bathroom, releasing a cloud of steamy air and shampoo scent into the room, she found next to the PDA a pair of dark green sweats and basic flip-flops. Chandler, sitting in one of the comfy armchairs by the drapes, glanced away from the items, as if he'd somehow had nothing to do with their presence. He, too, had changed, from the sleekly tailored suit to plain

green fatigue pants belted over a heavy V-neck that
draped so beautifully over the hard planes of his chest
that she suspected it had to be silk. He told her, "Food'll
be up in twenty minutes, they said."

"Great. I'm starved." She looked at the sweats, looked
at him, and ran a finger down the sleeve at the edge of
the bed. "Nice," she said. "Thank you."

He lifted a shoulder. "The best the gift shop could do
on short notice."

"After hours, no doubt. You must have been convincing. And somehow they got one of my best colors." The
green brought out her eyes, always had. "Give it up,
Chandler…it was thoughtful. Or is it against the rule book
to be thoughtful to someone who's not on your team?"

He gave it up. "You're welcome." And then looked
directly at her, somehow giving her the impression that
he wanted nothing more than to get up from his chair and
come over for a closer look, a most intimate look…
although when she blinked, there he was, relaxed and
quiet in the chair.

Whew. Tired. Imagining things. Or possibly not, but she
didn't want to go there.

There was a second chair by the bed. She sat in it,
pulling the PDA over for a few stylus-scrawled words to
Barbara, which she prefaced with the symbol that meant
she wasn't in a position for video communication and
needed to stick to text. There were no intrusion alerts as
she fired up the PDA, so apparently Chandler had kept
his hands to himself.

Hmm. Perhaps not the best turn of phrase for the circumstances. Beth put her mind to business and finished
with the PDA, then scooped up the sweats, disappearing
into the bathroom to change so quickly the door barely
had time to latch. She finger-combed her hair—not doing

a thing to change the bed-head look—and emerged just as room service knocked on the door. With an about-face, she disappeared back into the bathroom, leaving the door casually half-closed and making sure she wasn't visible in the mirror. When she came out again, she attacked dinner with a vengeance. Venison loin over a cinnamon and butternut waffle...heavenly. Halfway through the meal, she looked up at Chandler and, with no premeditation whatsoever, said, "Who was it?"

He gave her a startled glance, as well he might. Placing his fork and its cargo of crispy duck at the side of his plate, he said, "Who was who?" and then winced. "Pretend I didn't say it that way."

She grinned at him. He wasn't so bad when he wasn't taking himself so seriously. She remembered his words, used them back on him. "What *fiery creative type* pissed you off so badly that you're still taking it out on the rest of us?"

"Ah." Instantly he sobered. He played with the fork a moment and then pushed the plate away. With obvious effort, he kept his voice light. He didn't fool Beth for an instant. He said, "Someone I was involved with. She made a decision without consulting me. I guess I still wonder...daughter or son? So did she, I gather...she couldn't face what she'd done, in the end."

Beth couldn't help her aghast expression. "She—" and then didn't finish. There was no point. It was obvious what the woman had done...and what it had done to him. She watched the play of muscle in his cheek and jaw and then said, "I'm sorry. I wouldn't have asked if I'd thought..." *If I'd thought I would get such a straight answer.*

He managed to look at her. "You owe me one, then.

Who was it? Who made you so resentful of us poor schmucks and our rules?''

''Oh, that's easy,'' she said, and smiled beatifically at him. ''Everyone. But at some point I figured out it never works when you try to play it someone else's way. You can't ever truly fit what it is they have in mind. Much easier to go my own way.''

''Lonely, I should think,'' he said.

Okay, that stung a little. ''Sometimes, maybe. But the price is too high to do it any other way.'' She flexed her bare toes and used a finely controlled foot to snatch the flip-flips from the bed even as she eyed the last item on her plate. Dessert. *Mmm, thank you for that.*

Perhaps she shouldn't have savored it so openly…every spoonful of the crème brûlée allowed to melt away in her mouth, relished to the fullest. She knew he watched, but only when she glanced up with the last spoonful in her mouth did she see the intensity of his gaze.

She thought he probably didn't do much undercover work. Not with his nature, not with the way his feelings showed so clearly on his face and on every line of his body. A second glance confirmed it. Oh, yes, every line.

Beth sighed. Another day, another mission, and she might not be so eager to get out of this room.

Or on the other hand, maybe she would. Spending time with Jason Chandler…she didn't think it could be just another fling. Not with that face, telling her everything she needed to know. Not with the way she felt herself responding to him, even now. That lovely sweatsuit suddenly seemed just a little too warm, and her pulse pounded in places that took her by surprise.

Lucky for her it was time to run. Not to make a big deal of it, as she put the food tray on the floor and shoved it aside with her foot so she could stand and bend over the bed, folding the dress away in a neat roll, and looping the heel straps of the shoes through the clip on the sling pack strap meant for keys. The PDA wasn't charged yet, but she unplugged it and stashed it away in its neat leather wallet. "You're not asking me questions," she said, and went into the bathroom to brush her teeth with hotel toothpaste and her finger.

He sounded a little strained, which made her smile around her finger. "You've made it clear you'll talk when you bloody well please. And I, like a civilized person, am digesting."

Yeah, a half-eaten dinner. Perhaps guilt had ruined his conversation, as well as recollection of his impulsive ex-girlfriend. *Tomorrow morning,* indeed. This was one spy-girl who'd be on her own by then. Again.

She almost made it without any incident at all. She came out of the bathroom still drying her hands, tossed the towel on the bed, snagged her sling pack and parka, and headed for the door. She caught him flat-footed, but not so flat-footed he couldn't bound across the room and stiff-arm the door closed just as it was wide enough to slip through.

"Ah, damn," she muttered. She rested her forehead against the door. "We've had this conversation before," she said. "Remember how it ended?"

"Bugger that," he said, his harsh breath stirring the hair at the back of her neck, raising goose bumps. He demanded, "Where do you think you're going?"

At that she whirled to glare at him, very like that moment at the dock. So close…but not close in spirit, oh not at all. "Don't even try to play that game," she told him, taking in the cold anger of his gray eyes and not quailing before it, not in the least. "'Tomorrow morning? See you then?' What happened? Aren't you used to women who can take a fast shower? When were you going to tell me about your little date? Is he bringing drugs for me, or just a new set of handcuffs?''

He came right back at her. ''I'm doing my best to protect you, damn it, and that means playing my own people just as much as it means playing you. I might have told you, and I might not have. I wasn't prepared to make the decision right then.''

''Well, thank you so much for your honesty. Goodbye.'' She would have turned, but his hand came off the door and pushed against her shoulder—not quite pinning her there, but making the point.

''Don't do this,'' he said, earnest and angry all at once, and all of it right there on his face, so close to her. ''You're wasting your energy evading me instead of accomplishing anything—''

''—or *you* accomplishing anything.''

He glared. ''Or that. But damn it, I don't want you out there alone!''

''That's your problem,'' she snapped back at him. ''Now let me go, or things will get downright hostile in here!''

He didn't. He moved in on her, reaching for her. Possessive. Only at the last moment did her fighting brain realize what had happened, and by then her kissing brain was hard at work. By then she'd moved in against him like she'd wanted to since...face it, since those first moments on the dock, fingers clutching his shirt at the shoulders, lips and mouth and tongue busy and happy and thrilling the rest of her body. He cupped the back of her head in one strong hand, protecting her as he pushed her up against the door, capturing her more thoroughly than any MI6 trickiness could ever manage. She didn't care. She liked it. She reveled in it. Her fingers explored the short, bristly hair at his nape and then the longer hair above his ears, feeling the texture of curl hidden by the cut. She found the hard-cut muscles of his shoulders, had the impulse to tug his shirt free of his belt—and wasn't quite quick enough. He slipped a hand down the tight curves of her body, down to her bottom, where he got demanding, pulling her in against him as he rocked into her. She groaned into his mouth, startled by the shock of pleasure.

And then he broke away. Resting his forehead against hers, breathing raggedly and with his fingers clenching in her hair with the effort of the self-control, he said, "There, now you won't be alone. You'll bloody well take some part of me with you."

After a stunned moment, a moment when both her mind and her body gasped in response, she gave a laugh as ragged as his breathing. "Don't tell me—it's a new superspy technique."

"Yes," he said. "Absolutely. Can't fool you."

She took a deep breath. A steadying breath. A thoughtful breath.

She didn't think him capable of such fervent deception. Differing objectives, yes—but he'd been up-front about that, even to the point of immediate honesty when she'd confronted his intention to bring in a colleague the next morning. This mission had turned into a confusing muddle of morphing objectives, newly discovered enemies and a frustration of lost time, but of one thing Beth was sure.

He'd meant every bit of that kiss.

And so had she.

Her expression gave him hope. She hadn't rejected him, laughed at him or injured him. Face flushed, mouth swollen and definitely been-kissed, she considered him. Her lips parted slightly, words she wasn't quite certain of hesitating there a moment; she licked them and looked away. But...

Still thinking.

All *he'd* been thinking was about how close she was, and how he didn't want to let her go. And in how, having little choice, he wasn't going to miss his only chance to taste those lips. It hadn't turned out badly at that. Not badly at all. Crucial parts of him still twitched with reaction. He turned away from her, smiling slightly.

Headlights flashed through a gap in the curtains; for all there were three layers, they hadn't meshed neatly. He reached a hand up to twitch them into place and caught a glimpse of the well-lit parking lot, of several hurried figures tumbling out of a dark sedan. Another look confirmed it; he swore, dark and low.

She understood immediately. "Come with me," she said, even as she slipped off her flip-flops. Preparing. "This room is no longer secure." She eased her hand into the sling pack and removed the Sig's discreet carrying case, belting it around her waist and unzipping the pocket; then she slid into her lightweight parka.

Jason took it in on the move. He reached the desk in one swift stride, jamming the laptop in its briefcase, not bothering with anything else but the Browning and its ammo. Where he'd go from here was almost irrelevant; he—*they*—had to get out of the hotel first. "Whoever they are, they're not shy of using up resources to keep track of you," he grunted, jamming his arms through the shoulder holster straps, double-checking the two ammo pouches to make sure they were occupied even though he'd inspected the rig upon taking it off as a matter of course.

She waited by the cracked-open door, both patient and impatient as he snapped the rig together and settled the

Browning in place. Her face held no fear, only alert readiness. She said, "If Egorov's man is in the CIA as Lyeta said, and the CIA also thinks I shot Lyeta, then the mole would have no trouble committing resources to my capture."

More information in one casual sentence than he'd managed to pull from her all day. He took it in stride, refraining from comment—although if he'd known the agency and not a smaller wanna-be organization had been behind the earlier foray in the hotel lobby, he would have been more circumspect about bringing her back to the room. No doubt they'd paid off the desk clerks and the concierge and even the bellboys to keep an eye out for Beth's reappearance. And while he and Beth had been circumspect upon return...

Someone, somewhere, had obviously seen them.

The CIA. Compromised.

If he'd known.

It was an old phrase from an old song.

He tucked it away for another time, accepting that he, too, bore some responsibility; he hadn't learned the identity of those whose arses he'd kicked so readily in the lobby. He'd concentrated on finding Beth, rightly figuring that they were after her, not him, and wrongly figuring that they would continue to focus on her, not him. But the CIA had the resources to do both.

Obviously.

He made a hasty job of pulling his motorbike jacket on, coming up against Beth's back as she carefully checked the hallway. "They're frustrated by now," she said. "I'm sure they expected to have me before this. They didn't go straight for their weapons the first time, but I wouldn't care to assume they'll do the same in the future."

"We won't," he said, visualizing the hotel floor plan. Like so many of them, the halls wound around themselves in a confusing maze with exits to fire stairs at crucial points. "They can't cover the elevators and all the stairwells. I say we make for the exit on the other side of the floor and head down. There's a bizarre lower passage leading to the parking garage from there."

She glanced back at him, her lips still soft but her eyes hard and ready. Eager, almost. "You know the way?"

He nodded, and she immediately moved aside. "Your lead, then. Time to blow this joint."

"Lovely idiom. Let's avoid taking it too seriously," he suggested, giving a quick glance down the hall in both directions and then moving out at a fast clip. She came behind him, silent on her bare feet and close enough to cover his back, not so close as to impede him. He realized instantly that in spite of their differences, he could count on her to work *with* him and not just near him, actively partnering in a way made him grin fiercely. *Me and thee against the world.*

Once they passed the bank of three brass elevators, Jason picked up the pace considerably, startling several blithe hotel guests who chose just the wrong moment to emerge from their rooms. Beth effortlessly kept pace, flip-flops in one hand, the other ready to dive for the Sig. "Just around this corner," he said, turning his head just enough so she could hear him.

Just enough and too much, as from the corner of his eye he saw a body in motion. He reacted instantly, diving away but brought up short by the opposing hall wall, still fully exposed—

And this team had come in aggressively, ready to extract what they wanted and kill whoever got in their way. Even from the corner of his eye, Jason had recognized the lump of a sound suppressor at the end of the pistol aimed his way. Heard the sharp double *phhut* of the gunshot, and jerked at the astonishing burn as metal drilled through his biceps and into the wall, leaving blood splatter along expensive wallpaper. Bracing for a second impact, he scrambled to get out of the line of fire even as he reached for his gun—and then heard a third shot, a strange noise that didn't quite seem right.

Because it wasn't a gunshot at all. It was Beth, bounding in with those silly flip-flops, smacking them across the gunman's fingers, using her momentum to twist around and roundhouse the man's face with her bare foot, her legs long and lean and wielded with astonishing control. The man's head bounced off the wall. In the mere instant that he sagged, she snatched his gun, smashing it into his temple and barely hesitating to watch him go down. "You on your feet?" she asked, glancing back only for an instant before riveting her attention on the stairwell they'd been aiming for.

"Good to go," he said. "Looks like they have more manpower than we anticipated."

"Looks like they're not holding back this time, either." She nodded at the stairs. "These? Or a different set? And I ought to mention that from the sound of it, we have maybe fifteen seconds before someone comes through that door."

Bloody hell, that hurts! "We've lost too much time— this is it."

"Fine. Leg up?" She gave his arm a quick, questioning look.

He tried to flex it fully, failed, and offered her a quick grimace as he looped his hands together anyway, bending to offer her a stirrup even though he wasn't quite sure yet what she had in mind. "At least it's not spurting."

"None of that nasty jaggedy bone sticking out, either,"
she said, using his hand stirrup to launch herself up, and—
I don't bloody believe it!—climbed from his hands to his
shoulder and upward to crouch lightly on the stout door-
closing mechanism, balancing on one bare foot with just
enough room to fit under the extra-high ceiling. Jason
eyed her only long enough to convince himself she'd done
it, then put his back to the wall just beyond the turn with
the Browning in his hand.

Moments later, the doorknob snicked and turned; the
quickest of glances showed him Beth, with incredible
flexibility and balance, riding the door open with her free
foot and jamming the stolen, silenced pistol down on the
bald head just coming through the opening. A second man
took aim at her from within the stairwell but by then Jason
was in motion, squeezing the trigger on a round that
slapped the man down. A massive explosion of sound
echoed up and down the stairwell.

"Bugger," he said, and to Beth, "Sorry."

For the sound would bring the rest of them running,
and the three they'd conquered would be as nothing unless
they got out of here, *now*.

"Considering you just literally saved my ass," Beth
said, "I forgive you." Within the stairwell, the wounded
man moaned. She glanced to see his weapon had fallen
out of reach and ignored him, keeping her attention on
her captive. "Let's get this guy secured."

Standard-issue cuffs scavenged from the two wounded
men did the trick. Beth leaped lightly from her perch as
Jason did the honors, and at no time did the aim of her
weapon on the bald man deviate in the process. As Jason
pushed the man up against the wall, Beth got right in his
face. "Listen up," she said. "If you're Egorov's man, it's
time to back off. You're blown, and the word's about to

come down—I'd take flight if I were you. If you're not Egorov's, then you're plain old CIA being led around by the nose. Get off my back and start looking within your own ranks for the very poor sniper who killed Lyeta." And without a second look at the man, she jerked her head at Jason—*let's go*—and entered the stairwell.

Jason grabbed his laptop case and followed, but when she looked back at him she stopped short, jamming the silenced gun into her parka and backtracking impatiently to the wounded man. She produced a knife from... somewhere...to cut the man's suit jacket sleeve off and then the fine linen sleeve of his dress shirt. "You're leaving a blood trail," she murmured, splitting the end of the sleeve in two as she approached him.

"Ah," he said, holding his arm away from his body so she could work. "Your concern touches me to the core."

She hesitated as she wrapped the sleeve around his arm, glancing up as if in spite of herself, with enough worry in those exquisite blue-green eyes to startle him and, in the midst of gunplay and danger and hard decisions, to touch him. Then she grew fierce, an expression to which he was more accustomed. Doubling one of the sleeve's split ends back to tie off the bandage, she said acerbically, "Bleed slower. We don't want to leave them any bread crumbs."

"That's better," he told her, surprisingly chipper. And why not? No more stalking around on her trail, no more trying to outguess her, no more *waiting* for something to break on this assignment. They'd joined forces, they'd hit action—always his best thing—and damn, they were good together. He gave her a grin and was even more pleased as she returned it with a feral glint in her eye and led the way down the stairs.

With the bottom passage in sight, they heard the stairwell door open several floors above them, followed by the heavy tread of fast downhill footsteps, fast enough to include gaps where the pursuing agents skipped steps and ominous thuds as they jumped to the next landing. "Go," Beth said to him, already lost in concentration as she steadied her borrowed gun on the railing where it bent to follow the landing and the final tier of stairs before the passage. "I'll catch up."

Jason watched her try one angle, then another, and when she opened her mouth to urge him on, he said, "I damn well think not."

"Which of us is losing blood?" she snapped, choosing her vantage point and settling in. "Which of us is the better shot? Go!"

Jason glanced at the makeshift bandage and found it soaked, found fresh stain seeping back down the heavy material of his shirt. If nothing else he'd be leaving bread crumbs again, and soon. "Sod it all," he muttered viciously. He gave her a warning look—a *don't get killed* look—and headed down the stairs.

He made it only as far as the final landing. As right as she was, he couldn't bring himself to leave her. He looked up in time to see her take calm and steady aim, carefully squeezing the trigger twice in quick succession and then giving the borrowed pistol a startled look as the slide jumped back and stuck there, the magazine empty.

He'd heard bodies fall, but a third man came on. Beth swore a heartfelt oath and dove for the stairs, jumping the entire flight and lurching forward at the bottom to smack into the wall opposite them. Jason lifted the Browning just in time to drill her pursuer before the man targeted Beth. The man's wayward bullet hit high on the concrete block wall of the stairwell as he tumbled loosely down the stairs.

Beth wiped the silenced pistol clean of her prints and

dropped it on the man's twitching body. "Five freaking shots in that clip," she said in disbelief. "Who goes into a firefight situation with a half-full clip?"

"Not you, I'm sure," Jason said. "Let's not find out if there are any more of them. 'Out' is this way." But the stairwell swooped around him, and although he thought he'd stayed upright Beth quickly grabbed his good arm, shoving her hip up against his. Deftly relieving him of the Browning, she shoved it back into its holster, grabbed up his abused laptop case, and got them moving. "I'm okay," he said, unconvincing to his own ears. "Just need a place to sit down." He glared at the world as he stumbled along, muttering, "What a cock-up."

Beth snickered. If she was worried about his condition it didn't show, and he found that oddly reassuring even if she *was* laughing at him. "Oh, right," he said, unrepentant. "Different implication for you Yanks."

"Just a little," she said, still smiling as they entered the parking garage, discovering no sign of pursuit or surveillance. "Come on, then. I have just the right place. It's absolutely meant for sitting."

Chapter 7

Fast food has taken over the world. "Thirty thousand franchises in one hundred twenty-one countries," Beth told Chandler, handing over a paper-wrapped burger. "Forty-six million customers per day. Now you're one of them. Eat up, you need protein." She gave her own burger a skeptical look. "Guess I'm not sure just how much actual protein is in one of these things."

He sat in the otherwise empty theater with her—front row seats, of course—and automatically took the burger she proffered. In a moment she'd pilfer the theater's first-aid kit and rewrap his arm, but as long as the food was still warm and he had that pasty, used-up look on his face, they could just sit here in the barely heated auditorium munching burgers and fries. The franchise had been on the way, and she'd sat him down at one of the children's miniature picnic tables while she ran in to throw rands at them and grab the goodies.

Not that it had been so long since their last meal. But

Beth was making up for lost time and Chandler needed to make up for lost blood. Far too much of it. At the moment he just sat there, looking around the dimly lit theater with what was meant to be a practiced eye, but she could see he wasn't really tracking. She gave him a slanting glance as she reached for her milk shake, and pulled the straw out just far enough to make a series of horrible slurping noises. He started, immediately focusing on her.

"There," she said, meeting his surprised look without concern. "If there's anyone here, that should bring them running, don't you think?"

"You said there wouldn't be."

"And there won't. But you don't believe me yet, so I thought I'd give you a little demo. See? No one." She took a big bite of her cheeseburger, pretending it was actually juicy. "I know it's a big comedown from that hotel food, but do you know how many calories they pack into one little French fry?"

"No, but I'll bet you can tell me." He offered her something close to a rakish grin, an expression she hadn't expected to see from him. His hair, conservative as it was, still managed to look rumpled and even a little scruffy, and it went perfectly with that grin.

"Five hundred and forty total for a serving that size," she informed him, pretending to be unaffected. *Yeah, and that kiss didn't curl your toes, either.* "You can use 'em right now. So eat."

Normally she wouldn't worry about her curling toes. She wouldn't worry about her response to him at all—she'd just let it happen and enjoy the moments. But Chandler...her reactions to him ambushed her. Repeatedly. When she'd seen him in that hallway, the instant she knew he'd been shot but not just where—

She'd almost lost it. She'd almost rushed to him instead of disarming the shooter. Superbly trained, highly experienced, and all she could see was the stunned look on his face as the bullet hit. Not a good sign, that distraction. Not good sign, the depth of her response to him. She thought she'd left those feelings behind when she'd walked away from her long-discarded fiancé, but now they hit her hard.

So she worried about her toes.

Chandler was oblivious, wrapped up in his pain and his sweat and his distraction. Thinking about their situation, no doubt. As a good spy should. He unwrapped the crinkly paper just enough to expose half the burger, and took a healthy bite. "I know this is an active theater. I don't understand why—"

"Because they're just gearing up for production. I should know, I auditioned here a few days ago. Waiting for callbacks, now. They do the auditions in the morning, fight over them in the afternoon, and leave the theater to me in the evening. Not that they know about it. But honestly, did you think I'd bring you to a place I hadn't checked out? Or bring *me* to a place I hadn't checked out? This theater is perfect."

"It's hardly secure," he pointed out. "We pretty much walked right in."

"*This* part of it isn't." She stuffed a fry into her mouth and sucked the salt off. Ooh, so bad for her. No wonder it tasted so good.

He gave her a baffled look. "Backstage?"

Beth laughed. "You haven't been around theaters much, have you? They're wonderful when you want to disappear. This particular place has storage worthy of *Phantom of the Opera*. Once we go below, we're off everyone's radar." A final bite of the burger, and she balled the paper up and stuck it inside the bag. "Lean this way," she said. "I'll fix that arm up while you eat."

"Not the best combination of activities." But he did it, and she opened the kit on the seat beside her, twisting into a yoga-inspired shape to get a good working angle as they sat side by side. He said nothing as she worked, cutting the sleeve open and cleansing the wound. The natural distinct definition of his biceps had given way to swelling, and she wished she had antibiotics.

"Thank you," he said when she had finished, although she was certain she'd hurt him. Sweat daubed his face, gathering in the well-defined groove between his nose and lips. She snatched her hand back as it rose to follow an impulse, fingers drawn to trace those lips. The upper lip looked a little stern, but the bottom lip...sensuous and full and waiting for more kissing. *God. What timing, Riggs. The middle of a cock-up mission.*

Oblivious to her wayward thoughts, he said, "It's time to talk, Beth. *Is* that your name? Beth?"

She hesitated, then nodded. And required no more prompting. He was in this with her one way or the other— he certainly wasn't going to make any further easy contact with his handler. She didn't think he'd noticed it yet, but while the first round fired had hit his arm, the second had gone astray and cored the laptop case. She said succinctly, "I met Lyeta to give her sanctuary in exchange for information. She was shot as we spoke. She told me she had a copy of the master security keycard that would give us open access to Krystof Scherba's computer network. You know Scherba built Egorov's system, right?"

Okay, not the entire truth. Nothing about the mini CD that Beth already had, and no hint of a definition of *us*— Stony Man. But all the same he seemed stunned to realize he was, at last and in one swift conversational dump, getting the information he'd been looking for. She waited until he nodded, and until his expression turned faintly eager at the thought of the keycard. Then she said, ''All I know is that she stashed it somewhere to which the words *Blue Crane, under,* and *table* all apply.''

Chandler plucked a French fry from the bag between them; a smile showed in the quirk of his lips as he chewed. ''And so I found you crawling under tables at the Blue Crane Winery.''

She shrugged, feeling her own amusement. ''It was as good a lead as any. I've got a complete list of possibilities, but they're extensive. The big problem is that we can't find any record of where Lyeta spent her time the night before. If I could find that location, it might narrow things down considerably. If I could *search* it...''

Chandler smiled the kind of smile that shouldn't be coming from a man at the end of a fight-and-run scene and who still bled from a bullet wound. ''You may have gone to meet her at that dock, but *I* followed her there.''

He'd known? He'd known all along?

He just hadn't known it mattered.

Beth said it out loud just to be sure, fighting the impulse to jump up right then and there, demand the information and run off into the night. ''Then you know where she came from. Where she spent her last night.''

In spite of her restraint, Chandler saw the impulse. ''Easy there,'' he said. ''The answer is yes, as much as anyone knows. But now is not the time to act on it. You're exhausted—you're going to make mistakes. So am I, and I don't trust myself to cover anyone's back in this situation, not when we have options. Besides, the location doesn't come with lighting, and nature won't provide any until nearly six in the morning.''

The location. "You're not going to tell me," she said flatly, narrowing her eyes at him.

He winced. She didn't know if it was from his arm or her glare and she didn't care. He said, "As a matter of fact, no. Unless you tell me I'm wrong. Tell me you don't want to dash off into the night and do something about it."

She bounced up out of the theater seat and into the aisle, where she shed the flip-flops she'd worn on their hurried exit from the hotel and put her foot up on the back of an innocent seat in lieu of a stretching bar. He wasn't wrong. She *did* want to act, and to act *now*. But that didn't mean she *would*.

"I thought as much," he said, jamming the litter from the meal into the bag it had come in and wadding the entire thing up with enough pressure to turn it into a diamond. "Don't get a strop on about it. I had you pegged from the start. Why you think it's perfectly fine to make impulsive decisions without consulting the other people involved—"

"Get over it," she snapped at him, straightening from the tight straight-legged stretch, unaccountably wounded by his words. As if she cared what he thought. "Your attitude is exactly why I know better than to trust rule-book boys. You think you have the right to control every-one else, and if a thing isn't done *your* way, it's wrong no matter what."

As if she cared what he thought.

Evidently, she did. To judge by the wrench of the anger within her, the hot pain deep in her throat…evidently, foolishly, she somehow cared a lot.

He had his mouth open to say something; she cut him off. "As it happens, you're exactly right and exactly *wrong*. I wanted to run off and check the place out. But

I wasn't going to. It's the middle of the night, we're exhausted, and you're hurt. Do you even know how much blood you've lost? As it happens, I was going to *consult* you about how you wanted to proceed. So you can just—'' *Go to hell,* she'd been about to say, except she realized how revealing it was, how personal she'd let things get. Beside herself in what would no doubt be labeled an impulsive little temper, she let her foot fall from the seat and stalked down the sloped aisle and then up to the stage. She had no particular purpose other than putting distance between them, enough distance so she had time to cool off. Official retreat, hiding the very personal retreat beneath.

She couldn't make it *too* personal. She still had to work with him, to wait until morning and start the chase again. In spite of her anger, the anticipation gave her a little thrill—finally, Lyeta's keycard, her dying legacy, and the tool that would allow Stony Man to target not only the remains of the dying Egorov's legacy, but master hacker Krystof Scherba.

That Chandler would be there had nothing to do with it.

Damn toes. Stop curling.

She sat cross-legged at the back of the stage, massaging her feet. Dancer's feet, flexible and pampered and at the same time always just a little bit abused. Tough and tender. *Like he is,* said an unbidden little voice in her head, and with some irritation she slapped it away. *Controlling,* she told it, arguing with herself. *Unyielding.*

It made her glad for the deep shadows. Even with the various curtains drawn up in preproduction openness, the low light of the theater—a light she'd have to remember to turn off soon—barely reached her. It hid the stacks of flats leaning against the interior brick and the selection of scrims off to the side and it hid her, although not so much that Chandler wouldn't know she was there. He'd know she hadn't committed some impulsive fling of a decision and left him there.

Impulsive fling was perhaps not the best phrase to plant in her mind just now.

Beth sighed and switched feet, massaging each toe individually, letting her mind go blank, or trying to. She concentrated on deep breathing, dispelling anger and making way for relaxation. There. That was better. She stood, hand against the painted brick wall for balance, and lifted her foot high above her head, pulling down on her toes. Stretching again. What she always did when she needed moments of calm.

But when she looked away from the self-imposed focus point in the stage right wing where the dimly visible call board hung empty in preparation for the first list of callbacks, she found Chandler standing on the stage apron, immediately in front of the first row of seats. Gentle light from the auditorium limned his head and shoulders, leaving the rest of him in shadow. Amazing how much she could tell from that simple silhouette. That it was a non-confrontational stance, slightly hip-cocked; it lacked the precise squaring of the shoulders she'd seen him affect before action or argument. His arm bothered him; she could tell that, too, the way he unconsciously held it away from his body; in another moment she thought he'd tuck his thumb in his belt.

Just standing there, looking at him, balancing in her stretch, Beth felt a familiar curl. It had migrated from her toes to her lower belly, and it hovered there, pulsing quietly. *Ohh, I am in so much trouble...*

* * *

Quietly he said, "Dance for me."

That's not what he'd meant to say. He'd meant to say, "I don't want to argue with you," and "I'm sorry, I jumped to conclusions," and maybe something else besides, but when his eyes finally adjusted to the shadows of the stage, he lost those words entirely. She stood, stretching in a way to make her legs look impossibly long and her bottom impossibly firm. Instead of ballerina elegance she moved with lithe feline strength. Not a swan, but a panther—except that impossibly long, graceful neck. A *kiss me* neck.

And so he lost all his important words, his body stirring. His pragmatic nature fled before her, and his mouth said *Dance with me*.

Slowly she lowered her leg. She took several pantherish steps his way and said, "What?" in a wary, puzzled tone that let him know she'd heard him...she just didn't know what to make of it.

He should just shake his head at her, and go back to his plan. The "I don't want to argue with you" plan. The one where he didn't embroil himself any further with a woman whose nature was so contrary to his, who was sure to rip new wounds over old scars.

Except that wasn't fair, was it? If it was entirely true, he wouldn't have come up here to apologize for jumping to conclusions. She *was* creative...and impulsive and fiery and all the things that made his pulse pound in places other than his arm as he grew hard, painfully hard and painfully fast. Just thinking about her.

Sod it all, I am in so much trouble...

He said again, "Dance for me." Part demand, part request, with an edge to his voice that she'd first thought was anger and now realized was anything but.

Beth looked at him a moment, then closed her eyes, tipped her head back slightly, and listened. Waiting for the right music.

"What?" he said after a moment.

"Shh," she told him. "I'm listening for the music. Your music."

Quiet strength in waiting. Low music, maybe cello with subtle drum work as foundation. She drew herself up and started in *adage,* in slow, controlled movements that showed his order, his structure, but also his strength. Strength in following the rules without giving up the passion of his goals, an aspect of his character that she only this moment truly understood. Strength in waiting for just the right moment to act. And when that moment came...

The drums shifted to a slightly higher pitch, and violas joined the cellos; a whisper of wind music layered in the background. Her movements quickened. She saw not the backstage, not the dimly lit auditorium, not even Chandler's form downstage of her. She saw only her mind's eye, where he came alive with the charm of his grin and the unexpected dry lick of words, British humor in wry sarcasm. She picked up the tempo, adding quick-footed chassés and a few jazz undulations—nothing too developed, but understated. Held within.

But only until he burst into action. The drums turned heavy and fast, the strings sweepingly full. She leaped into a fan kick, coming down into a series of turns and jumps and falls, all economical but powerful, three men scattered around a lobby at his feet. Only when she turned to their most intense moments together, that scorching more-than-just-a-kiss against his hotel door, did she release herself into full expression of movement, full-flung leaps and tight spins, eloquent arms flung wide to expose her body at its most vulnerable...riding the energy to completion.

Beth came down from a final leap to land before him, a perfectly balanced halt. Breathing heavily but not harshly, her muscles flushed with warmth and exertion. She had a glimpse of his face, an expression she couldn't quite identify. Something profound...something touched. Something beyond verbal communication.

Wordlessly he reached for her. He cupped one hand around her cheek and kissed her. Kissed her deeply, unhindered by her panting breath; working with it. When she needed to come up for air, gasping at exertion and arousal both, he moved on to her cheek, her earlobe, the soft outside corner of her eye. He'd shaved before the wine tasting; his scant stubble scratched her face only enough to create tantalizing friction. He tipped her head slightly and ran a line of kisses down her neck, murmuring against it, "Cor, I love this neck."

Beth lost herself to the exquisite sensation he created along that neck, the tingling that rippled down her spine and along her shoulders and somehow gathered at her breasts and at her loins. She found his ear, nibbled it, and smiled when he stiffened from head to toe, right down to the fingers twining in her hair. That was a good spot, was it? Delicately she licked the inner cusp of that ear, and he growled into her neck. The sound undid her. Mr. Controlled MI6, growling in helpless lust. Her mind and body spun closer to that place where nothing in the world mattered but their hands on each other and their bodies locked together.

But before she grabbed his shirt to bring him in closer, before she lost herself altogether, she put a hand on either side of his neck and ever so slightly held him off. He responded immediately, if not without effort, his eyes looking lost and dazed and slightly fevered. She said carefully, "I know what I'm doing—" *As if. You won't be able to walk away from this one, Bethany Riggs. Not without leaving something of yourself behind.* She could live with that. She'd have to, because it was already too late. But this…this couldn't be something *he* regretted. Or that he thought had been her decision. She waited until he'd focused on her eyes, though his body remained quivering and attentive, barely restrained. "Do you? Know that you truly want this?"

He didn't answer right away. He pushed her hair behind her ear, ineffectively smoothing the mess he'd made of it, slightly clumsy with the want of her. He looked at her long enough to make it clear he'd heard her, and then very deliberately leaned over to take her mouth and plunder it so thoroughly as to leave her breathless all over again.

Her entire being sighed with relief. And still— "Come with me," she said.

"I plan to," he muttered, one hand busy finding its way up the soft fleecy sweatshirt he'd bought for her, letting a tunnel of cool air rush up against her spine in delicious contrast to the heat of his hand.

She giggled, a rare sound that suddenly felt like freedom. "Downstairs," she said, catching his hand as it found her bare breast, leaning into it with luxurious greed. "Mattress. Privacy. A place to throw your clothes when I rip them off your body."

Not that she cared about the privacy per se…what was a Stony Man agent if not a thrill-seeker? But for two spies on the run…two spies about to become intensely, irreparably distracted…privacy meant safety.

Understanding crossed his face, followed close on by

impatience. "Bloody well hurry, then," he said, sliding his tantalizing hand down her stomach and across her flank as he removed it from beneath her sweatshirt. Instantly she ached for its return. The parts of her body he hadn't even touched yet ached for its return. She found that hand with her own and swiftly led him to stage right, where the discreetly set stairs awaited. She drew him down in unseemly haste, laughing quietly at herself and yet nearly bounding with anticipation.

Chandler's body. Her body. Heat and slick skin and coarse chest hair against her soft skin. Oh God, and they hadn't even reached the room yet. "In here," she said rather desperately, and led the way into the small, dark chamber, closing the door with one absent foot to then push him up against it with an assertiveness that first surprised him and then inflamed him. She tugged his shirt free and ran her hands beneath it, finding that crisp smattering of hair she'd anticipated, following the muscled ridges of his stomach up to the flat planes of his chest. She hardly noticed when he pulled her sweatshirt off, aside from those few seconds the soft material enveloped her head. Then she was free and returning the favor, albeit with much care as she disentangled his wounded arm. He didn't make it any easier, tipping his head back with fierce pleasure and using his good arm to pull her hips against his. Distracting. He seemed to realize it, making the supreme effort to hold still until she finished. "No-no-no," she murmured, pushing herself against his erection, making them both gasp at once. "No stopping."

"This isn't going to go easy," he said, by way of question as his fingers dug into her bottom, clenching reactively. Not a soft, gentle loving, but fierce and wanton.

"It's not meant to," she told him, finally freeing his shirt, quickly working his belt free. Damn military slide belts…ah. There. Only his briefs between them, because she made short work of her sweats and panties, naked in the cool darkness but flaming hot within.

"Wallet," he reminded her with effort. "Always be—" But his words cut short in a hiss as she groped her way around him in the dark, finding places to linger, parts of him to fondle. In the end he was the one to dig out his wallet, first making crinkling noises and then disgusted noises. "Not meant to be done in total darkness."

"Here," she said, sounding wicked even to her own ears. "Let me help."

Slowly, attentively, she applied the condom. Slowly, while her own loins grew wet and hot, she made him tremble, his fingers closing hard on the curve of her hip, his legs threatening to buckle, his injured arm making helpless attempts to reach for her. "Hurry," he told her through gritted teeth. "I'm about to whimper, and that would—*ah!*—be embarrassing."

"All done," she said sweetly, with a final caress. He growled and he grabbed her hips, pulling her in, pulling her up. She wrapped one leg around him, giving him access. Opening to him, until they came together with a mutual cry of satisfaction. His legs did give way then, but she merely went down with him, ending up astride his lap while he sat back on his heels. One-armed, all fierce passion, he pulled her close, nuzzling her, gasping and groaning and clutching and thrusting while fire and lightning gathered along her nerves and built to unbearable—

He cried out, abandoning all his control, stiffening until his muscles corded and then abruptly pulsing within her. It tipped her over the edge into climax; they milked each other into fiery satiation, their cries mingling in the darkness.

Long moments later, Beth heaved a great happy sigh.

He ran his hand down her spine in wordless agreement, a gentle touch after the roughness of their lovemaking. With some chagrin, Beth said, "I think I bit you."

"I bloody well think you did at that," he responded. "I hope it scars."

She snickered gently into his neck, then licked the offended spot. He shivered. She felt the goose bumps rise up under her hands, and reluctantly and gently separated herself from him. "Brr," she said. "A little heat would be nice."

"We just generated a fair amount of it," he said.

"I noticed that. Where'd you throw my—never mind. Got it." She slipped the sweatshirt back on, glad to snuggle into its warmth, though she'd rather be wrapped around Chandler. *Jason,* she thought to herself, trying it out.

Nah.

"There's a mattress down over here," she said, groping around for her bottoms and giving up. Come morning the light would filter in the tiny window up by the ceiling, leaking in around the hanging bicycles. Nothing more than dim at best, but enough for finding undies. There was also a light switch in the hall, but it would show along that same window, quite thoroughly giving them away.

"All well and good," he said, pushing himself to his feet with a grunt, "if I could see *over here* and didn't have my pants down around my ankles."

She laughed and went back to him, finding him still a little shaky and leaning against the door. Guilt assaulted her. He'd lost blood, he was in pain, he'd—

He'd made his choices. And he'd enjoyed them. She smiled in the darkness and bent down to draw his pants up, careful of those things that might get caught in zippers. He gave a little laugh himself. "You're...not like anyone I know."

"Probably not," she agreed, finding his hand, although not without running her fingers over his bare chest and down his arm to do it. He already held his shirt—he'd found it somehow—and she entwined a single finger around one of his. "Come over here. We can keep each other warm, and get some of that rest you were talking about."

She heard his grateful sigh as he sank down on the mattress; she followed him down, snuggling inside the curve of his body. His arm fell carelessly from her hip until his hand landed on her breast, and she put hers over it, welcoming his quiet touch.

They breathed together.

After a moment he said, "She went to an obscure trailhead at the base of Table Mountain. That area's covered with thick, stumpy trees...I have no idea just where she spent the night. I picked her up on the way out to meet you at the dock."

Beth stopped breathing a moment. "The sleeping bag," she said. *"Table Mountain."*

"Yes," he admitted. "Probably the table you've been looking for."

She felt it again—that stark, sudden impulse to jump up and run out into the night. But...

Thick, stumpy trees. An unknown trailhead. The middle of a long night. Chandler, wounded and in need of rest. Beth herself, sliding into exhaustion. Out loud she said, "Don't worry. Not being impulsive, here."

He kissed the back of her neck in reply, sighing deeply. Still satisfaction, but more than an edge of fatigue. And when he shivered again, it had nothing to do with her hands on his body.

"Our jackets!" she said abruptly, pulling away from him. He gave a monosyllabic protest, but she dashed out into the hall anyway, up the stairs in a sweatshirt and nothing else. She found their jackets, the sling pack, and his briefcase, and gathered them up in a huge armful that threatened to break free all the way back to "her" room.

Chandler already slept, offering the hint of a ragged snore, curled up against the cool air. Beth wasted no time. From her sling pack she extracted the night vision scope and carefully located not only her pants, but a folded lump of stage bedding. In moments she had the makeshift bed covered, and she crawled in to reclaim her space—but only after setting her watch to wake them an hour and a half before dawn. A mere four hours of sleep. It would be enough.

Carefully she rearranged Chandler's injured arm into its original position, this time clasping her fingers through his, gently kneading them. His were strong hands. Strong in action, strong and confident as they lay claim to her body. She'd seen for herself the strength in the man behind them. The persistence. *The rules.* She wished she didn't think that when push came to shove, just like all the others, he would try to mold her to his way of thinking.

To change her.

Because it wasn't going to happen. She'd gladly have the world's longest-distance affair, she'd find ways to meet him between assignments and make love to him in every exotic locale she could manage.

But she wouldn't change the essence of Bethany Riggs. Not for him, not for anyone.

Chapter 8

In the end Beth slept poorly. Chandler's thighs against the back of hers, his hips against her bottom, his breath soft on her neck. His physical presence kept her aroused; his emotional presence kept her worried. She slipped out of his embrace before her watch alarm went off. No need to wake him just yet. She twitched the heavy French knot bedspread back over his shoulders, wishing she could take a peek at the bloody bandage. She thought she could smell it, but couldn't discern if it was infection or simply the smell of so much dried blood. No telling, in the darkness. Instead she ran her hands along his back, from the swell of his shoulders to the sculpted taper of his waist and then to the sweet curve of his ass. Very nice. He had a sturdy physique—not whipcord lean, not beefy. In between. Just right.

But her touch failed to garner anything but an appreciative sigh, and with a wry smile she gave him a final pat, kissed his shoulder through the bedding, and gifted him with a little more sleep.

And then she got busy. They were both targets now; she didn't want to be recognizable when they left the theater. Nothing she could do about the yellow BMW, but she could certainly find ways to distract anyone's attention from the bike itself. *Hiding in plain sight.* She grabbed her sling pack and went out into the hall, where she extracted a small flashlight and the nightscope and went to work. First a little cleanup—a splash of water on her face, a quick application of her toothbrush, and already she felt more alert.

Then she started in on the theater wardrobe collection. For Chandler, she found a greasy-looking wig of dark blond hair that would hang in his eyes, obscuring their sharp gray color and his equally sharp gaze. Leather pants, a pair of scuffed boots that might be a little big but ought to work, and a ripped biker tee. His own jacket wouldn't do—far too staid. She found a leather jacket with lots of studs and chains, and even a pair of studded gauntlets.

He was going to hate it.

For herself she picked out a punk-tart look. Ultrashort black leather mini, shiny boots with hateful heels, a denim jacket over a black slashed top. And the wig. Spiky lime-green. No one would look at that BMW yellow as long as she wore the spiky lime-green hair. She hung up the dress and shawl from the night before, smoothing the wrinkles as best she could, and then did her best to smooth out the other signs of her presence. At seven that morning the auditions would start again, this time for the principle dancers. They had no reason to come down here, but sloppiness could cause problems if they did.

She hauled the goods back to their room, judged it close

enough to dawn to be worth the risk, and turned on the hall lights.

Chandler lay sprawled on his back, his hair scruffed up and his mouth slightly open. Very much a morning look. She would have found serious amusement in the contrast between this and his waking self's careful attention to neat detail, had he not also looked so unwell. Beneath the scruffy hair his face seemed grayer that it ought, even in this light. Strain painted itself in shadows under his closed lashes and a certain hollowness in the strong bones of his face.

Nor did she imagine he normally slept so deeply, deeply enough that he had not even twitched at her comings and goings. No doubt he needed more of it.

Well. Maybe later. They had a keycard to snatch. She didn't know if Egorov's mole and his CIA patsies had any notion of the keycard's existence, but she figured it to be a good bet, given their persistence in pursuit.

She gave Chandler a few more moments' rest, perching at the edge of the mattress to send Barbara Price a message of the tersest sort. After a moment of thought, she removed the mini CD from its latest hiding place and stuck it under one of the bicycle seats, an easy location to describe…and then she made sure Barbara knew.

Beth tucked the PDA away, checked that the sling pack was otherwise ready to go, and crawled onto the mattress beside Chandler. He stirred but didn't wake, and she took the opportunity to lean over him and apply a slow, deep kiss. He responded almost instantly, and Beth lost herself in the gentle, dreamy contact until he gave a sudden start, and she knew he'd finally actually woken up. She smiled, knowing he'd feel it, and drew him back into the kiss until she felt an urgency quiver between them. Then she pulled back and said, "Good morning."

He glanced look around the cluttered room—his first actual look at it—and then gave a rueful shake of his head. "I'm not sure if that's the best awakening I've ever had, or the most tormenting."

"Think of it as the most enticing," she said, tracing the straight, dark line of his eyebrow to smooth the little frown that had immediately appeared there. Pain, she thought. "The sooner we get that keycard, the sooner we can revisit this moment. Are you up for it? You look like hell."

I feel like hell. Gritty eyes, his arm hot and heavy, his energy bottomed out. But he didn't say it out loud. No doubt she was perfectly capable of whipping up some devilish means of restraint for his own good, and running off to hunt out the keycard on her own.

On the other hand, it was hardly fair to pretend he was perfectly functional and have her depending on him for a level of backup he couldn't provide. He didn't have to look under the crusty bandage to know all was not well there. But he also knew just how far he could push things and still rebound quickly once he got the care he needed. For now, a few words with Bear would net him the antibiotics he needed to stave things off. He glanced around the amazing chaos of the tiny room again, seeing with dry amusement that if they'd been able to make it only another step or so past the doorway the night before, they could have made love on this mattress in the first place. Draped over the mattresses still leaned against the wall were a couple of outfits he gathered Beth had picked out for them, complete with wigs.

He hoped the lime-green one was for her.

"Where—" he started, looking for his laptop, but Beth gave a quick shake of her head.

"It's behind me," she said. "But I'm afraid you weren't the only one to take a bullet yesterday. If that's your means of communication, you're going to have to hunt up an alternative."

Ah. Immediate contact with Bear not an option. Jason could call in as soon as they ran across a public phone, but Jason had the distinct feeling that by the time that happened, events would again be in full swing. "It's just you and me, then," he said, and then looked over at the outfits again. "Or some version thereof."

"Yes," she said, still running a gentle hand across his brow, along his cheek. Tempting, just to close his eyes and let her do that for another day or two. Instead he shoved the covers off and carefully sat. As flexible as ever, she sat back not on her heels but with her ankles splayed to the side. It made him wince. So did the look on her face—concern mixed with determination. She said, "The question is—is it you and me? Are you ready to go? Because you know as well as I that I'm better off on my own than depending on a partner who can't come through."

He rubbed his hand over his face and through his hair, scrubbing it into what must have been an interesting mess, to judge from the amused look on her face. He was not in the mood to be amused. "Sod it," he said under his breath. "Look, there's no way I'm staying behind. I'll let you know when I'm no good to you."

She gave him a small, grim smile. He suddenly realized she'd expected nothing less from him. In that moment he had a fleeting moment of trepidation—not about hunting out the keycard, but about what had happened between them. *Jason Chandler: does not fall hard and fast. Stays far, far away from creative whirlwinds.*

Until now, apparently. Big mistake, asking her to dance. He'd seen her heart...and he loved it.

"Hey," she said, prodding him, her eyes narrowing until they were shadowed into deepest green.

"Just thinking," he said.

"Think later. Dress now." She rose to her feet, somehow not looking at all awkward in spite of her splay-legged starting position. Tossing his outfit at him, she started to strip, not the least bit self-conscious.

Jason gave the wig and clothing a wary glance. "You're quite clearly a tart," he said. "What am I, a biker?"

She snorted, pulling the black leather miniskirt up over her hips and fastening the wide red leather belt. Jason felt a clear case of early-morning stonker coming on. *Bad timing,* he told it, but couldn't bring himself to look away as she picked up her shirt. She said, "A biker? On that yellow banana you've been riding? No way. You're a biker wanna-be. I even have a couple of pathetic stick-on tattoos for you."

"Like playing dress-up, do you?"

"That," she said, displaying her torso in all its toned and firm beauty as she pulled the tight black and lace baby-doll tee over her head, "is something we can talk about later. Now come over here and let me take your pants off."

Riding the banana-yellow bike behind Beth did nothing to ease Jason's body, but he found himself remarkably relaxed, trusting implicitly in her skill with the bike as his hands rested right at the level of that low red belt, possessing her hips with remarkable familiarity. She hadn't even considered the thought that he might sit behind the handlebars, but had taken his keys, hiked back to the hotel and appeared half an hour later with a big grin and even spikier lime-green hair than she'd started with. He guided her with nudges and a word or two, and soon enough they traveled the winding tree-lined road at the base of Table Mountain, coming up on the small parking area for the trailhead with a strong dawn rising over the mountain itself. She slowed the bike, downshifting, before he had a chance to point out the gravel pull-off.

A dark sedan already occupied the small lot. He felt Beth tense as she, too, spotted it, but she pulled the bike into the lot as though it made no difference, scattering a little gravel as might be expected from a green-headed chick and her biker wanna-be.

"Don't see anyone," he said into her ear.

"Someone's watching," she said, lifting her leg over the front of the bike and hopping off. She spent a moment beside him, mussing his fake hair and bestowing a nice public display of affection. This was purely work; he knew it and she knew it. But he didn't fail to note how naturally it came to both of them. As he dismounted the bike, she shifted her low-slung fanny pack to one side and carelessly left the sling pack over the bike's handlebars, ambling in a hip-swinging way over to the protected trail board at one end of the parking area. "Cor," he said, catching up to her. "You *are* a tart. I consider myself lucky you didn't happen across any gum. You'd be popping it at a rate to drive me mad."

She smiled sweetly at him. "You betcha. So this is where you saw Lyeta?"

"Taxi dropped her off. She had a small kit and she didn't use a flashlight—she must have done a recce before I started tailing her. So I haven't the foggiest where she went." He hooked his arm in his belt, hoping to look macho but probably just looking stiff and pained.

It drew her attention from the board. "Are you sure—"

"Quota," he said abruptly, and then at her puzzled look explained, "You used your quota up on that question. Look, Beth, forget about it. When we're through here, I'll reach Bear and he'll send in a doctor we trust. Until then, I'll make do. Don't let it distract you."

She gave him the most skeptical of looks and returned her attention to the board. Shortly thereafter a slow smile spread over her face. "Why, look at this," she murmured. "Blue Crane trail. At the base of Table Mountain. Imagine that."

Jason caught her fierce blue-green gaze and grinned back at her. At last...the hunt was on.

The thrill caught Beth where it always did, just above her heart. She glanced at Chandler and saw that he felt it, too—and realized then that she couldn't recall sharing that particular thrill before.

It felt good.

"Gonna get my takkies," she said, in a perfectly fine South African accent and just loud enough for their unseen but inevitable observer to hear. Her *takkies* were not, in fact, her choice of footwear for scrambling around in the woods. They were meant for a dance floor, not this rugged terrain with its dense foliage, most of which was stumpy shrubbery as Jason had described but also included bona fide trees. Add in the rocky, variable terrain and it made for all sorts of challenges. Hard to see who was watching you, hard to keep your eye on anything but where your feet might land. Hard to find small, probably hidden items like a computer keycard. They were here, but where to begin?

And almost more importantly, where was Egorov's mole and his recruits? Did they have the same clues? Or like Chandler, had they simply followed her here and then to the dock, seeing there the opportunity to get rid of Lyeta and set Beth up as the killer?

She wondered if the bad sniper from the dock was here. She almost hoped he was. She had a good sneer stored up for him.

At the bike, she gratefully pulled off her boots—they'd set her character perfectly, but weren't anything she wanted to inflict on her feet any longer than necessary—and slipped into her dance sneaks, tying the laces with a flourish. Then she slipped the sling pack over her tart's jacket. She had Wyatt in the fanny pack, and Chandler had his shoulder rig on under the T-shirt—another strategic rip had served to obscure it quite nicely under his jacket. She also carried a few backup tricks, although Chandler had not had the chance to return any of the things he'd taken from her parka.

They were as prepared as they could be. And they knew they had company—whereas with luck, the company—no doubt CIA—had not seen or known the bike, and thought they were a couple of slackers come out to hike an easy trail. Except—she glanced at Chandler as she left the bike to join him at the trail board, and gave a mental eye-roll. "Slouch," she hissed at him as she went by, patting his ass fondly in her tart character.

"I *am* slouching," he said, offended.

"It's over here," she told him, heading for the spot where the Blue Crane trail should start. And, under her breath, "You're straight as a military stick. Think about how much your arm hurts and *slouch*."

"I *am* a military stick," he said, still offended. But he altered his posture into something less stringent and struck the trail with her.

As out of the way as this place was, the path still wound

clearly through the landscape, turning out to be less difficult to follow than Beth had supposed. It looped back upon itself as it climbed the hill, and in glancing up she saw snatches of the trail here and there above them. But she didn't like the terrain…it was nearly indefensible. The strong breeze rustled leaves, as did the ground birds and the small creatures who scampered off in front of them. If the misled CIA agents were here, she'd never hear them. And she didn't like how quickly Chandler grew flushed and out of breath. Even with her scant experience with him, she knew it was way off the scale of normal. Just knowing he was SAS-trained would have told her that. She slowed her pace, although the path wasn't wide enough to walk side by side. Every so often, they passed a stake by the side of the path with a gracefully stylized line carving of a Blue Crane. Trail identifiers. Handy.

Blue Crane. Bottom. Table.

She stopped short. "Hold on," she told him, unable to shake the feeling that this trail had far too many opportunities for ambush and observation from the brush. "I dropped something." She ran back to the little signpost they'd just passed and crouched by the side of the trail, feeling around the ground and then just coincidentally along the signpost itself. Nothing. Quickly she picked up an ordinary pebble and stuck it into her pocket, trotting back up to where Chandler waited, looking gray and muzzy. Pretty much like a biker wanna-be with a hangover, which worked out fine except he'd be better off if that were actually the case.

Lighten up, Riggs, she told herself. He was perfectly right. Whether they found something or not, they'd have ample opportunity to get to a "safe" doctor once they finished here. To Chandler, she said in her airiest tart voice, "Gotta remember to take off the gems before we go on a jaunt."

He gave her a patient boyfriend look and gestured her ahead on the trail. "At least you found it."

At the next trail marker, she found a plant to exclaim over. By the next, he'd figured out what she was up to, and pointed out a nonexistent lizard.

Taped to the back of that little signpost was the computer keycard, snug inside a clear waterproof plastic case.

Yes! She palmed it, stuck it inside the front fanny pack pocket, and took Chandler's hand to lead him farther down the path, giving it a little squeeze of excitement. *We found it.*

He stumbled. Not in the plan.

Enough then. She turned back to give him a little moue of a pout, and said, "This trail's longer than it looked on that board. I'm tired." She put a little whine into it. "We've got that party to make tonight, you know—it's all the way in Tierkloof."

"Turn back then," he said, sounding realistically surly. "I'm not stopping you."

There was enough rustle to warn them, not enough time to do anything about it. One of the nondescripts moved out from the hillside beside them, very L.L. Bean in khakis and a flannel shirt and—

A rifle.

Beth narrowed her eyes at the sight. Sniper rifle. A Model 85 if she saw rightly, a basic U.K. weapon he'd probably bought right here at the Cape.

"Hey," Chandler said, put a protective hand on Beth's shoulder, drawing him back to her. "We don't want any trouble. Just taking a walk."

The man grinned. He wasn't so nondescript up close; his eyes were set too narrowly and his nose rose between them like a sharp blade. He said, "Drop the act, Chandler. You shouldn't have teamed up with her. You were safe until you did. Now you've both got a lot of questions to answer." He lifted a small radio to his mouth and said, "Got 'em both. We're on the way in."

You don't have us *yet,* Beth thought, glancing back at Chandler and giving a quiet inner smile when she realized he'd squared his shoulders up again. *You don't have us by a long shot.*

And speaking of long shots...the man's weapon was hardly meant for this range. As powerful as it was, balanced the way it was...he'd have a hell of a time using it for anything but the steady shoulder weapon it was meant to be.

She said, "Well, if the game's up, I'm ditching this wig. It itches." And with no further ado she plucked it off her head and flung it into nondescript's face. A quick kick disarmed him, and by then the man was free of the wig and he and Beth closed in in earnest as Chandler grabbed the rifle and flung it out of reach, his own gun coming quickly to hand.

The rifle guy was quick and strong but not precise. Beth found herself on the defensive, evading blows and knowing if she took them, they'd land hard. She found an opening, landed a quick series of lightning-fast kicks without ever bringing the leg back in for balance, and then heard Chandler's bark of a command, "Get *down,* Beth!"

She threw herself aside and rolled, getting enough of a glimpse to know Chandler had his Browning trained on their new friend—except in the next instant there was a great rustle of brush and from off the trail came a second nondescript. This one plowed right into Chandler, smashing his wounded arm with obvious intent. Chandler went down with the kind of gagging, involuntary gasp brought on by deep agony, and the second nondescript snatched and flung the Browning away, snapping at the first, ''We want them able to answer questions!'' as he leaped for Beth.

And oh damn I'm on the ground already—

Beth surged upward, knowing it was too late and running headlong into the truth of it. She took a blow to the head, a second to her shoulder, hard enough to knock her completely off balance. She tried to roll but they both ended up on top of her, one trying to restrain her while the other groped roughly around her body, taking punishment from her knees and feet, clearly astonished that she had the ability to reach him with either. He found the clasp for her fanny pack and ripped it from her, plundering it for the keycard and then flinging the pack far from their struggle. He tucked the card away just as Beth nearly managed to free herself, and with some irritation turned his attention to subduing her, pounding her with a quick series of blows while the first man held her—and though she never stopped fighting back, she felt her strength and coordination seep away beneath their fists—

Until something snarled. A whirlwind entered the fray, jerking the rifle guy away and kicking the second man off her in the same instant of combined attack. Beth rebounded into the fray, back up on her knees, sweeping a leg around to take the second man off his feet as he came back at her. He went down, he tumbled downhill—and when he got up it was to reassess the situation, close a hand around the pocket with the keycard, and run down the trail.

''Damn!'' Beth muttered. He'd done the smart thing, taking no chances with his prize, but she was too staggered to catch up with him, and Chandler—

Chandler had rifle guy down and out, but had paid the

price for it. He swayed on his knees, his face pasty white, hunched over his arm. Blood dripped out of his jacket sleeve and down his hand; blood dripped from his face.

Hell, she realized. There's blood dripping from *my* face.

He spoke though gritted teeth, but still managed to put a dry English spin on the words. "Remember I said I'd tell you when I was no good to you?"

"Wrong," she said abruptly, scrambling for the spot where he'd thrown the rifle and snatching it from the brush when she found it. "Stay right where you are." She gave the weapon a quick once-over—the adjustable walnut stock was too long for her, no time to do anything about it. Bolt action—she levered a round into the chamber, swung around to snug up against Chandler's back, kneeling one knee down, the other up and under her elbow. "Ten-round capability—let's hope this guy actually loaded it to capacity." She rested the stock on Chandler's shoulder. "Rest down on your heels. Steady. Breathe evenly." She put her eye to the scope, found the crosshairs…and found the spot where the trail looped back below them, shifting slightly until the natural point of aim rested there and double-checking by relaxing her muscles to make sure the rifle didn't move. "I don't know how he's got this scope sighted in," she said. "If it's off, I may have to take a second shot. This thing's got a nine-hundred-meter optimal range and we're at the edge of that. You'll probably jump when I fire, but I need you to come right back to this position." She made a swift adjustment for the downhill trajectory and then—

Nothing to do but relax. Waiting. Chandler said nothing, hadn't ever said anything, but she felt his breathing, as soft and shallow as a man struggling for breath could make it, growing gentler by the moment. She synced her breathing with his, trusting him, her finger caressing the trigger, waiting, waiting...

There!

A quick flash of motion to the left of target was her only warning. She hissed softly to warn Chandler and, leading out on the target, squeezed the trigger.

He jumped at the explosion of noise even as she absorbed the force of the rubber recoil pad against her shoulder; he couldn't help but jump. But as she'd asked, he swiftly put himself back in position.

No need. She swept the area with the scope and immediately found the man down—twitching, alive as he should be with the thigh shot she'd taken, and giving up after his first few attempts to rise. She'd aimed for the high meat of the thigh and with any luck, had broken bone. He'd be there until someone hiked him out on a stretcher.

Instantly she dismissed him, her mind racing ahead. There was a third man somewhere, the one who'd been on the receiving end of the radio call. Possibly the one behind all this. Egorov's man who'd burrowed into the CIA, the one who'd had Lyeta shot, who'd put Beth on the run, who'd had them ambushed not once but three times. The reason Chandler sat drained, full of pain and at the end of what looked to be considerable limits.

She worked the rifle bolt, climbing to her feet, her eyes narrowed and focused on downhill.

How well he knew her already. "Beth, no," he said hoarsely. "Secure this one, get the card from the other. I'll stand lookout. Or *sit* lookout." That dry humor again.

It wasn't enough to take her gaze off the path down to the parking area. "You know he's Egorov's man," she said, absently wiping at the steady trickle of blood from a cut under one eye. Nondescript number two had worn a ring, damn him. "He's the one running this operation; he wouldn't be the one in the thick of it."

"You're right. But we've got two of them. They'll talk. Especially if you're right—if they're bona fide CIA, they're going to want Egorov's man as badly as you do. As *we* do. But neither of us have the resources to go for him right now. It's—"

"I know." She gave him a quick glance over her shoulder, relinquishing her glare at the unseen foe below for one of resentment. "It's SOP, right? It's procedure. It's by the book."

He hesitated. He no longer sat on both heels, but had brought one knee up before him and leaned back on his good arm. The other he had tucked against his body, looking useless. But beneath the blood on his face, some already drying and some still welling anew, his expression was resolute. Resigned, but resolute. He nodded.

"Damn," Beth muttered, and sighed hugely. She released the tension she'd been holding and turned to eye him. "Just so you know, I'm about to stamp my foot." Which she did, adding another entirely heartfelt and frustrated, "Damn!"

He watched her with an expression she could only call wary, and she shrugged. "You're right," she said. "Never mind procedure or rules or whatever...you're right. We've got the keycard, we've got the guys Egorov's man roped into working for him...sooner or later, we'll get him, too." Carefully she leaned the rifle against a tree at the edge of the path, rotating a sore shoulder with annoyance. She pulled a slim knife from its equally slim sheath inside her tarty red belt, eyeing a flexible, thorny vine growing in a terrible tangle at the foot of another tree. "Excellent," she murmured, and carefully cut off a generous length of it. The lime-green wig lay not far off, and she retrieved it on her way back to the rifle guy. "Let's get him up against one of these trees."

"That's it?" he asked. "You're not going to run off and chase Egorov's man down anyway?"

"Do I look like I'm running down the hill?" she asked with a grunt, preoccupied with the effort of dragging rifle guy. The man roused himself, and she fixed him with a sharp look and pointed him at the tree. He moved as if he had broken ribs—and she was almost certain his jaw had been broken, separated at the chin—but moved he did, showing no sign of fight. "Besides," she told Jason, "I'll bet he's gone by now."

The man gave her a dazed but frowning look, and mumbled indistinctly to Beth, "He said *you* were Egorov's—he had authority to deal with you. I was aiming at *you* next on that dock."

"Surprise, surprise," Chandler mumbled back.

Beth raised one arching eyebrow and said, "Guess what. He lied. And you're a terrible shot. And you know, maybe we're all going to get along in the end, but until then..." And she plunked the wig down on his head backward, blinding him, and wrapped the thorny vine around his wrists and waist, then stepped back to eye him with satisfaction. He looked like an alien. "I'm going to get that keycard," she informed him sweetly. "And true, your feet are loose, but if you get up and stumble around with that wig over your face, before you get yourself sorted out, you're going to fall on those broken ribs of yours, and those vines will rip your wrists to shreds. Got it?"

"Not going anywhere," the man said, even more indistinctly through the wig. "Think we need to talk. Will you let me check in with my people?"

"Actually, we'll do that for you," Chandler said. "After we get you and your friend to medical treatment."

"After we get *you* to treatment," Beth said, wiping off the last drip of blood from her own face. She could feel the bruises puffing up, hot and pulsing. "As for me...I could do with an ice pack." Then she twitched the wig more firmly in place over rifle guy's head and looked down the hill; time to grab the keycard and check the condition of the second man. If she hadn't hit his femoral artery, he would be just about ready to curse her a blue streak.

But on her way she detoured by Chandler, wiped a clean spot on his face, and leaned over to give him a careful kiss. He grabbed her before she could move away, gave a blissfully admiring look to the wig-faced, vine-bound agent, and then pulled her down to take her mouth, a kiss as demanding as either of them could offer. When he let her go, he murmured, "Now *that* was teamwork."

She went to get the keycard with a smile playing around the edge of her lips and wicked thoughts in her heart.

Chapter 9

"Oh, he's here right now," Beth said, and looked up from her PDA to give Jason a little smile. "He's dying with curiosity. Loves my toy."

He made a face at her and sat upright against the head-board of the bed in their hotel room, his legs crossed and his lap covered with their notes about Egorov's mole. *Their* hotel room, a new room in the Peninsula Hotel along Beach Road, with all of Beth's cheerfully scattered belongings mined from the theater and her original lodgings, and Jason's neatly stashed travel kit. She was back in her low-cut jeans and a cap-sleeved stretch shirt that kept inching up to show her lean, toned midriff. He was dying, all right, but not with curiosity. He shifted uncomfortably on the bed and decided it might be time to take one of the antibiotics he'd been given, and then couldn't tear himself away from the conversation. Besides, his wound had been flushed clean, X-rayed and prodded while he sat in the back of a certain unprepossessing clinic and soaked up IV antibiotics until he thought he'd pop. Now it was bandaged, in a sling, and fast on its way to becoming yet another scar.

Beth, too, bore the signs of their adventure together—bruises on her face and arms and even on that delectable midriff, just now coming to full bloom in an excruciating rainbow of colors. The cut under her eye had taken a stitch, and had already closed into a thin, barely detectable line.

She saw him looking and wiggled her toes at him. Her toes were quite fond of him, she'd said. He'd never realized he could gain so much power over a woman with the simple act of a foot massage, but he wouldn't forget it. To her mysterious contact on the intriguing device she called a *toy*, Beth gave no sign of their exchange. "We're waiting pickup now, don't anticipate a problem. But about Egorov's mole in the CIA...I want him. *We* want him."

The response was muffled at this distance; Jason suspected Beth had the sound turned way down. But she got a wicked grin and said, "Hey, *you* were the one who suggested we work together if possible. Turns out...it's possible."

More than possible.

They'd already gotten the basic story from the two CIA agents, who remained nicely contained at that same clinic, their own needs tended. Egorov's mole had gotten the authority to take his team into Cape Town and after that, the agents had received communication only through the mole. The man's name was of little account; by now he had another. But Jason and Beth were building a dossier based on their interviews, and they were well and beyond ready to start the hunt.

"Oh," Beth said, flicking her gaze at Jason and offering a smile to both her contact and to Jason at once. "He's free enough—he's on sick leave. Turns out he isn't allowed to come back to active duty just yet.'' The smile turned wicked. ''Rules have their uses, it seems.''

A gentle knock sounded at the door. Beth alerted to it and said, ''K's here. I'll check back later,'' before swiftly shutting down the PDA. She pointed a finger at Jason. He recognized it for what it was—I'm still worried about you. Stay where you are to make me feel better—and acquiesced. But when Beth opened the door she flung it wide enough to expose him, so her contact could see the entire room before choosing to enter.

The woman hesitated in the doorway a moment, just long enough to sweep the room with her gaze, and then sauntered in. Like Beth, she had confident and self-possessed demeanor, but the similarities ended right there. Blond to Beth's espresso-dark hair, with a trendy, choppy shag haircut and eyes that were discernibly green even from a distance, this woman gave an impression of lushness next to Beth's spare, aesthetic beauty. And although she moved like an athlete, the new arrival had curves that didn't quit. Curves a man—*any* man—couldn't help but appreciate. ''Can't linger,'' she said to Beth. ''Gotta stunt gag scheduled in an hour. Everything on track?''

Beth glanced back at Jason, giving him a wry smile. She said, ''They all look at her like that, you know.''

The blonde gave him a cheerful grin, and Jason grinned back with no apology. ''Everything's on track,'' he said, and nodded toward the small, gift-wrapped package near the foot of the bed. Just the size of a medium jewelry box, it held both the keycard and the mini CD, and was covered in a cartoonish child's birthday wrap. MI6 hadn't been pleased to know that neither Beth nor her mysterious organization would relinquish the prizes outright, but Jason had expected nothing less. He also believed Beth when she said the pertinent details would be shared. But the truth was, Beth had taken the CD from Lyeta and hidden it from Jason the entire time. And Beth had taken down the agent who fled with the keycard on his way to meet up with Egorov's mole, and been the one to retrieve it. Jason himself was just satisfied enough to know the information was in allied hands and would be put to good—and aggressive—use.

Beth handed the little box over to her counterpart and said, ''We're after the mole.''

''Got the go-ahead? Good.'' The blonde gave the room another look, this time focusing on Jason's things, and then on Jason. ''The two of you? The odd couple, I'd call you. But whatever works…''

Jason didn't blame her for the obvious curiosity and even her reservations. Not with free-spirited, creatively driven Beth on the one hand and his neat, crisp military approach on the other. But she'd learned he could be flexible, and that he would back her up in an instant even when he didn't understand her immediate intent. And he knew she wouldn't go haring off on wild, precipitous impulse…that she'd listen to other opinions while on the cusp of action, and even respond to them. Looking at her, thinking about her…

Made him very glad for the paperwork covering his lap. ''Cor, yes,'' he said to the blonde. ''It works.''

Beth grinned back at him in a way that made him twitch happily, a look that said just exactly what he was in for when that door closed again. He caught a whiff of her scent, and couldn't help but breathe deeply of its natural freshness. No more illicit sniffing of parkas for him—he had the genuine article right to hand. He barely believed it, but he had…

Beth.

Her grin took on a particularly wicked glint not meant for their visitor at all. Meant for him. *Oh, God, close that door and go away,* he thought fervently at the blond woman even as Beth told her in a gentle takeoff of his own Brit accent, "Not only does it work, but it works damn bloody well."

The blonde laughed and said, "I'll leave you to it, then. Happy hunting."

By the time the door latched, Beth had pounced, tossing away Jason's paperwork. About to get fiery and creative.

Jason flung away his rules and joined her.

*   *   *   *   *

THE GET-AWAY GIRL

Meredith Fletcher

* * *

This one is for Leslie Wainger, who invited me aboard.
And for Mary-Theresa Hussey, who provided
many kind words and a lot of laughs.

Dear Reader,

I was talking to a writer friend just the other day, discussing the book you now hold in your hands (hopefully appropriately intrigued by the title!). She asked me what the book was about. I quickly replied that the book featured three mystery women.

Well, much to my chagrin, my friend took me to task over that attempt at a simple clarification. According to my friend, all women have elements of mystery about them. It's part of our arsenal, along with being bright, resourceful, independent and having the uncanny ability of being right most of the time.

After having that pointed out to me, I resolved to be—like the three women you will meet in this collection of stories—more on target. The women in this book are all operatives of a supersecret agency. They lead lives of danger and deadly pursuit—being the hunter or the hunted, sometimes *both*—in the dark shadows of the world's deadliest places while playing for the highest stakes.

Secret agent Kylee Swain uses her cover as a movie stuntwoman to travel around the globe while on an undercover assignment. In "The Get-Away Girl," Kylee follows up on information passed along from a fellow agent. Her quest puts her on the trail of Krystof Scherba in Prague. Unfortunately, the action also puts her in the crosshairs of Scherba's ace bodyguard and ex-CIA agent bad boy, Mick Stone, who takes his job very personally.

I hope you enjoy meeting Kylee and our two other lovely ladies, who will definitely acquaint you with a life of danger, introduce you to three of the sexiest and most dangerous men in the world, and will earn their designations as *Femmes Fatale!*

All best,

Meredith Fletcher

Chapter 1

Kylee Swain stood steeped in the night's shadows that draped the Charles Bridge as she surveyed her target. Excitement and anticipation sharpened her senses. And maybe more than a few of those feelings centered on the tall man in the dark suit who stood in the prow of the boat she'd had under close but distant surveillance since getting this assignment two days ago.

She didn't know his name—there had been no way to identify him through the long-range lenses and all-too-brief snooping sessions she'd been able to put together during her present shooting schedule while working on the action film she was stunting in. Added to that, the man never appeared in public unless his employer, Krystof Scherba, appeared in public. Creepstof, as Kylee had taken to calling the man, rarely put in public appearances, even aboard his boat.

But the man in the dark suit was interesting. He moved

like a panther, always calm and controlled, always watching. Totally predatory.

Anyone who stepped into that man's territory after something he protected was in for a fight.

Kylee knew that. And she was looking forward to the coming event. Creepstof Scherba was the chief computer-programming wizard behind terrorist mastermind Kapoch Egorov's international crime cartel. Creepstof was the target Kylee had been assigned to by Stony Man Farm mission controller Barbara Price, and moving against him was going to put Kylee full in the sights of the mysterious man who protected him.

Me and you, she mused, thinking of the man's controlled and confident movement aboard the boat. She hated the immediate feelings of competition that seemed to spring up. But if all went well, she'd be into Creepstof's computer before Mr. Mystery knew about it. All she needed was a few minutes with the encrypted disk she'd received as part of the assignment to download data concerning the terrorist network's personnel and Egorov's hidden agendas.

Getting a Stony Man Farm assignment always brought out the best in her, but it also brought out the worst. Being born in between four brothers who were competitive and physical, then stepping into her father's stunt team against the best wishes of her mother, had sharpened her own competitive instincts. Her brothers and her male counterparts didn't hold back so she could stay up—they struggled to keep up with the pace she set.

She turned her face into the cold north wind, feeling her senses surge in response. Her anticipation had a knife edge to it.

Below the bridge, the dark waters of the Vltava River cut through the heart of Prague, heading north till they bent east around Josefov, the Jewish Quarter of the city. Tourists and residents crossed the bridge behind Kylee, the former taking in the sights while the latter made their ways home from their night jobs. A few entertainers with puppets and hucksters peddling trinkets and keepsakes stubbornly lingered, although most of their paying crowd had departed for clubs and hotels. Strains of music from a half-dozen guitarists threaded through the slight breeze that came from the south.

The three predators who'd followed Kylee from the disreputable bar she'd found in the twisting alleys of Old City on the east side of the bridge remained only a short distance away.

Talking it over, Kylee realized. Getting their courage up. She felt the adrenaline zooming within her, and she couldn't help but smile. There was nothing like that feeling, like she was standing on the edge of a bottomless pit about to step off.

And tonight that analogy was true. Despite Barbara Price's trepidation about Kylee's plan, tonight was going to be a great goof. *Too bad you're not going to get to tell anybody about it, Kylee.*

Describing the situation to the stunt people and gaffers she worked with and considered her friends would have been fun. Her mother, of course, would have had a cow if she knew about the whole stuntwoman/secret agent career choice Kylee had made. Even if Kylee hadn't been sworn to secrecy, she would never have told her mom.

"So," Kylee said softly, imperceptibly, "have you figured out who our mystery guy is?" She wore an earpiece that connected to a satellite phone hidden within the big and warm but unflattering coat she wore. The coat was necessary to cover the gear she needed for the goof, but the garment didn't scream "tourist" the way the money she'd been flashing in the industrial metal club had.

"Not yet," the Stony Man mission controller admitted.

The satellites used by the top-secret antiterrorist group peered down onto Prague from a distance of 23,000 miles. Looking down presented no profile possibilities. Identification of unknown subjects was difficult. Kylee had spent a short time earlier tagging the subjects aboard the target vessel before going trolling for potential muggers.

"Maybe while I'm on board I can get you a few pictures," Kylee offered. "He's a good-looking guy. We can share mug shots."

"Don't press your luck," Barbara advised. "What we want is access to that notebook computer."

Okay, Barbara, so maybe humor isn't exactly your style, but some of us like to have a little fun with our spying. In the same moment that she thought that, Kylee pushed the thought away. During the past year and a half that she had known Barbara Price, the Stony Man mission controller had never been as detached or overly demanding as the National Security Agency case officers Kylee had previously worked with. Barbara was money in the bank with an agent in the field, and she never backed away from a hard call or an op that turned into a busted play.

"Right, chief," Kylee said. "I'm keeping my eye on the ball." She adjusted the magnification of the Zeiss microbinoculars she used to spy on the ninety-foot catamaran striped in light green and white. She swept the boat's three decks again and her gaze was magnetically drawn to the guy she'd been asking about.

Mr. Mystery stood on the top deck just where Kylee knew he would be. Never far from Creepstof. Mr. Mystery was tall and solid, but he was long bodied and didn't give the appearance of height until he was standing near other people attending Scherba's gathering. Those times were seldom because he kept himself separate from the group of revelers that roved the catamaran's three decks.

As Kylee watched him standing there, as implacable as a mountainside, she couldn't help wondering if he had a voice as sexy and as daring as she imagined it would have to be to accompany the predatory roll that he used while moving through the crowd to stay close to Creepstof.

That line of thinking, she knew, was totally unprofessional. But she excused herself because she, and Barbara, knew how antsy she got if she had to wait around too long during an assignment. She wasn't the waiting type.

Mr. Mystery wore a dark blue suit and a black turtleneck. His chestnut-brown hair hung in ringlets, and the deeply tanned skin offered mute testimony to the fact that he spent much of—at least, his recent—life outdoors. His face was square and chiseled, the face of a man who had been down some harsh roads.

The face of a man, Kylee had been thinking, that would be worth getting to know. Of course, she'd come across several handsome faces that had only run blocker for cheating hearts or served to mask a deep and abiding self-interest. Hollywood was full of guys like that, and so was the spy business.

Besides that, at this particular juncture, Mr. Mystery was definitely the opposition. Pulling off a get-away meant never getting too close to the fire or hanging around too long. If she pulled the mission off right, there wouldn't even be a fleeting introduction.

"I believe he's working security for Scherba," Barbara said.

"Why?" Kylee checked on the three men who had followed her from the headbanger club. They were still there, still talking. *C'mon, guys. We don't have all night.* She was amped up and ready to go.

"We tagged him early after you pointed him out," Barbara said. "We've been following him. I like to cover the variables. He never gets more than ten feet from the principal."

The principal was Krystof Scherba, the man whose notebook computer Kylee had been assigned to steal. Scherba, who had been identified from the Intel Bethany Riggs had turned up on her mission in South Africa, owned the catamaran. *Guilty Pleasures* was registered in Prague and flagged for international waters. Scherba maintained a home in Prague, but he often entertained aboard the catamaran, as he was doing now.

Kylee was grateful that Scherba was presently on the catamaran. From the information package the Stony Man mission controller had sent her via e-mail, Kylee knew that Scherba's home in the mountains outside Prague was literally a fortified castle. Breaking into his home would have been much harder than getting aboard *Guilty Pleasures*.

The fact that the catamaran was currently crawling with people in full party mode would have normally been daunting. However, with the goof Kylee had planned, the number of people was going to be helpful.

Before she could stop herself, she wondered if Mr. Mystery would be impressed by her stunt. Of course, there was a better chance of him being impressed if he wasn't going to be one of the main victims of the goof.

The party aboard *Guilty Pleasures* had been going on since eight o'clock. It was currently midnight, the witching hour. During those four hours, small boats had constantly carried caterers, food and drink to the catamaran. A five-piece band on the second deck pumped out bluesy jazz music that spread out over the Old City and the Lesser Quarter. The music wasn't something Kylee would have expected from her potential quarry.

Kylee adjusted the binoculars, zooming out with the touch of a button, and picked up Scherba. Besides being powered, the Zeiss lenses were also packed with light amplification circuitry. Some of the things that she liked best about the spy biz were the toys. They were almost as good as those she got to play with in the movies she worked on. And Stony Man Farm always provided some of the best toys.

Pallid and grungy-looking, Krystof Scherba didn't look like an internationally known and feared computer cracker. His razored black hair lay in disarray. Facial piercings along his eyebrows, nose and mouth glinted in the lights ringing the catamaran. A red dragon tattoo covered nearly all of the left side of his face. The fantastical creature's head nestled over Scherba's left eyebrow and its tail reached down to coil around his neck.

Shifting her view back to Mr. Mystery, Kylee wondered what connected the two men. Mr. Mystery had a certain rough charm about him, but he knew how to wear a suit. But why wear a suit?

Almost immediately, the answer dropped into her head: Mr. Mystery was creating distance. The suit was like armor, a posted warning to the rest of the party goers aboard *Guilty Pleasures* that he stood apart from them.

You didn't have to do the suit, Mr. Mystery. You would have stood out from that crowd anyway. Or are you normally a suit-and-tie kind of guy?

Scanning the crowd aboard the catamaran again, Kylee decided that the man didn't fit in at all with the young bohemians that filled all three of the vessel's decks.

*You're the hired help, Mr. Mystery. Security, definitely.
But how good are you?*

The thought floated another smile to Kylee's lips. The
adrenaline inside her burned a little sweeter. She was a
throwback, her mom had told her on more than one occasion and with more than a little mortification and ire,
to the Highland rogues and rascals in her mother's family
tree. Sometimes Kylee acted chastened, but she secretly
loved the thought that she was so much like her mother's
people.

Well, we'll see, won't we?

He presented a challenge because he kept watch over
the boat. Taking the notebook computer Barbara Price
said was aboard wasn't quite the same as ferreting
Scherba away from under the mystery guy's nose. That
would have been a goof worth pulling off.

Another time.

"He's not going to be a problem." Kylee shifted and
put the microbinoculars away. From the way she had been
standing in the middle of the bridge next to the statue of
Saint John the Baptist, one of thirty statues of saints along
the structure, no one could have seen the binoculars.
"When this goes down, his first order of business is going
to be to protect his boss."

"If the principal happens to go belowdecks where the
computer is—"

"He won't. The show's going to be out here." Kylee
checked the three men that were keeping her under surveillance.

All of them were young and gaunt, festooned with body
piercings and tattoos, and wore thick coats that had seen
better days. The three men turned and looked away, afraid
of meeting her gaze.

Oh man. That is so not good. Kylee felt exasperated.

Three guys, and you still don't feel like you can take one woman.

Part of it, she was certain, was that the three men had wanted to take her in Charles Alley before she reached the bridge. She hadn't allowed that and had stayed ahead of them.

The three men were hunters. Kylee was sure of that. During her travels on Stony Man missions, as well as working on films as a stunt person around the world, she had seen plenty of men like these three that had singled her out in the bar. She had sought them out for that reason. And like natural predators, they wanted the security of the dark and the advantage of their home ground.

"I've got to go," Kylee said. "I've got to make this thing happen. I'll be back in touch with you as soon as I'm on board."

"Affirmative," Barbara said. "Be careful. If you're caught—"

"I won't be—I'm never caught." Kylee palmed the earpiece and shoved it into the waterproof pack she had strapped to her left thigh under the long coat.

The three men stopped talking and watched her.

Weaving a little, as if she'd had too much to drink and the effects were just starting to hit her, Kylee walked toward the three men. She hoped they didn't turn and run.

"Hey," she said. "Do any of you guys speak English?"

They all just looked at her.

Rocking on her feet, putting on a look of exasperated disgust, Kylee said, "English. *English.* I'm lost. I need directions. Man, you guys watch American TV over here on your satellite dishes. Surely you can speak the language." Her words were designed to provoke, to push the men into doing now what they were waiting to do later.

One of the men, a lank individual with long hair, took a hit off his evil-smelling cigarette. He shrugged, then nodded. "Yeah. I maybe speak English. A *little* English."

"Good." Kylee walked toward them.

Automatically the three men flared out, forming a triangle around her like wolves getting set to take down a lamb that had wandered from the protection of the flock.

"Where you want to go?" the man asked. The cigarette coal glowed orange against the creased, pockmarked face.

"Kampa Island," Kylee said, slurring her words just a little. "I'm supposed to meet a friend at the John Lennon mural." She intended to see the murals on the island before she left with the film crew.

"Ah." The man grinned. "Finding Kampa Island, that is very easy, yes." He pointed. "Other side of bridge in Mala Strana. You know Mala Strana?"

Pointing toward the west side of the bridge, Kylee said, "I know Mala Strana. It means Lesser City." She pointed to the east end of the bridge. "Stare Mesto. That's the Old City."

The man smiled, but the effort looked like the hungry attention on a wolf gone gaunt with winter. "Yes."

Kylee hiccuped and covered her mouth. "I just got turned around looking out at the river, that's all. Thanks for the help." She started to walk away, knowing she needed to get closer if the men didn't take advantage of the moment.

"Wait," the man called.

Kylee looked at him, her body gearing up, getting more ready for the goof.

"Finding Kampa Island," the man explained, performing the wolf's smile again. "Very easy, yes. But finding mural…" He spread his hands. "That maybe not so easy."

"Do you know where the mural is?" Kylee asked.

"I draw you map, yes."

"All right," Kylee agreed.

"Come here." The man took a small pad of paper from his shirt pocket. "I draw. I explain."

Knowing she was stepping into a trap, actually relishing the amount of danger she was in, and knowing that Barbara Price wouldn't exactly be happy with the fact that she did or knowing that she enjoyed it, Kylee stood at the man's side.

He took out a pencil and started to draw, talking about directions to occupy her attention.

From the corner of her eye, Kylee saw the man on her left slip a short-bladed combat knife from his coat pocket. The way that the man on the right moved told her that he had also pulled a weapon.

Spreading her feet slightly, Kylee felt the adrenaline pushing through her. Every movement she made felt oiled, loose and exact. Her brain, working with muscles that had trained for split-second timing for years, choreographed her next moves.

Just as the man on the left started to move forward to place the knife at her back, Kylee blocked the movement with a sweeping left forearm, planted her left foot, twisted her torso, then brought her left arm back around in a whipping motion that slammed her left elbow forward into the man's face.

The guy's nose broke with an audible snap. He staggered back, blood streaming down his face. By the time he landed on his butt, Kylee had stepped back and thrown her right arm out, catching the second man under his left arm. Whirling again, she hip-tossed the man and brought him down with smashing force against the stone bridge. A kick to the temple stretched the man out prone.

These days, with all the kick-butt action movies and television action shows featuring women, a stuntwoman wasn't worth her salt unless she was familiar with martial arts. Kylee's four brothers had been very involved in sports and had joined her father's stunt team out in Los Angeles. She'd grown up physical and had gotten into stunt work, despite her mother's wishes and her father's chagrin.

The third man tried to break and run. The pad he'd been drawing on fluttered over the side of the bridge.

Kylee grabbed the front of the man's coat and yelled loudly. "Help! Muggers! Somebody call the police! Help!"

The man tried to get away from her, pushing at her hands. Fiercely she held on. He cursed. Kylee didn't have much more than rudimentary knowledge of the local language, but she knew most of the words the guy used. None of them were complimentary. She shifted and twisted her wrists, easily breaking his frantic attempts to get away.

"Help!" Kylee screamed again. She stood an athletic five feet nine inches tall and carried more weight than her build would suggest, all of it in toned muscle. From all the fight scenes she'd taken part in, she knew how to hold her own.

But the man she was detaining was driven by sheer terror at the moment. Possibly he was afraid of being picked up by the Czech police for outstanding warrants, but more than likely he feared the madwoman that had grabbed hold of him.

"Help!" Kylee screamed again. She stayed close to the mugger, knowing that the passersby who turned to look would believe the man was assaulting her.

A tugboat passing in the river below shined a spotlight

on the bridge. The ellipse of white light sliced through the night and tracked along the bridge.

The man cursed again and threw a hard right fist at Kylee's face.

Twisting, Kylee slipped the blow like she'd learned to do when she was eleven and her older brothers had practiced their stunt skills on her. She'd always been a quick study when it came to muscle memory.

When the man drew his fist back to try again, Kylee ducked forward and head-butted him in the nose. He shuddered and would have gone down but Kylee propped him up against the bridge's low wall.

The conscious mugger with the broken nose got to his feet. He hesitated as if torn between fleeing and helping his comrade. The tugboat's spotlight flared over the man, causing him to instinctively throw up his hands, then he turned and ran like a vampire avoiding daybreak.

A man's voice, strong with insistent authority, blared from a PA system aboard the tugboat.

"Let me go, you stupid bitch!" the man demanded, trying English. He pushed at Kylee's hands but she kept slipping his grip. He didn't try to hit her again.

When the tugboat's spotlight fell over her, joined by at least three others almost instantly, Kylee knew she had to close the show and sell the goof. Timing was everything in stunt work.

"Get away from that woman!" someone cried in a British accent. A quartet of tourists, two men and two women, all of them young and obviously scared and half-drunk, halted a safe distance away.

Kylee feinted another head-butt, causing the would-be mugger to lift his hands in immediate defense. Then she kneed him in the crotch, a quick burst of movement that remained hidden in the shadows left by the explosion of light from the beams pouring over the wall. The man sagged toward her, his legs completely going out from under him now. Instinctively he put his hands on her, trying to get her to stop, trying to find some kind of support.

In the bright light, though, Kylee knew the situation looked like the man was pushing her. She screamed again, then fell back over the low bridge, whirling her arms and kicking her legs to make the dismount more dramatic.

Thankfully, the maneuver caught the spotlight operators by surprise and they weren't able to track the beams after her as she expertly turned the fall into a headlong dive. She thrust her hands in front of her, fingers outstretched, and reached for the dark river twenty feet below her. The tugboat was less than a dozen feet away. Her peripheral vision revealed at least three crewmen scrambling across the forward deck.

Then she dove deeply into the dark, cold water. *Here I come, Mr. Mystery. Ready or not. I've got my game on.*

Chapter 2

Helpless frustration filled Mick Stone as he stood in *Guilty Pleasures'* bow and watched the rescue effort taking shape under the Charles Bridge. Everything in him cried out to go to the unfortunate woman's aid. But that was primitive instinct, and he recognized the impulse for what it was. Tough and seasoned as he might think he was, he wasn't any more proof against the deathly icy chill of the Vltava River than the woman who had plunged over the bridge's side.

And, as a sailor, he was aware that the men working the river knew the current and the location better than he did. He would have been in the way even if he'd gotten to one of the outboards tied up astern of the catamaran, and that knowledge rankled him. Mick Stone wasn't a man accustomed to feeling useless.

"Is there a problem, Stone?" Krystof Scherba's voice was calm and controlled, the quiet stillness of water sluicing between two rocks tightly jammed together.

Making certain his features were neutral, Mick turned to face his present employer. *Damn, I hate this job. I should have never taken it on.* The thought wasn't a new one. Mick had experienced similar lines of thinking since he'd entered his present employ. But he hadn't been able to take one more empty day on the quiet Pacific Ocean. He'd craved excitement and the chance to measure his skills and his ingenuity against others.

And in the end, when the job offer had come to watch over Krystof Scherba, he'd taken the assignment on for those reasons rather than for the money. He had three older sisters in Australia, all of them married to good men, but since their parents had passed away a few years ago, he had always envisioned himself as the family patriarch, always striving to put money away in case they ever needed it. None of them had, but he still felt responsible.

Krystof Scherba stared almost blankly. The dragon tattoo near his left eye glowered malevolently. He sipped his drink. "You're supposed to be a professional, Stone," the computer cracker accused. "Yet you find your attention divided between me and the woman who fell into the river."

A small Prague police car eased down the length of the Charles Bridge. The whirling light ripped away the night's shadows over the statues of the saints along the bridge as the vehicle passed.

"No," Mick replied. "I've had my eye on you the whole time we've been up here. Even during this bit of confusion."

"Still, as highly recommended as you have come as a bodyguard, I would not have expected you to be so hypnotized by the sight of a woman plunging from a bridge. From what I understood of your background, death was a constant companion."

"Aye, sir," Mick said. He caught his response too late to stop it. *Aye.* As though he was a sailor instead of a professional bodyguard.

But that had come from months between jobs when he'd taken his houseboat to the open Indian Ocean and made his way up to Singapore and Macao for extended visits. Those places had netted small security or recovery jobs, violent and nasty bits of business, and he had needed them. Not for the money so much, because he had enough of that tucked away for a while, but because he had craved the action.

The action was the only thing that staved the periods of melancholy and loneliness that caught up with him. He'd needed the sea, needed to feel the harsh pull of her beneath him and to be kissed by the wind and warmed by the sun to remember that he preferred being alone in his life. Time in the boat allowed him to get away from the seemingly endless procession of prospective dates his three older sisters threw at him.

At first the job Mick had taken with Krystof Scherba had seemed like the answer to a lot of prayers. Scherba had a lot of enemies, and most of them did not wear badges. Authorities in several countries—and Scherba had given Mick a list of those countries—still had warrants out for his arrest regarding some infraction of cybernetic espionage.

Even more than that, though, were the wheelers and dealers of the shadow world, born of greed and savagery, that wanted information Scherba had or could get for them with his skills. Terrorists and criminals alike wanted Krystof Scherba. If the man had possessed any common sense at all, he would have gone into hiding in that fortress of a castle he had outside Prague. Instead, Scherba seemed determined to flaunt himself at his potential enemies.

In the five weeks he had been on the job, Mick had foiled three attempts to kidnap or kill Scherba. The attempt just before Mick had taken over had resulted in the death of his chief of security. Despite that, Scherba still didn't see fit to heed Mick's advice and warnings, or even consider giving him an agenda.

Within the past few days, something had happened in South Africa, perhaps in Cape Town if one overheard fevered whisper was to be believed. Mick still didn't know what that event was, but he knew it was big and people had been killed.

Scherba's eyes were cold as ice. "The people I got your name from said you were resourceful, dedicated and brutally rash. Even to the point of jeopardizing your job."

Mick felt a wave of shame course through him. He had been told all those things before. Sometimes the principals he had been bodyguarding had meant the observations in a kind way, and other times the statements were inflammatory accusations. Those qualities were what had helped him find work before the CIA had also added *intractable* to his dossier and work—at least, work he would agree to—dried up. A year ago, he would never have taken the job with Krystof Scherba.

Out on the river, one of the fishing boats unfurled a net and dragged it through the water. With the slow, lazy movement of the river through the heart of the city, the net would probably come up with the body in a short amount of time.

A police boat was in the water downriver. The lights whirled as it sped through the river traffic. Pleasure crafts, offering drinks and a late-night buffet, crawled slowly out of the way.

"Krystof," a cultured voice said.

Mick was aware of the man making his way toward

Scherba. Instinctively, he placed himself between Scherba and the new arrival.

Suave and urbane, Shane Dellamer stepped from the crowd. He wore a long black leather coat against the chill. Below his high, broad forehead, his gray eyes stood out starkly in the ruddy darkness of his face. He had a wide, generous mouth and was known in the media for being an entrancing orator. His face was blunt and squared-off as a trenching tool, and looked a good ten or fifteen years younger than the fifty-one his file had him clocked at. At an inch or two over six feet, his height didn't really make him stand out in the crowd, but he carried himself like a lion, regal and apart.

As CEO of Dellamer Enterprises, Dellamer was fantastically rich. With those enterprises lodged firmly in electronics, pharmaceuticals and munitions, Dellamer's interests were also spread across the globe. The multimillionaire industrialist also worked at his rebel image, which was—Mick assumed—one of the reasons he'd come to Scherba's party tonight. Dellamer had been in the news a lot lately as he prepared for a bid at a political position in his home state of New York.

"Yes, Shane," Scherba responded. "Stone, please."

Only somewhat chagrined, Mick stepped back. His gaze raked the river as the fishing boat trawled along. A second police boat had joined the first. Lights aboard the second boat showed divers hastily pulling their gear on.

Seeing the divers bothered Mick. He had witnessed the battle aboard the bridge. At the time he'd been caught up in the drama of the moment, but now that the presence of the divers made him think back, he realized the woman had dispatched two of her attackers rather handily.

Like a pro. The thought burst into Mick's brain like a direct napalm hit. Three guys. She disables two of them.

And the third manages to put her into the water? He glanced around at the crowd thronging the railing as the feeling of unease soaked through him. *Not exactly shrimp on the barbie, eh, mate?*

Dellamer and Scherba were in deep discussion regarding background checks the computer cracker had finessed regarding some of the recent pharmaceutical mergers and acquisitions the industrialist had his eye on in the European theater.

A silent alarm jangled the handset inside Mick's jacket. He felt the vibration and reached into his pocket. Intimate knowledge with the device and the way the security zones had been set up aboard *Guilty Pleasures* told him the alarm had been set off in Krystof Scherba's private berth aboard the vessel.

But it was the *secondary* alarm, not the primary. Whoever had penetrated the secondary alarm was good. But he or she was also in a hurry.

Mick raised his left arm and exposed the pencil mike secured on the inside of his wrist. "Josef. Radu."

"Yes," Josef Szekeres replied. From Hungary, he was a bodyguard known for his nerve and methodical nature. Ten years older than Mick's thirty-two years, Szekeres was an accomplished mountain climber and often worked security on high-profile extreme sports figures. He was compact, five feet eight and one hundred sixty pounds, a man who was often overlooked because he appeared so commonplace.

Mick had worked with Szekeres three times before, all of those times with the American Central Intelligence Agency. When he'd been given the present gig, Mick had brought Szekeres into the assignment.

Radu Galca was the local Romanian bodyguard Scherba had worked with for three years. Radu was a mountain of moving muscle, a steroid freak who lived in a gym and hunted bar fights when he wasn't at post on a security detail. Galca and Scherba went back to the cracker's beginnings of international attention. At twenty-seven, he was the same age as Scherba. But where nature had bestowed a keen intellect on Scherba, Galca was, as Josef put it, dumb as a box of hammers.

"I am here," Radu said, mimicking the voice pattern of Arnold Schwarzenegger in *The Terminator.* He was smooth-shaven and in the habit of always wearing sunglasses, fitting in with the grunge crowd that Scherba hung with.

"Stay with the principal," Mick ordered. "I'll be back as soon as I check out this alarm." Seeing that Josef and Radu both moved immediately to Scherba, Mick got into motion.

"Trouble?" Josef asked.

"Don't know if we have trouble, Josef." Mick shoved through the crowd, trying to be as polite as possible. He drew a multitude of curses but didn't leave any broken bones and only a few bruises behind him. "Got an alarm tripped, mate. Think I'll nip down and have a look-see."

"An alarm?" Radu repeated. "You shouldn't go by yourself."

"Probably just one of our *guests.*" Mick said the word like a curse. He stepped through the foyer of the main doorway and stepped into the empty room.

Light glinted across a bright trail on the carpet. The carpet was a tight Berber weave that held up to heavy traffic and repelled water. Diamond-bright droplets captured Mick's eye and created a trail across the floor. Most people would not have noticed them, and if he hadn't been looking for something out of the ordinary, he knew he wouldn't have noticed them either.

Kneeling, he put a hand to the wet carpet. He dragged his palm across the nap of the Berber weave. The water was cold to the touch, colder than it should have been if it had been there for a while. The trail was evident. For a moment, a scene from one of the old black-and-white monster movies he'd watched as a kid came to mind. One of his favorite scary movies had been *The Creature from the Black Lagoon.* If the creature had been real, it would have left a trail like this.

Or, Mick thought, remembering how the woman had plunged over the side of the bridge, someone who has dragged himself or herself from the river just a few minutes ago. There were no guarantees that the ''woman'' on the bridge had really been female.

He reached inside his jacket and curled the fingers of his right hand around the butt of the Colt .45 M1911A semiautomatic pistol he'd carried for years. Accurate to fifty yards and more, the pistol fired a big, slow-moving round that could be easily silenced and carried a tremendous amount of knockdown power.

Reaching into his inside jacket pocket, he removed a custom-made silencer and threaded it onto the pistol barrel. If someone had broken aboard *Guilty Pleasures* with killing on his or her mind, he intended to put that person down quickly.

Pistol in hand, Mick followed the carpet trail to the stairwell and went below. He stopped at the door to Scherba's room and listened intently while he examined the locks. Nothing seemed to be amiss, but he thought he heard movement inside the room.

He tried the door and found it unlocked.

Now that, mate, he told himself, *that definitely ain't right.* He took a firmer grip on the pistol and let the weapon lead him into the room.

Shadows cloaked the berth.

Mick moved immediately, stepping to the right so he wouldn't be skylined against the doorway. His heart rate slowed slightly, the way it always did when he was under stress, like a shark gliding through the ocean just before a lightning-fast strike.

He noticed the prone figure swaddled in bedclothes first. Remaining in profile, the pistol gripped in a modified Weaver stance the way he'd been taught in the military, taking small comfort in the bulletproof vest he wore, he held his position.

Remember, mate, he told himself, *a vest doesn't cover your head.*

"Hey," he said.

The sheet-covered figure didn't move. Lying on her side as she was—and Mick was definitely sure it was a *she* he was looking at because the hips, though slim and compact, held definite womanly curves—she was turned away from him. One naked shoulder and an arm showed outside the bedclothes. The light from the open doorway turned the skin alabaster, milky smooth and sleek.

Asleep, passed out or dead, Mick thought. After weeks of seeing Scherba at work, he knew any of those was possible.

But it was also possible she was playing possum, waiting for him to go away. *Someone* had left the wet trail through the upstairs room.

"Hey," he said in a louder voice.

When he'd set up security on Krystof Scherba, Mick had known the people gunning for him would be coming after the man himself or the work that he did. Scherba had secrets, and secrets were worth money. The computer cracker never went anywhere without his notebook computer. Mick had persuaded Scherba to allow the secondary alarms to be put on the computer as well as on the desk.

The desk alarm had lit up, indicating that the computer had been tampered with.

Using his peripheral vision to keep an eye on the woman lying in the bed, Mick glanced at the computer. Green lights danced and flickered across the front of the machine, indicating that it was in use.

No way would Scherba leave that little beastie running unattended.

Then the wet pattern in the computer chair caught Mick's eye. The rounded pattern was wide hipped, definitely feminine, and he would have bet the contours fit the vixen lying abed.

"Nice try, darlin'," Mick said. "But the computer's running, and I know my principal wouldn't allow that to happen. So why don't you come up out of that bed and we'll have us a chat."

"Krystof?" The voice sounded plaintive and whiny.

But the voice also sounded sexy as hell. The accent seemed to be American, but that could have been put on. There was nothing more attention getting than the soft, sexy voice of a woman just roused from sleep.

Only he was certain that this particular woman hadn't been sleeping, and that she was gutsy enough to try to pull off the act proved she was dangerous. And if that wasn't enough, there was still that little swan dive from the bridge while struggling with assailants to keep in mind.

"Not Krystof, love," Mick grated. Irritation stung him. Even though he'd captured the woman, he was certain there would be hell to pay because she had managed to get aboard the catamaran.

Scherba was a man who expected perfection. He found

it in the computer work he did, and he demanded the same capability from the people who worked around him.

Languidly, making no sudden movements, the woman sat up in bed. The blue silk sheet slithered down her athletic body, revealing rounded shoulders sculpted by serious dedication in the gym. She was tall, Mick realized as he tried to gather all the details and remember if he'd seen her near or around Scherba in the past few days.

Shadows gathered in the hollow of her throat as she regarded him with a sleepy gaze. The sheets continued skidding down her body, holding just for an instant at her breasts, then cascading over those as well.

Inadvertently Mick's gaze went to those breasts and the back of his throat dried immediately in response. She was definitely full figured in addition to being athletic. Her breasts were firm and proud, defying gravity. The pale pink nipples stood out darker than her white skin. No immediate attempt was made to hide the lush femininity.

She lifted her knees and wrapped her arms around her legs, trapping the treacherous silk sheet and hiding the voluptuous body in an economy of motion.

Mick had to resist an immediate impulse to rip the sheet away and reveal the rest of her. Catching her like this, with her pants down so to speak, made her his conquest. And a beauty like this one brought out all the primitive instincts that lingered in the back of a healthy, red-blooded man's brain.

No, Mick corrected. *Not a man's brain. Someone like this, she took a man's brain right out of the bloody equation.* His breath tightened in his chest and he felt his pulse pound at his temples.

Swallowing hard, Mick pushed his primitive response away. Still he stared at the outlines of her breasts where they curved out from the shielding protection of her crossed arms atop her sheet-covered knees. *Let her feel naked,* he thought. *It'll make her less likely to feel confident about this whole situation. I'll get the answers I need.*

Her lambent green eyes—despite the darkness Mick was certain they were the green of the Pacific—held amused lights in them as she regarded him. Damp and matted to her head, her hair could have been any color, but he was certain it wasn't dark or red. She was a woman who could steal a man's breath away.

Or a computer cracker's secrets, he reminded himself.

"Are you going to shoot me?" Her tone was too light, too in control for someone facing another person down the length of a pistol pointed in the wrong direction for personal comfort.

"I might," Mick growled. "And if it wasn't me, there are men aboard this boat who would shoot you." Even as he said that, recognized it as truth, he felt badly for her. Scherba's regular security people would probably have come in blasting.

And in that moment, Mick Stone realized he might be the woman's only chance of getting off the boat alive.

The young woman's eyes widened somewhat, but Mick got the definite feeling that it was all put on. She wasn't scared. Even staring down the barrel of his pistol, she wasn't scared. *Stupid sheila,* he thought. *You should be afraid right now.*

"Whatever would they want to shoot me for?" the woman demanded.

"For being here."

"I'm a guest."

"Like bloody hell you are," Mick growled. He hated the fact that the young woman looked so vulnerable in the bed. His gaze kept flitting to her breasts, and he couldn't resist wishing he could see the whole package.

"Krystof isn't going to like how you're talking to me," she insisted.

Mick shook his head. He had to hand it to her, she didn't cave easily even when a situation was going against her. "Smooth as you think you are, darlin', there are a few things you messed up on."

"Ah," she said, arching an eyebrow. "A critique then."

Despite the tension of the situation and the fact that Scherba would take him to task later, Mick liked the woman. He liked her bravado in the face of certain disaster and he liked the skill she'd obviously had to get aboard the boat. None of the women his sisters had foisted on him over the years had that quality.

Here he was, facing a woman who had actually piqued his interest, and she had to be a damn thief.

"You got wet swimming through the river," Mick said.

The woman wrapped her arms around her shoulders. Her breasts jiggled suggestively and Mick couldn't help wondering how they tasted and how they felt. Heavy, he guessed, heavy and solid and definitely feminine.

"Very cold," the woman said.

"You left a trail across the main foyer."

She shrugged, and her breasts pressed together and deepened the cleavage. "Couldn't be helped."

"You left a wet spot in the chair."

The woman's eyes drifted to the chair. "Now that," she said, "that I did not think about." She looked back at him. "But I'll remember in the future."

"And your hair is wet, Goldilocks," Mick said. "Meaning you're my girl no matter what little story you decide to trot out."

"Looks like you have it all figured out, Father Bear." She trailed her fingers through her damp hair, revealing one bounteous globe that hung tantalizingly before him. "I have to admit, you didn't catch me at my best."

Mick appreciated the insouciance in her tone and couldn't help paying attention to the way the muscles of her shoulders moved as she touched her hair. And he couldn't help wondering how that tanned skin would look under the warm kiss of fragile moonlight.

Or how her lips would taste and feel.

Roughly Mick shoved the thoughts from his mind. Above all things, he was a consummate professional. Except that the reaction his body was presently showing didn't advertise that.

"But the thing of it is, darlin'," he growled, "I did catch you." And the hell of it was that he didn't know how he was supposed to keep her whole—or maybe even alive—when Scherba discovered she'd broken in.

She smiled sweetly at him. "The trick is, Mr. Mystery, keeping me caught. You see, I specialize in get-aways." She tilted her chin up, her tone definitely flirting, and blew him a kiss.

Then she closed her eyes.

Mick didn't realize that he had seen her close her eyes until after the explosion of light and sound filled the berth. He was stunned, deafened and blinded by the thunder and blistering light. For a moment he thought she had been a suicide bomber, there to take Scherba down at any cost, killing them both in the blast designed to rip the bottom out of *Guilty Pleasures* and send the boat to the river bottom.

Then he realized he was still standing.

Just a flash-bang, mate, he told himself. He was familiar with the disorienting effects of the pyrotechnic grenades from his stint in the military and considerable exposure to them since.

He also realized that the woman would try to make her escape as well. He still had a chance to stop her. But he was blind as a bat.

Chapter 3

As soon as the flash of light faded from her eyelids,
Kylee snapped her eyes open. Even though she'd had her
eyes closed, there was some residual loss of vision. Black
spots whirled in front of her. Excitement flared through
her, accompanied by unwanted stirrings she had seldom
felt. Mr. Mystery had been much more handsome than
she'd been able to ascertain through the long-distance
lenses.

She blinked her eyes, wishing she could see, wishing
there was a better time to just look at the man. But she
knew her vision wouldn't recover completely in time. She
took some solace in the fact that the battery-powered
minicam she wore on her wet suit shot footage of everything in front of her. The fish-eye lens would make certain
she got it all.

As bad as her present condition was, though, she knew
she was light-years ahead of Mr. Mystery. He opened and
closed his eyes rapidly, striving desperately for some re-

turn to normal vision. That would be minutes in coming, though. The F/X box she'd planted on the wall behind her when Barbara Price had warned her that the man was coming had strobed directly into his eyes.

Still, the light in the room was enough to reveal the hard, handsome planes of his face. He had high cheekbones and a square jaw, the features of a man who had shaped his life through determination and grit. And the ringlets of hair drew her attention. She couldn't help wondering what it would feel like to trail her fingers through those ringlets.

Get away! Get away! The impulse roared within her.

Trouble had always been easy for her to get into. Escaping trouble was the trickier part.

Getting aboard *Guilty Pleasures* had been easy. Under the cover of the river, Kylee had slipped a small miniscuba from her coat and swum to the boat. Everyone aboard had been pulled forward by her dive into the river, drawn by the plight of the drowning woman. Besides the miniscuba, she'd also carried several of the F/X boxes set up to respond to the miniature remote control device she carried.

Once aboard the boat, Kylee had fitted the earpiece to her ear and throat again, then let Barbara Price guide her to Scherba's stateroom with the thermographic capabilities of the spy-satellite Stony Man was using for the mission. A digital electronic lock pick had gotten her past the locks on Scherba's door.

Inside the room, Kylee had used the encrypted disk Bethany Riggs had turned up in Cape Town, South Africa, to bring up the hidden operating system lurking inside Scherba's notebook computer. A spare satellite phone plugged into the notebook's modular connection had provided the link Barbara and her team needed to access the computer's hard drive.

Everything had been going great till Barbara had reported that Mick Stone had decided to come belowdecks. A quick check then revealed the secondary alarm booted directly to the computer that Kylee had missed earlier. By then, it had been too late to run.

She'd pulled her wet suit down to her waist on the theory that the sight of a naked woman temporarily rendered most men unable to think for several seconds at a time, then crawled into Scherba's bed. The ruse had been an excellent on-the-fly idea. Too bad it hadn't worked. If she hadn't had the F/X box rigged and ready to go, getting out of the room could have proved much harder.

And you're not out of here yet, she chided herself.

With easy athletic grace, Kylee rolled from the bed, fully expecting Mr. Mystery to start blasting with the big silenced pistol in his fist. The fact that he didn't surprised her.

However, he did shift, clearly moving by memory, and came to a stop in front of the doorway. That was something she had not planned on. His economy of movement, the sheer grace of his course of action, was expected after seeing him so many times in motion aboard *Guilty Pleasures*. But she hadn't expected him to think so quickly to block the doorway.

Now that she was this close to him, had felt the heat of his cerulean-blue gaze, she couldn't help wondering how good he was physically. She was a trained martial artist, but he looked like a bruiser who survived on sheer strength and ferocity. Unfortunately, he also looked like a man who could clear out a bar of Hell's Angels by himself.

He stood in the doorway, raising his open left hand to

block her. He blinked his eyes rapidly, continuing to try to bring his vision back to normal.

That's not a place you want to be, Mr. Mystery, Kylee thought. She rose to her feet in front of the computer table, glanced to check that the satellite uplink was still functioning, and estimated the distance separating her from the man. Now she pulled the wet suit back over her shoulders and zipped up.

Taking one long step, Kylee launched herself into the air in a flying kick. Some preternatural instinct must have warned the man, some ghost of a sixth sense that had survived the prehistoric times. He was in motion before she could stop her attack, dropping into a defensive crouch.

Instead of striking his chest as she'd intended, the heel of her left foot collided with his face. She hated that, hated thinking of the swelling and the bruises that would surely mar those handsome features for the next few days. The impact drove him backward, but he turned to allow some of the kick to glide past him. Kylee slid with it, ending up in a spilled tangle of arms and legs and heaving bodies.

He cursed at her. "Stupid, sheila. Even if you get past me, how do you expect to get by all of those guards topside?"

Kylee didn't waste her breath. She slammed an elbow under his chin, snapping that handsome jaw shut and hoping she wouldn't break any of his teeth.

He slapped at her with his free hand when she grabbed his other wrist and tried to break his pistol free. Putting pressure on the man's arm was like trying to squeeze an iron bar.

For a moment during the skirmish, she was on top of him, her legs straddling him as she fought to control his gun arm. Her pulse thundered at her temples, and she knew the increased pace and pressure weren't only from the exertion and the excitement that flared through her. She felt the hard length of his body pressed against hers from underneath, felt the heat of him as he struggled against her. Her breasts molded to his chest as he circled his free arm around her upper body and tried to lock a hold on her. She drew back a fist and punched him in the nose hard enough to snap his head back. She'd never hesitated to hit her brothers during a stunt session that called for it.

Mr. Mystery snarled curses at her in the same thick Australian accent he'd used only a moment ago. He maintained his grip even as she shifted, grinding her hips into him to get the leverage she needed, and drew back her fist again. This time, though, he dodged and she slammed her knuckles into the floor. The carpet wasn't enough to cushion the blow. Bright, broken pain shivered up through her wrist and she hoped she hadn't sprained it.

"Give it up, sheila," the man yelled. "They'll kill you."

"And you won't?"

"No."

"Sorry. I don't believe you." Kylee slammed her forearm into that stubborn jaw again.

In the end, though, the same wet suit that had given her away in the chair also proved too slick for the man to maintain his grip on. She slipped away even as he tried to squeeze her and restrain her. Kicking her feet against him, she slid across the threshold on her back.

On the other side of the doorway, Kylee tried to get to her feet. Her ribs felt bruised, but she couldn't help smiling. *I'm better than you, Mr. Mystery. I came onto your home turf and captured your flag.*

Pushing himself over onto his stomach, his blind eyes

still searching the immediate area around him, the man lifted the .45 in his right fist.

"Hold up, sheila!" he roared. But his aim was off by a few inches, letting her know that he still couldn't see properly.

Rolling onto her side away from the man, Kylee swung her right arm back, catching the man's gun wrist and knocking the weapon loose. The big .45 struck the wooden flooring, dug a scratch in the finish and slid away.

The man caught Kylee's right ankle in a grip that felt like iron. Instinctively she rolled so that her ankle turned in toward the man's thumb. Years of martial arts training had taught her that turning a trapped limb toward the opponent's thumb was the easiest way to break that opponent's grip no matter how strong he—or she—was.

Her ankle turned now, but she was certain she'd lost some skin and would wear a ring of bruises around the ankle for a few days. She stamped with the other foot, catching the man's elbow and breaking his hold.

Kylee rolled away. The catamaran crew would be alert now. Her escape window was closing by the second. She pushed herself to her feet, surprised that the man was getting to his feet at the same time. He threw himself forward, seeming to fill the middle of the room as he got to his feet between her and the spiral stairs that led to the catamaran's main deck.

The man drew up in an openhanded martial arts stance. He also turned his head to the side, using his peripheral vision instead of trying to look at her directly. The temporary stun effects of the F/X box would take out direct vision, but peripheral vision wasn't affected quite as much and recovered more quickly.

Kylee closed on him, trying to muscle her way past him.

His hands flicked out in a series of slaps and punches. If any of them had landed, Kylee was certain she'd have been knocked down. She ducked and bobbed, blocking with her open hands, using her hands and her forearms to turn the blows aside.

You're good, Mr. Mystery, Kylee silently conceded. *You're quick and you're dangerous.*

She ducked beneath a strike that would have flattened her nose if it had connected and fired a punch into his midsection. Her fist connected with the Kevlar vest he wore, but she could also feel the hard muscle that lay beneath. The punch didn't even faze him.

If it hadn't been for years of martial arts training and stuntwork, seemingly unending days of being a mock punching bag for her brothers, Kylee knew she wouldn't have lasted more than a few seconds against her opponent. Even then, she suspected that the man was holding a little back, maybe to protect himself or maybe because she was female.

And with each passing second, the man's vision grew better.

In an all-or-nothing move, Kylee dropped quickly into a crouch and threw a leg out to sweep the man's feet from under him. She pushed herself up again as he fell. By the time she reached the spiral staircase leading up to the catamaran's main cabin, she'd taken out the earplug that had protected her against the loud noise of the F/X box and put the earpiece into place.

"Are you there?" Kylee asked in a breathless rush. She grabbed a coat from the rack near the door as she entered the stairwell, shrugging it on to cover her wet suit. She ascended the stairs in a rapid, driving rhythm.

The man cursed behind her as he got to his feet. He

ran forward and slammed into the spiral staircase by mistake. The structure shook.

"I'm here," Barbara answered. "You're in a bad spot."

"And assessments off the cuff like that are what a mission controller does?" Kylee quipped. "I think I had that one."

"The good news is your button-cam got a picture of Mr. Mystery. We may be able to identify him."

Kylee stopped at the entrance to the main cabin. The room was filled with buffet tables and elegant lounge furniture. "What about the room?"

"Four guys. All armed."

"Security?"

"Two confirmed hits on the database we built on the op," Barbara agreed.

"It's a safe bet on the other two, then," Kylee said. The stairwell vibrated beneath her, letting her know Mr. Mystery was up and about and in hot pursuit.

"I'd say so."

"The computer connection?"

"We're working it."

Desperate, Kylee peered out. Four men stood in the room with pistols in their fists.

"Over there!" one of the men yelled. "In the stairwell!"

Kylee ducked and at least two bullets ripped through the stairwell above her head. "Don't shoot!" she yelled. "Please don't shoot!"

Thankfully, the vibrations coming up from belowdecks halted as well. Maybe Mr. Mystery thought she was going to be coming back down.

Despite the seriousness of the situation, Kylee couldn't help feeling jazzed and amped up. She *was* a throwback to the Highland rogues, as her mother had feared. Situations like this always brought out her worst. At least, that was how her mom would have looked at it.

God forbid that she ever find out, Kylee thought.

One of the men spoke in a guttural language that Kylee thought she recognized as Czech. However, with an earplug in one ear, and with gunshots still ringing in the other, she wasn't sure. She hoped the translation was roughly, *Hey, that was a woman. Don't shoot.*

Taking a deep breath, she stepped out into the cabin with her arms away from her body. She still had the remote control in her left hand and kept the device concealed. Looking down the barrels of four pistols, she discovered it wasn't hard to look scared. She held her hands up immediately.

"Who are you?" one of the men demanded in accented English.

"Down there!" Kylee gulped and glanced nervously at the stairwell. "A man with a gun! He's killed them! He's killed them all!" She decided then and there that if Barbara Price ever offered to let her see any video or hear any audio recording of tonight that she would flatly refuse. Playing the ingenue was *so* not her best suit.

"Killed who?" the man demanded.

"Them!" Kylee screamed in terror. *Come on, guy.* Them *are always getting killed.*

She glanced over her shoulder at the stairwell. So far, Mr. Mystery hadn't put in an appearance. She hoped he wouldn't get hurt. Besides being quick and dangerous, Mr. Mystery was also quite dashing. In a rough-hewn kind of way.

The men seemed undecided. All of them kept their pistols pointed at her. Maybe they hadn't immediately moved her into the *potentially datable, don't shoot her in the head* category that most men seemed to lump attractive women who appeared suddenly before them.

It's the hair, Kylee thought. *Definitely the hair.* She hated having a bad-hair day, but having a bad-hair day at gunpoint was *so* much worse.

Deciding to up the ante before she lost all control, Kylee said, "There he is!" She screamed, pointed and dove for the floor.

One bullet cut the air over her head, missing her by scant inches. *Okay, good thing I wasn't holding pat with the bluff.*

Gunshots cannonaded inside the cabin. The trapped noise swelled to enormous proportions. Curses in a half-dozen languages rent the air.

Kylee scrambled across the floor on elbows and knees, driving herself forward with her head down. At least one of the gunners was stubbornly targeting her. Bullets chopped through the buffet table, smashing plates and knocking vegetables and bowls of dip to the floor.

Unfortunately for his teammate, the man's targeting efforts also lined him up with one of the other security guys. A bullet caught the other guard in the hip and sent him crashing to the floor.

"More people are coming outside," Barbara said over the headset.

Of course, Kylee thought grimly. *Can't wait around forever for the drowned woman to be scooped from the river. Maybe take in a gunfight as an intermission.* She was of the definite opinion that Creepstof Scherba didn't know any decent people.

"Cease fire, damn you!" Mr. Mystery's deep bass voice thundered through the crash of gunshots. "Cease fire!"

Kylee pushed herself up at the edge of the buffet island.

She took an F/X box and lobbed it over the table toward the man who had chosen to shoot at her. She saw his feet shift as he turned toward the device, then turned quickly away.

Probably thinks it's a grenade, Kylee told herself.

The gunfire stopped.

"It's the woman!" Mr. Mystery roared. "Stop the woman!"

Everybody hates a tattletale, Kylee thought. She closed her eyes and pressed the remote control.

In response, all the F/X boxes blew, filling the back end of the catamaran with light and thunder. There was enough noise to make most observers believe the boat was under attack.

Kylee rose into a sprinter's position on her knuckles, then hurled herself forward. She stayed low as she charged for the door that let out onto the catamaran's stern. She counted her steps, a habit that came out of her stunt training because everything there had to go by the numbers. Counting during action was second nature; first for safety during the gag, then for the cameras to make the director happy.

Only a few of the gunmen were on their feet. The rest of Creepstof Scherba's guest list that had wandered to the catamaran's stern in search of entertainment had dived to the floor. Most of them carried guns as well.

Kylee decided the computer cracker must have been giving weapons away as party favors. As she ran, she was forced to step on the bodies of the frightened people lying on the floor. She didn't hesitate because the biggest risk was that she would slip and twist an ankle before she could get clear of the boat.

Five feet from the stern, she leaped into the air and spread her arms as she dived over the side. She kept the dive shallow, quickly arching back up for the cloth bag tied to the boat's ladder that contained the swim fins and the miniscuba she'd secured there when she'd come aboard.

By the time she had the scuba in her mouth, search-lights around the catamaran had flared to life and started tracking the river's dark surface. She dove lower, swimming less than three feet from the bottom.

The light cones from the powerful searchlights illuminated fish swimming close to the surface, but they never touched her for more than an instant, a glance of contact that never allowed the men looking for her to find her.

Mick stood in the bow of the catamaran and stared into the dark water. Ellipses of yellow-white light from the boat's searchlights skipped across the river water.

Twice, men from Scherba's regular security team fired into the water. The bullets slapped against the water with flat cracks that let him know the 9mm rounds had ricocheted from the rolling river surface.

"Cease firing," Mick snarled. Anger flooded through him, but it was a mixed thing. He was actually relieved the woman had gotten away. Even if she was a thief, hired by one of Scherba's enemies, she didn't deserve the fate Scherba would have had in store for her. From the talk he'd heard from the other security guards, Scherba wasn't a man who suffered enemies long after they'd made a move against him. But Mick was most angry with himself because, if he'd been truly effective at his security post, the woman would have never set foot on the catamaran. She would have never become a danger to Scherba. Or a danger to herself.

"Over there!" one of the security guards yelled. He pointed his pistol and fired.

"Cease fire," Mick roared again. "The next person who fires a weapon is getting his damned head busted."

The regular security detail stared belligerently back at Mick. He knew he was confronting a pack of wolves, all of them needing only a moment of courage or a leader to turn against him.

"Stone."

Glancing up, Mick saw Scherba standing on the deck above. "Yes, sir," Mick said.

"I'm told we had an intruder aboard." Scherba leaned on the bow railing and glared down.

"Yes, sir."

"How did that happen?"

You parked us in the middle of the bloody river, mate, Mick thought. *Left us exposed as all hell.* But he said, "She swam underneath the river and climbed up on the back of the boat during the confusion."

Scherba scowled. "This is the quality of security I can expect?"

"You're alive, Mr. Scherba," Mick replied. "That's what I guaranteed. If that changes, I'll know I made a mistake."

"Your humor is not appreciated, Stone."

"No, sir. Probably not. But neither is the fact that I'm having to try to do my job tied up in the middle of this river like a sitting duck."

By now Mick fully well intended to tender his resignation. The woman hadn't been one of the hardcases that he'd turned away from Scherba three times in the past. Despite the fact that she was a damned thief, she hadn't tried to kill him. If she'd carried a gun or a knife downstairs when she'd set off the flash-bang, he knew there was a good chance that he wouldn't have survived. He'd let himself get too distracted by that expanse of bare skin and soft curves.

"Did you see the person who boarded my boat?" Scherba asked.

"Yes, sir."

"Who was it?"

"A woman." There was no reason to hide that fact from Scherba. Other security guards had seen that.

"You didn't recognize her?"

"No, sir." *But I will if I ever see her again.* She was that kind of woman: the kind that left an indelible mark in a man's mind.

Flashing blue lights strobed over *Guilty Pleasures* as a Czech police boat cruised over to them. The loud-hailer barked. Even though Mick didn't understand the language, he understood the intent. He dropped the pistol to the deck and raised his hands. He wasn't worried about the authorities, though. Prague law enforcement was corrupt enough and Scherba was wealthy enough that tonight would be only a matter of a few hours' haggling before an agreement on a price to drop all charges was made.

He stared out at the river, knowing he wouldn't see the woman, but unable to keep from looking for her all the same. Memory of the soft and supple body on top of his wouldn't leave his thoughts. The pain in his bruised face reminded him how good she'd been. He grinned. *You're a looker all right, sheila. Just make certain you stay the hell away from my operation.*

Even as he thought that, though, Mick knew that the woman wouldn't if she hadn't gotten what she had come for. Before coming up the staircase after her, he'd unhooked the sat-phone plugged into the notebook computer. Whatever program had been running hadn't finished.

She hadn't gotten whatever she had come for. If she had any sense, she'd stay away. But she hadn't backed down, and Mick had the definite impression she wasn't the kind of woman who would. That meant she would return, and she would find Scherba's bloodthirsty crew waiting for her. They wouldn't hesitate to kill her.

Mick hated the thought of that beautiful body getting savaged by bullets. He sighed in resignation, knowing what he had to do. Until he knew the woman had been properly warned off, he couldn't leave the bodyguard detail with Scherba.

Chapter 4

An hour later, Kylee stood under the hottest spray she could coax from the shower in the bathroom of her hotel. The hotel was billed as having old-world charm. In the three days that she had been there, Kylee had learned that description loosely translated to "ancient and rusting and relatively overpriced." But the studio was picking up the tab, she had an excellent view of the Vltava—and *Guilty Pleasures*—and the small café around the corner from the hotel served excellent pastries.

The water temperature never truly reached hot and she had to settle for a little more than lukewarm. Still, the shower was hot enough in the coolness of the room to make steam and that was at least psychologically uplifting even if the chill persisted.

She leaned on her palms against the tile wall and let the water cascade down her back. Mr. Mystery continued to claim her thoughts, filling her with desires and needs and images that danced unwanted through her head. Actually, they weren't unwanted, she had to admit. Since she'd first stepped into the shower and started having them, she had elaborated on them. She'd slowed down the action in Scherba's stateroom, relived the pressure of Mr. Mystery's body against hers.

And the want and need that the confrontation had instilled in her deepened into a bout of near-frustration. She took a deep breath, then tilted her head up into the gentle spray. Okay, maybe the explosive contact with Mr. Mystery had driven her pulse up and turned into a first-class case of frustration. It had happened before.

That was a lie and she knew it. She'd been attracted to men she'd known before, and even drawn to some of them like a heat-seeking missile after a few days of working with a guy who was confident and good at what he did.

But she'd never before felt a full-blown surge that had so totally made her senses come alive like this one. Standing there in the shower, she could have sworn she felt the individual beads of water tracking down her flesh. It was tempting to think of them as Mr. Mystery's fingertips.

Okay, frustration it is, she told herself angrily.

Giving up on the shower, unable to steam the chill of the Vltava River from her bones or get Mr. Mystery's memory to fade the hell away, Kylee toweled off and put her hair up. In the bedroom, she pulled on a soft cotton Los Angeles Dodgers baseball jersey she'd swiped from one of her younger brothers six months ago when he'd made the mistake of leaving his laundry out while she'd been visiting her parents.

Kylee curled up in the huge four-poster bed and stared at the rugged face on the notebook computer monitor. *What kind of person are you, Mr. Mystery?*

Upon returning to the hotel room after hauling herself from the river, Kylee had accessed the remote Web site that the Stony Man intelligence people had established for her so she could review the people and the events she had seen, then add details or ask questions as necessary. She had flipped through the video footage taken by the button-cam she'd worn on the wet suit until she'd found a good still of the man.

She could still hear his smoky voice, Australian accent and all. *And your hair is wet, Goldilocks. Meaning you're my girl no matter what little story you decide to trot out.*

She stared at his image on the notebook monitor, at the square-cut chin, blue eyes, and chestnut ringlets. Fast and dangerous and dashing. That definitely summed him up, but—remembering the way their bodies had been briefly locked together—other qualifications came to mind as well. The wet suit had been formfitting, and the slacks had been thin.

Too bad, Mr. Mystery, Kylee thought. *It would have been fun to give you another chance.*

The line of thinking was unusual for Kylee. A few guys had been of interest to her, but she'd found most of them too shallow to be interesting, too insecure because of her profession to hang around, or too married or otherwise involved to be available. Even the good, decent guys her brothers, two sisters-in-law, and her mother had tried to set her up with had lacked that spark to keep her interest. True to her nature and her work in stunts and in spying, she'd always made a fast get-away.

Kylee didn't lack for male friends. The stunt work and the real and deep friendships she had with her brothers made certain of that. Twenty-six years old, around the jet set of the movie crowd as well as down-to-earth guys who worked as set carpenters, studio horse wranglers, and guys who worked marine salvage, and she'd never found a special guy. Nobody had ever turned her world upside down.

Not that she was looking forward to the experience. She liked her life as it was, liked being able to make her own decisions.

One of her best friends—Sammi San Giacomo, a fellow stunt person—accused Kylee of being too unwilling to let someone sweep her away.

And maybe there was some truth in that. Every time Kylee had been vaguely interested in a guy, she'd seek— and find—a reason why he wasn't Mr. Perfect.

You have your warts, too, Mr. Mystery, Kylee told the image on the screen. *Number one: you're working for the bad guys. I'll bet there are plenty of others. Which we won't be discussing.*

Still there was something about the Australian security man's rugged good looks that struck her in a way she hadn't been struck before.

Must be that first impression, she decided. *Peering over a gun barrel and all.*

The satellite phone on the small nightstand by the bed rang.

Kylee picked the phone up and said, "Oz?"

"Oz?" Barbara Price asked.

"Great. Wise. All-Knowing. You know, *Oz.*"

"Funny." The tone implied the nickname was anything but. "You're still awake?"

"Yes. I gave up on soaking out the chill and settled for a good shampoo and some time well spent with a loofah sponge. I can still taste the river, though, thank you very much."

"We have a problem."

That got Kylee's attention immediately. The satellite phone was heavily encrypted so she felt safe talking about events without masking identities or events.

"The notebook computer didn't give us access to the files we were hoping for."

Kylee took that in, knowing in the space of a heartbeat what that meant. "So we have to crash Creepstof Castle." She sat up in bed, forgetting the chill that plagued her. A chance at further clandestine action focused her instantly.

Also, there was the added benefit of chancing another face-to-face with Mr. Mystery. The thought warmed her blood more than the shower did. She should have felt guilty, but she didn't. For a brief moment, a vague unease touched her. He was good. She had barely gotten away. Then she smiled at the face on the monitor. *I can beat you, Mr. Mystery. I can get away from you again if I have to.*

"Possibly. I'm working on getting another team into the area."

"Whoa, Oz," Kylee protested. "This is my gig. You brought me into this. I don't play as a second-stringer."

"You also don't play a full-blown guns-and-ammo type op, Kylee." Barbara's voice sounded resolute. "You're strictly finesse work. In and gone before the bad guys know it. The team I'm talking about shakes down the house."

"Creepstof might not keep the information you're looking for at the castle," Kylee said. She hated the idea of being cut out of the mission.

"I know," Barbara admitted. "That's one of the reasons I haven't reached for the other group of players."

Kylee knew from experience that Barbara ran two or more wetwork teams, so-called because they handled the down-and-dirty and bloody business of counterterrorism that left behind body counts. Kylee had been an advance scout on three missions for those teams before.

She took a deep breath and blew it out. "If you want me sidelined, Oz, I'm sidelined. I'm a team player." A stunt person had to be.

"I appreciate that," Barbara said. "We'll see. For the moment, I want you on the inside of the op."

Mind flying, Kylee turned over the possible parameters of the continued op. "Getting close to Creepstof could be hard after tonight. The face-to-face with Mr. Mystery probably blew that out of the water."

"I agree. However, there is another angle we can exploit."

Staring at the rugged face on the notebook computer monitor, feeling a mild—and definitely unwanted—blush of arousal and interest, Kylee said, "Mr. Mystery."

"Right." The smile was audible in Barbara's voice. "You might be able to get close to him."

Now there was a delectable thought, if somewhat self-destructive. "I thought he was one of the bad guys."

"That's open to debate."

"How much debate?"

"A lot. He's cashing checks from a known technoterrorist."

"Maybe he's got a good heart." Kylee smiled.

"We've identified him."

Interest flared through Kylee. *A name for Mr. Mystery?* "So who is he?"

"Mick Stone."

"Australian?"

"Very."

"What's his background?" Kylee asked.

"Covert ops for the CIA and a few other international players. Usually as a bodyguard. As good as we are, I don't think we have it all. Yet. Interesting guy. I'll forward his brief so you can look it over."

"You want me to meet him?" The possibility brought *way* more excitement with it than it should have.

"If we can arrange a meeting."

"I'll need a cover ID," Kylee said.

"We're putting one together. I'm thinking along the lines of posing you as an international recovery expert specializing in stolen software."

"The geekspeak might be hard to fake," Kylee said. Her computer skills were decent, but she couldn't sling programming tools or hardware specs well enough to fool anyone versed in those things. All things computer were Victoria Grayson's specialty.

"Not with Stone," Barbara said. "He's strictly old-school. A by-the-book kind of operator. From his file, we know that he plays with security toys, but he doesn't go that deep into tech."

"I kind of got that from the Colt .45 he shoved in my face tonight. Another guy might have used an MP5 machine pistol, which would have made my F/X boxes just the last hurrah before he blew my lights out."

"Tough guy talk?" Barbara asked.

Kylee rolled her eyes. "It's the action film I'm in. I've been reading the script."

"So," Barbara said, "do you think Stone got a good look at you tonight?"

"Are you kidding? Everything aboard that boat happened too quickly." Kylee still remembered the slap of bullets striking the buffet table and the floor as they missed her. "He won't know me if I'm in a disguise."

But I'll know him. She knew, at least for the moment, that she had the man locked into her personal radar. The trouble was, she also had him under her skin.

Now aren't you the brazen one, darlin'? Mick Stone thought as he stared at the long-legged blonde walking over to the dark green sports car parked in the center of the street that had been blocked off by the American film crew. Bright interest flamed inside Mick, and he knew the feeling was more than just from confirmation that he'd found the beautiful thief who had engineered a dramatic distraction to steal aboard *Guilty Pleasures* in the dead of night.

The sheila filled out the catsuit in a way that left damn little to the imagination, and left him breathing just a little shorter and more than a little tight in the groin. Her shoulder-length blond hair whipped around her pretty face as she threw a leg through the open window of the Aston Martin Vanquish and clambered aboard.

You should have kept running last night when you started, darlin'. Just kept running and never looked back. The fact that she hadn't, that he'd been able to find her when she'd thought she was so clever, made him angry. She was a target, a beautiful target, but a target nonetheless, and she was acting as if she didn't know that.

"Oh, look," one of the young women in front of Mick said. She pointed excitedly. "There she is. There's Destiny Cranston."

"I see her. I see her." The two young women hugged each other.

"Excuse me," Mick said.

They both turned to look at him.

"Are you referring to the woman in the car?" he asked. "Is that Destiny Cranston?"

"No," the brunette replied. "Destiny Cranston is sitting there by the director."

"Ah." Mick nodded. "Then who's the blonde in the car?"

"Probably Destiny's stunt double," the other young

woman answered. "I was here yesterday and I saw Destiny wearing the same outfit."

"Oh, I don't think it was the same outfit," the brunette said. "That woman is a lot heavier than Destiny."

"If she's any heavier," Mick said defensively, "it's only because she's four or five inches taller than that little slip of a thing in the golf cart."

"Destiny is a strict vegetarian," the brunette said, obviously miffed.

"And you don't know a healthy specimen of the feminine persuasion when you see one," Mick retorted.

Definitely offended now, the two young women moved farther down the fire escape landing.

Mick ignored them, then got mad at himself. He wasn't in the crowd to be remembered. A bodyguard served best when he or she was nondisruptive, when he or she could step into a principal's life and take care of that person's safety without interfering in day-to-day business. Normally he was one of the best in the craft at that.

But this mystery woman—damn her eyes and his own treacherous libido, *and* her lack of common sense to get gone while the getting-gone was good—had thrown him off his usual course of action.

Bruises covered his face where she'd kicked and hit him last night. Other bruises lined his legs and arms. She hadn't been gentle, hadn't pulled any punches, and she had brought the fight directly to him. He had to respect that.

The situation aboard *Guilty Pleasures* last night after her escape had been tense. Mick didn't think he had Scherba's trust anymore, not even a grudging amount of it. But the computer cracker had let him stay on in his bodyguard capacity, and hadn't said a word when Mick had taken his normal time off this morning.

Money had changed hands with the Czech police last
night. Quite a lot of it. Over the past five weeks, Mick
had learned that Scherba never traveled anywhere without
a lot of cash from a dozen different nations. American
and Canadian dollars, Japanese yen, Russian rubles,
German marks, French francs and British pounds sterling
were only some of the slush fund that Scherba carried.
That had been the only thing that had kept most of
Scherba's security staff from jail after they had indiscrim-
inately fired into the river after the fleeing woman.

With the situation being what it was after last night,
Josef had talked to Mick that morning, suggesting that it
was time for both of them to head to greener pastures.
Both of them had reached the conclusion that Krystof
Scherba wasn't the kind of man they wanted to work for.
But the money had been good for Josef and his large
family, and the work had temporarily broken the funk
Mick had found himself in since the CIA had severed ties
with him almost a year ago over the Black Dragon Triad
incident in Shanghai.

Mick had told Josef he was going to stay on for at least
a little longer, till he was certain the threat that the woman
had represented to Scherba was gone. Mick wasn't the
kind of guy who left unfinished business. Josef knew and
respected that. After all, he was a bloody professional and
depended on his reputation, which the damned CIA had
more or less scuttled a year ago.

But that wasn't the real reason he'd stayed. The real
reason was that Mick was afraid for the woman. Josef had
stayed because of Mick, and he'd known of Mick's concern for her. She'd been too cocky, too sure of herself.
Either she didn't know how dangerous Scherba was, or
she was grossly overestimating her own skills.

True, she had been good at what she did, but if Scherba

found out who she was—and Mick had every reason to believe that the man would, because *he* had deduced who she had to be from the moves she'd exhibited and the flash-bang equipment she'd left behind—she was dead.

The way Mick had it figured, he was maybe the only chance the woman had of getting out of the situation alive. Doing that put him at risk, though, and as he stood there on the third-floor landing, he was keenly aware of that.

A warning flickered through his mind. The feeling was something he couldn't have named, cultivated from years of close cover work and spending time with principals who were hunted and stalked by murderers and assassins.

Sweeping the street with his gaze, Mick spotted a man in the shadows of an awning in front of a small sidewalk café at an alley corner. The man was alert, tense. He lifted his left wrist and spoke. Mick knew the man was carrying a headset walkie-talkie, indicating that he was part of a team.

The man was also an unknown. Mick knew all of Scherba's people. Getting to know a principal's daily life and the contacts within it was standard operating procedure for a professional bodyguard.

A minute passed, and Mick spotted two other men at the end of the four-block run on the set. Those men spread out, and the way they moved told Mick they were armed. The man in front of the sidewalk café glanced up at the roofline.

Following the man's gaze, Mick searched the rooftops. He didn't see what the man was looking for, but Mick knew that whoever he was looking for up there was on-site. The first thing that came to Mick's mind was that the buildings were a perfect place for a sniper to hole up for a shot. He started making his way up to the roof, intending to get to the other end of the stunt run as quickly as he could.

Behind the Aston Martin's steering wheel, Kylee strapped herself into the five-point safety belt harness. She pushed her mind past Mick Stone and Creepstof Scherba, dismissed the cameras and the film crew on the other side of the window and focused solely on the gag. A stunt person without focus had about as much of a chance at a long life as a Christmas turkey on December twenty-fourth.

She drew her breath in through her nose, taking it deeply into her lungs, then blew it out her mouth. Nerves and instinct training and adrenaline all came together in a rush and gelled.

The radio mounted under the sports car's dash crackled and the director's voice asked, "Ready, Kylee?"

"Ready," Kylee said.

"Whenever you're ready, then."

Kylee twisted the key in the ignition. The powerful engine snarled to life. "Ready." She tapped the accelerator and felt the engine rev.

"And...action," the director said.

Kylee dropped the accelerator to the floor and popped the clutch. The Aston Martin's tires squalled as they spun against the street. Then the rubber found traction and hurtled the vehicle forward while slamming Kylee back into the seat.

She ran through the gears using the paddles built into the steering wheel. The Vanquish used six forward gears, and the transmission ratio was tight, allowing her to get through the first five gears before she had to make the turn.

The buildings at the end of the four-block distance

swelled into view, providing a solid unbreakable wall. If she lost the Aston Martin, she knew she'd end up smashed against the wall.

Downshifting from fifth gear to second, Kylee tapped on the brakes and threw the sports car into a controlled skid. The back end of the vehicle skewed around as she whipped the steering wheel into the direction of the skid and depended on the rack-and-pinion steering to pull her out of the drift. The second she felt the tires grab traction again, she let out on the clutch, stomped the accelerator and pulled the steering wheel straight. The car came to a rocking stop only inches away from the brick wall.

"Oh, man!" the director crowed. "Way to fire, Kylee! That looked great!"

The sports car burned rubber coming out of the tight turn, looking for all in the world like it had caromed from the brick wall. Heart pumping, adrenaline flooding her system, Kylee searched for and found the jump ramp two blocks ahead. The Aston Martin shivered beneath her like a big cat preparing to take flight.

"Get to speed, Kylee," the director urged.

Then there was no more time for anything. Kylee felt the world slow down around her as it always did when she was in the heart of a stunt.

The Aston Martin's front wheels hit the ramp. In the same instant, Kylee noted the shifting shadow at the roof-line of one of the buildings at the end of the four-block run. The figure brought a long bar-shape to its shoulder.

Kylee knew what the shape was even before Barbara broadcast a warning over her tiny earpiece.

"Sniper!" Barbara said. She had already let Kylee know that Mick Stone had put in an appearance in the audience. At first, the news had shocked her, but then Kylee had buzzed with excitement over the increased stakes.

But Barbara's warning arrived too late. Kylee was already into the stunt. Trying to turn back would have busted the gag, wrecked the Aston Martin, and required days of downtime on the movie to repair.

And if she stopped, she knew she would only be a sitting duck for the sniper.

The sports car's V12 engine roared in Kylee's ears, drowning out the noise of the rest of the world. She felt the slow thud of her heart in stretched-out explosions and knew that in real time, not the frozen time of the stunt, her heart was hammering.

Dim morning sunlight glinted from the sniper's telescopic lens as he took aim.

I'm in motion, Kylee told herself. *I am a moving target. I am one of the fastest moving targets in the world at this moment. Wile E. Coyote couldn't catch me with an Acme jetpack.*

She held the steering wheel steady as the rear wheels roared onto the ramp. The centrifugal force of the rapid ascension up the ramp shoved her back and down into the specially contoured seat.

Mick Stone, I know you're behind this, and I am so going to kick your ass when I find you.

Near the top of the ramp—moving at seventy-eight miles an hour as they had agreed on—confirmed by the digital speedometer on the dashboard, Kylee slid her forefinger over the button concealed under the steering wheel and pressed.

A rifle bullet shattered the windshield, throwing out small squared chunks of safety glass that peppered Kylee's face. For an instant she thought she had been hit, and kept waiting for the pain to ignite within her. Then the explosion rigged under the Aston Martin fired.

Carefully placed and measured, the explosion under the sports car's driver's side was designed to roll the vehicle in midair on leaving the corkscrew end of the ramp. A whipsaw motion heeled the car over like a small plane twisting into a barrel roll.

Snug inside the safety harness, trapped by the momentum of the stunt, Kylee watched the world revolve around her. The Aston Martin totally inverted, then continued rolling. If everything worked right, the sports car would hit an apex of twenty-three feet, go a distance of forty-seven feet, and land top down like an overturned turtle.

A second bullet ripped the driver's side mirror off. Fragments of the mirror's housing flew into the car and clattered against the car's side like beaks of carrion birds beating against the metal to get in.

Secured in the seat, Kylee flipped a total of two and one-half times as she came down into the street. Despite the heavy padding and the weight distribution design, the seat belts painfully cut into her shoulders. Another bullet cracked the windshield, letting her know that whoever was on the business end of the rifle was an excellent marksman.

The Aston Martin landed in a scream of tortured metal. Kylee hung from the seat belts as the car revolved and slid across the street. Sparks sprayed out in the sports car's wake, and fresh white scars tracked the street's stone surface.

And when the sliding stopped, Kylee was grimly aware that she was going to be a much easier target for the rooftop sniper.

Even with his lead and the pause she took between the stunts, Mick barely reached the last rooftop at the turn in time to see the bright green Aston Martin hit the end of the ramp. The sharp bark of a high-powered sniper rifle rang out during the snarl of the racing engine.

The sports car was still in the air when Mick spotted the sniper three rooftops away. The man was lean and ferret-faced, his rifle nearly as long as he was.

And there it is then, Mick thought in a cold second. *The sheila is the target.* Even though the man wasn't someone Mick recognized, he knew the man couldn't have come from anyone else. Scherba was covering his bases.

By the time the Aston Martin rolled two times, the sniper had fired twice more. One of the bullets had struck the driver's side mirror, but the other had gone wide of its intended target.

Mick pulled the Colt .45 pistol from the holster under his jacket. The distance made accuracy with the handgun more a thing of luck than skill. Still, the .45 made a hell of a lot of noise. He opened fire as the car skidded down the street on its top.

The bullets slammed into the tarmac beside the sniper and tore out fist-sized divots that skipped into the man. Startled, the man turned from his target, rolling sideways and looking for whoever was firing at him. He lifted the rifle.

Calmly Mick stood his ground and fired through the last three rounds of the seven-round clip. One of the bullets caught the man and knocked him backward, rolling him across the rooftop.

Then a hail of gunfire ripped through the air by Mick's head. The sniper had evidently had backup shooters in place on the ground.

The Aston Martin rocked to a halt but turned sideways like a good boxer slipping a punch for the camera. Kylee watched the world revolve slowly through the windshield. Two fist-sized holes showed in the glass now.

She hung suspended in the seat belts, but her hands sought out the catches automatically. The sweet, acrid scent of gasoline cloyed at her nostrils. Before long, she was certain the sniper would think about targeting the gas tank.

Designed to work even under the most hostile circumstances, the seat belts peeled away. Kylee fell, trying to take most of her weight on her shoulders.

"What the hell is going on down there?" the director bellowed over the radio.

"Somebody's shooting at the car," one of the cameramen called back.

"At Kylee or the car?" the director asked.

"I don't—"

"To hell with that," he exploded. "Are you rolling film?"

"Oh yeah."

"Because I'll have your ass if you aren't," the director threatened.

Terrific, Kylee thought as she squirmed out of the seat. *Nice to know I'm working with professionals.*

But the thought was only partly remonstration against the cold-blooded reality of the situation. The footage was real, and having it in the film would be a bonus, something the Internet film schemers and dreamers could talk about before the movie released. Emerson was definitely going to have a box-office smash on his hands because of the word of mouth over this one alone.

"Kylee," Barbara Price called over the ear bud.

"I'm okay." Kylee paused at the window. Little room remained in the sports car. At least the reinforcements had kept the top from collapsing and burying her in a twisted ruin.

"Oz," she said. Despite the rush of adrenaline she was feeling, a combination of the jump and being shot at, she was scared.

"I'm here," Barbara said.

"How many shooters?"

"We've tagged four."

Four! Four? Kylee took a deep breath. *Four isn't so bad. Now ten—ten would be bad.*

"What about Stone?" Kylee asked.

"He's there."

"I knew that. Was he the one shooting at me?"

"Negative," Barbara answered.

"Am I clear?"

"I don't know."

"You're the one with the satellite recon," Kylee pointed out.

"You've got a riot forming there. We've got a lock on the rooftop sniper, but we don't know where the other shooters are. Two of them shot at Stone."

"Why?"

"I have to assume it's because he shot at the sniper shooting at you."

"Doesn't sound like he's one of the bad guys," Kylee said. She couldn't resist the gibe. "I mean, unless he's a bad shot. An *incredibly* bad shot."

"Have you got time to talk about this?"

Kylee pushed her breath out. "Not really. Nope. Don't have any *Oprah* moments left." She rose into a sprinter's position in the blocks. "I'm moving. Paint me an escape route."

"When you're ready."

"Go!" Kylee slithered through the open driver's side window. Her palms scraped against the long scratches dug into the street stones, but she kept moving forward.

"Left!" Barbara commanded. "And down! Now!"

Without hesitation, Kylee threw herself left and down, rolling and coming up behind the Aston Martin. Bullets chewed through the car body as if it was plate glass, leaving a firecracker string of tears and dents as the shooter targeted her.

Automatic weapons, Kylee thought. *You gotta love automatic weapons.*

Another burst of autofire raked the side of the Aston Martin. The shooter had switched locations, or perhaps another shooter had taken up the slack. The bullets pushed Kylee to the other side of the sports car. Chunks of bright green metal tore loose from the vehicle. Broken windows rained chunks of safety glass. The left rear tire shredded and deflated in a rush.

Time to go.

Kylee gathered her nerve, leaped and heaved herself aboard the overturned Aston Martin and ran along the undercarriage. Surefooted as a gazelle, she sped toward the front of the car and made the leap toward the second-floor fire escape only six feet away.

She caught the wrought-iron railing with her right hand, managed a grip with the left and hauled herself over just as bullets chopped into the brick wall where she had been hanging. Rolling forward, she dropped into a prone position just as another blast of gunfire tore out the windows of the apartment overhead.

Kylee sincerely hoped no one was home, or that they had taken cover the minute the shooting began. As soon as the gunfire died down, she pushed herself up and ran forward toward the end of the fire escape. She put her hands on the railing and did a handspring, wrapping her arms around her knees and performing a full somersault and a half with a twist that put her facing the wall when she landed in the alley on the toes of the boots to avoid the treacherous spiked heels.

"Look out!" Barbara called. "To your left."

Wheeling, spreading her feet to set herself, Kylee saw a man with an Uzi turning toward her from the back of the alley.

So not good, Kylee told herself. Amped up and jazzed on adrenaline, she moved at once. She picked up the round plastic lid of a five-gallon detergent container and ran at the wall on the other side of the narrow alley.

The guy had the Uzi up and yammering. Bullets tracked the stone floor of the alley as Kylee reached the wall and ran up it three long steps. Feeling gravity starting to take over again, she kicked out and sent herself backward in a tight roll. She came down on the balls of her feet as the sharp cracks of the bullets splitting the stone of the wall filled her ears.

Whipping the heavy plastic lid back, she threw the lid like a Frisbee from ten feet away. The lid sliced through the air and slammed into the bridge of the gunman's nose.

Blood splattered and the man's head snapped backward. The Uzi went up into the air.

Having executed similar moves in movies for years, Kylee crossed the distance in three long strides and caught the Uzi as it fell.

"Okay then," Barbara said. "I didn't know you could do that."

"Me either," Kylee admitted as she started toward the back of the alley. "Don't you watch my movies?"

"I've seen you in real action."

''Well it doesn't get any more exciting than this.'' Kylee peered around the corner. ''Can you steer me clear of this yet?''

''We're working on it. The hardest problem is getting clear of the crowd so we can identify the shooters and keep you away from them.''

''I like that idea.'' Kylee stepped forward, moving into a quick jog through the alley. She had the vague notion that she was headed back toward the hotel, but that was the only thing she knew to go back to. She remembered that Mick Stone had drawn fire from the shooters. Thinking of him lying somewhere, wounded or dead, made her heart pound and filled her with anxiety. ''What about Stone?''

''He's alive.''

Relief loosened some of the knots in Kylee's stomach. ''Where is he?''

''We lost him in the confusion.''

Kylee turned right at the next alley, breaking free of a crowd that was headed in the other direction. The crowd separated and flowed around her, making an effort to avoid her.

''Going in the opposite direction as a fleeing crowd isn't exactly a good rule of thumb,'' Barbara said.

''I'm going where they aren't,'' Kylee said. ''I could use some solitude about now. Especially since I don't know who I can trust.''

Around the next corner, Kylee spotted the gunman the group had been running from at the same time he spotted her. He started to turn, a machine pistol in his fist. She lifted the Uzi and froze him into place for just a moment because she had the drop on him. Intending to put her point across more succinctly, Kylee aimed above his head and squeezed the Uzi's trigger.

The machine pistol clicked. There was no explosion of gunfire, no brass spilling from the ejection port, no jarring recoil.

The man grinned.

Uh-oh, Kylee thought.

Confident now, the man lifted his weapon and took aim in one reflexive movement.

Kylee turned to run, knowing the alley corner couldn't be more than a couple of steps away. Instead, she ran into a broad chest and saw the pistol in Mick Stone's fist as he thrust the weapon straight out.

Chapter 5

Staring at the big Australian, Kylee felt her pulse speed up even more. Standing there like that, he was indomitable, an irrevocable force of nature that would not be denied. In a flash of frozen time, she remembered how his body had felt under hers, how grim and certain he had been gazing across those pistol sights in Creepstof's private berth aboard the catamaran. He wasn't a man to turn from a harsh situation. No, she knew as she faced him that he would take any difficulty life gave him head-on.

Too bad you're working for Creepstof, she thought, then her conscious thoughts fled as the sharp sound of the pistol temporarily deafened her.

Mick Stone's .45 barked three times in quick succession, a cadence that included a double-tap rhythm and a single shot on the heels of those.

She took a half step back from Mick. Dropping the useless Uzi, she swung her left elbow into his forearm.

Numbed by the blow to the nerve cluster at the base of

his elbow, Mick dropped the .45. His face darkened.
"You're crazy, sheila! What the hell did you do that for?
I just saved your life!"

Kylee stepped back, holding both closed fists in front
of her face, ready to ward off any blows the big Australian
might want to send her way.

Mick reached for the pistol.

Sliding a foot out, Kylee kicked the pistol away, send-
ing the weapon skidding. A small bubble of delight
formed in her stomach when she saw the frustration and
anger in his handsome face.

"Now that's about the dumbest thing I've seen done
yet," Mick growled. He stepped toward the pistol.

Mirroring the Australian's movement, Kylee remained
in step with him, keeping herself between Mick and the
pistol. Her peripheral vision revealed that the Australian's
bullets had slammed into the other gunman, dropping the
man to a crumpled heap in the alley.

"What are you doing?" Mick demanded.

"Walk away," Kylee said. She felt drawn to the confrontation with the big man. He seemed like an elemental
force, a natural law of physics that she had to change or
alter or cheat her way around like she did with any stunt
that demanded her best. She wanted the chance to prove
that she could be his equal, or more.

His face became stern, as if it was shaped of iron.
"Like hell I will. That's my weapon. Damn me, but I
should have let him shoot you."

"He wouldn't have shot me," Kylee said. "I could
have gotten away if you hadn't been standing there. I
probably still could have gotten away."

"'Gotten away'?" The big Australian sounded as
though he couldn't believe it. "That's not how it looked
from where I was standing."

"Then you weren't standing where you needed to be."

Mick's jaw tightened and his dark rage showed in every line of his face. He started to move around her.

With no warning whatsoever, Kylee punched him in the face, snapping his head back and splitting his lip. With the way she had been mooning over his pictures in the hotel room last night, she felt a little vindicated.

Surprised, Mick stepped back. He knuckled bright red blood from his mouth. "I can't believe I risked my arse for some thieving sheila." He shook his head. "I really can't."

"I'm no thief," Kylee said.

"Oh yeah?" Mick looked doubtful. "Well, you got a funny way of showing that. I mean, what with breaking into people's places and such."

"I don't know what you're talking about."

"I'm talking about breaking into *Guilty Pleasures* last night," Mick said.

"That wasn't me."

A confident smile twisted Mick's lips. "That was you, sheila. The moves you've got, they're memorable ones. I saw you in action last night. I wouldn't forget that. We were up close and personal."

Get away! Get away! The voice sang frantically inside Kylee's head.

She turned to break away, intending to be gone before he even had a clue. Instead, a big hand clamped down on her shoulder and spun her back around. She went with the pull, sweeping her left arm in, then back and out to knock his hand from her shoulder. He'd been overconfident, thinking that his greater size and strength would allow him to dominate her. She balled her right fist and powered it into his jaw.

Unfortunately, Mick Stone's jaw appeared to have been

made of the same material as his surname. His head snapped around, probably partly because he gave ground before the blow to lessen the impact, but he moved automatically into a martial arts stance. He shook his head.

"You throw a pretty good punch, sheila," he growled. His hands came up in front of him. "I got to give you that. But I'm not going to stand here and be your punching bag like some damned newborn joey."

Kylee feinted another punch. Mick raised his right hand to block the blow. The move left him open for the front snap-kick that she slammed into his stomach. It was like kicking a stone wall. The Kevlar vest provided an extra layer of protection.

"You kick pretty well, too, sheila," Mick said with a faint grin. He punched at her head with his left hand.

Kylee swept her right hand across, catching his wrist and deflecting his punch. She wheeled on her right foot, coming around in a one-hundred-eighty-degree turn, then bringing her left foot around in a heel stamp to the back of his knee.

Mick's leg buckled and he almost fell. But he came back swinging faster than Kylee expected. She also noted the slight hesitation as he came around, recognizing the fact that he was unwilling to engage.

He's holding back, she thought as she let the blow skate less than an inch from her face. Her respect for his prowess went up. Normally the move would have stretched an opponent flat on his or her back and allowed Kylee plenty of time to get away.

The big Australian grabbed at Kylee and managed to get a fistful of the jean jacket. He reeled her in like a fisherman taking in a fish. She let him have her, knowing she couldn't break away from the denim. Drawn into his arms, Kylee found herself face-to-face with Mick Stone.

She smelled his cologne, the musk of him, and felt the strength of his arms as he held her. Being held with her body pressed close against his wasn't a totally unpleasant experience. In fact, if anything, the experience was entirely a little too pleasant.

He stood braced for an attack that she didn't deliver, evidently prepared to handle any assault and maintain his hold.

"Damn, sheila," Mick swore. "You're a true piece of work, ain't you?" He smiled.

"I don't know what you're talking about," Kylee insisted.

A roguish smile twisted Mick's mouth. "And stubborn. I like that in a woman."

Kylee wrapped her arms around Mick's neck and let her body rest more heavily against him. "What else do you like in a woman?" She stroked his neck and pressed a miniature audio bug into place under his shirt collar as she leaned forward and kissed him full on the mouth. She decided it was a good thing she had planted the bug first because the touch of his lips froze her mind.

He relaxed and gave himself over to her kiss, the soft, sensuous feel of her lush mouth.

Almost as tall as he was while wearing the stiletto boots, Kylee easily peered over Mick's shoulder. Movement drew her struggling mind back to the situation instead of the physical pleasure of the moment.

A gunman peered around the corner of the alley. His pistol came up.

Mick evidently read her change in body language. He knotted his right hand in her jean jacket as he wheeled around, placing himself in front of her.

The gunman's pistol sounded once. Mick took a staggered step backward as the bullet slammed into his chest. He growled like a bear, obviously in pain.

Kylee knew the pain was from the blunt trauma of the round striking home against the Kevlar vest she'd felt earlier when she'd kicked him. The bullet hadn't penetrated flesh. But it could have. If the gunman had shot higher, he could have shot Mick in the face.

Mick Stone would have taken the bullet for her.

The thought was sobering. As was the realization that Mick obviously wasn't working with the men hunting her. He had killed one of them, and the second had shown no compunction in the slightest of firing at him.

Kylee whirled and ducked out of her jean jacket. The maneuver was one of the simplest escapes to effect, and she was the get-away girl. She had a reputation to uphold.

And she had a mission to finish.

Thinking quickly, she drew the pop blaster from the drop-rig holster on her thigh. The weapon looked like it could have launched disruptor bolts that would have brought down star-cruisers.

The gunman scrambled behind the alley corner.

Mick turned around, the abandoned jean jacket in one fist. He looked at her, then at the .45 lying a few feet away.

"No choice," Kylee said.

Growling inarticulately, Mick launched himself at the pistol as the gunman spun back around the corner and started firing again. Mick brought his own pistol up and fired twice, driving both rounds through the center of the man.

Before Mick could get to his feet, Kylee turned and fled down the alley, using her long legs to eat up the distance, tossing the prop pistol aside to get her arms into the rhythm.

"Talk to me, Oz," she said as she rounded the next alley corner. "Where am I going, and how am I going to get there really fast?"

Kylee stood inside a gift store across the street from an open-air café in Prague's Stare Mesto district. Long-bladed ceiling fans swept through the sluggish air of the noonday heat.

The sniping incident was almost four hours old. The Czech police were still investigating the scene, and Kylee Swain, Hollywood stuntwoman, was being sought after for questioning. Mostly the police seemed concerned for her safety, and the studio PR people were stating they feared that a terrorist cell had kidnapped Kylee. Barbara Price briefly considered closing down the mission, but no one else was in place to pull off the operation.

Creepstof Scherba remained a necessary link to finding out what Kapoch Egorov was up to. So far, Creepstof had remained aboard the catamaran.

Across the street, Mick Stone lounged at a table under the shade of a brightly colored umbrella. He'd been there for over three hours, for no apparent reason. *Like a lazy hound dog,* Kylee couldn't help thinking with a mixture of disgust and frustration and anger.

Still she didn't mind looking at him. Just lounging at the table, Mick was a sight to behold, and one that accelerated her pulse in a way she had never known before. Her lack of control infuriated her. No sane woman could possibly look at a man so potentially harmful to her with that kind of desire.

So okay—lust, Kylee thought angrily. *If you're going to think it, call it what it really is. He's just a momentary bit of weakness in an otherwise orderly and sane life.*

Well, somewhat orderly. And definitely sane. This, this is just an aberration.

All she needed was a day or two of separation from his immediate proximity and she'd be fine. Maybe a week. Surely no more than a month.

But she still felt her emotions warring within her.

A server in a tight blouse and an exposed midriff approached Mick's table. She was obviously into heavy metal music, judging from the piercing and the tattoos on her ankles and the small of her back. Her dark hair, streaked with crimson and blue, stuck out around her head.

Mick talked and joked with the young woman. She stood in front of him, partially obscuring Kylee's view, one hand on a deliberately outthrust rounded hip. They seemed content to talk forever.

Are you that shallow, Mick Stone? Kylee asked. She crossed her arms over her breasts. *She is* so *not your type.*

And Kylee had to ask herself when she'd gotten so sure of what type of woman the Australian bodyguard would want. Then she had to admit that was just wishful thinking because she didn't really know him at all.

Except that he had stepped in front of her when the man had fired at her. Kylee didn't know many men who would have done something like that, and even fewer who could have reacted fast enough to handle the threat.

Bottom line: he'd protected her.

Kylee sighed in disgust. She didn't know what she was going to do with Mick Stone, but obviously the one thing she couldn't do was ignore him.

"Is something wrong, miss?" the elderly shopkeeper asked at her side.

"No," Kylee said.

"You see something you like?"

Kylee stared at Mick Stone. "Yes."

Across the street, Mick threw his head back and laughed. Kylee was incensed. He was working for the bad guy. How dare he sit out there so carefree...and so, so, so *available.*

"Do you want me to wrap it up for you?" the shop-keeper asked.

"I'd rather you bash his brains out for me," Kylee replied.

"Miss?" Confusion registered in the old man's voice.

"I'll take this." Kylee pointed at a delicate arrange-ment of glass flowers. The piece was actually striking. She'd noticed it when she'd first entered the shop.

"Wrapped?"

"Please." The package would complete the touristy disguise she'd put together at the safe house Barbara Price had guided her to after the shooting incident. Returning to her hotel hadn't been possible. She wore a dark wig, jeans and a printed blouse.

When the piece was paid for and packaged, Kylee tucked it under her arm and walked out of the shop into the heat of the day. She cussed under her breath, glad the earpiece was safely tucked into her handbag for the mo-ment because she didn't want Barbara to hear what she had to say. Mostly she cussed Mick Stone because he just didn't seem to fade into the woodwork as he should have, but partly she cussed herself for being so interested in him.

I mean, so what if he has those moody cerulean-blue eyes and buns of steel and a smile that's so close to a smirk I just want to pinch it off of his face while he's looking at that waitress?

As directly as she was heading for him, Kylee fully well expected Mick to become aware of her at any second.

Instead, he seemed captivated by the young server who had launched into a salvo of body language hints that she was not only single but she was also definitely interested.

The server broke eye contact with Mick first, turning her gaze to Kylee. "Ah, Mr. Stone," she said, "this must be the party you said you were waiting on."

Mick looked at Kylee and smiled. "Actually, she is."

"I'm jealous," the server went on, giving Kylee a head-to-toe sweep of inspection with her eyes. "But she is as beautiful as you said she was."

Beautiful? Kylee froze. *What's going on?*

"What would you like to drink?" the server asked.

"Hot chocolate, please."

"Chocolate?" The server raised one pierced brow in mock surprise. "Chocolate is supposed to be good when you're feeling...how do you say, *certain* frustrations." She smiled at Mick. "I don't see how you could be with such a man and have *those* frustrations."

Kylee glared at the server. "Let's just say that he doesn't live up to the image he presents."

Mick looked a little uncomfortable. He shifted in his seat and rubbed the back of his neck with a big hand.

"Ooh," the server said. "How terrible. For you both." She sashayed away, obviously not put off at all by Kylee's warning.

Of course, disharmony in paradise might just trigger her interest in Mick even more, Kylee thought.

"So," Mick said, his mouth twitching in a small smile, "here we are."

"Yes." Kylee folded her arms over her breasts, certain that Mick's gaze behind the sunglasses rested on her there.

"Shopping?" Mick nodded at the package Kylee had placed on the table.

Kylee shrugged and looked around at the café. "Sitting?"

Mick scowled and let out an irritated sigh that was definitely male, something Kylee had heard her father do on numerous occasions. "I thought we might meet and talk things over," he said.

"And how did you think that would happen? This is a big city."

"Maybe it wouldn't have. But I knew you weren't at your hotel room."

"And how did you know that?"

"I was there. The Czech police were there. Scherba's men were there. And probably some of the guys from the team that tried to whack you this morning."

"That must have been a regular circus." The thought chilled Kylee. She was being hunted. She had to refuse the impulse to look around. Barbara had warned her that meeting Mick here could mean she was stepping into a trap.

"It was," Mick agreed. "The only thing missing was the clown."

"Funny."

"Not terribly so." Mick sipped his drink as the server deposited Kylee's chocolate in front of her.

Kylee took out money.

"Put your money away, sheila," Mick growled. "The least I can do is buy you a drink."

Disgusted, Kylee put the money under the chocolate, which she intended not to drink.

"I'll buy my own drink," Kylee said.

"With your ill-gotten gain?" Mick asked.

"I'm not a thief."

"No, you're an American stuntwoman—"

"Stunt *person*."

"—who breaks into people's boats."

Kylee hesitated. "Creepstof Scherba is not a nice guy."

"Creepstof?" Mick's lips twitched again.

Kissable, Kylee thought. *Those lips are definitely kissable.* "My pet name for him."

He scowled, which was definitely no improvement, but Kylee still thought the overall effect was sexy. She felt the immediate pull toward him. Sitting there across from him like strangers who had just met, it was easy to fantasize that they had just met. She wondered what it would be like to run her hands across the hard, sculpted planes of his chest, to kiss him, to feel the heat of him against her as he—

"Are you listening, sheila?" he asked.

Kylee snapped out of the daydream, irritated with herself for allowing her attention to lapse. "Yes."

He shook his head. "You are definitely in the wrong line of business. Or is this your first foray into the burglary?"

"I got away from you last night," Kylee pointed out.

Mick cursed. "Pet names for your targets. Electronic gadgets and gizmos. You act like this is some kind of game."

"I don't think it's a game," Kylee objected, but she knew that part of her did.

"Yeah, you do. That's why you met me here."

"I didn't meet you here." Kylee put some fire in her voice. She pointed at the shop across the street. "I just happened to be shopping and saw you."

"You're behaving like a stupid little girl, sheila." Mick pulled his sunglasses off and looked at her with smoldering eyes. "Meeting me here was one of the stupidest things you could have ever done. For all you know, I

... out in
... attention of sev-
...

... felt self-conscious. How could she
... attracted to such a man? He was a jerk. It had
... be the assignment.

Mick recovered. "I know my principal is a bad man.
That's why I came here to warn you."

"Then why are you working for him?"

"That's my business, sheila, and none of yours."
Mick's face looked stony. "It's time to stop playing
games, darlin', and go on home."

"I'm not playing games."

"Yes, you are. But the thing is, I don't know if you're
more greedy or more driven by the thrill of it all."

"There's no thrill in meeting you," Kylee said, and
she knew that she was lying so badly all she could do
was hope he didn't see right through her.

"You're busted, sheila," he grated. "They know who
you are, and they'll be looking for you now. Scherba is
concerned about you. I saw that in him last night. And
not only that, but I don't know who this other team is that
you've dragged in."

"What other team?"

"The men that tried to snipe you today."

Kylee felt confused. "Those were Creepstof's men."

possibly be

Kylee immediately

eral people around them, then he broke

harsh, derisive laughter that attracted the

Mick was frozen for a moment, then he broke

at him. "And you, too,"

"Because," she said, winging it,

"And why not?"

snipers would have taken your sniper out." She pointed

"I wasn't worried about that," Kylee said, fee

cold prickle between her shoulder blades.

around us."

wicked ... these

they get yo ... l see, just as

dead."

"I'm doing all ri

"Wrong. You're jus ... or greedy to know you're so far in over ... hose men who came for you today, I figure the ... ck. They won't quit. And if you bring them around ... principal, you're just going to make my job harder. I can't allow that."

"Maybe you don't have a choice."

Mick leaned forward in his seat. "I have a choice, darlin'. That's why I came here and waited for you."

"You don't want to get too close," Kylee warned. "If you make any sudden, overt moves, my snipers will take you out." She'd acted in a similar situation in a movie a year ago. The dialogue came naturally.

"I don't, do I?" Mick's tone was daring.

"No." But Kylee knew her reply didn't sound convincing. She wouldn't have believed herself.

"You're right, sheila," he said. "I don't want to get too close. But I can."

Before she could move, Mick leaned forward and kissed her.

Get away! Get away!

The voice screamed in the back of Kylee's head, but again she ignored it and gave herself over to his kiss. She felt his hot lips against hers with almost bruising intensity. And she felt her body responding, growing warmer and tingling. She had to stop. But she didn't. She opened her mouth and allowed him entry. His hand curled behind her head, stroking the back of her neck. Her senses swam and she knew some of her alertness dimmed. She was suddenly the most vulnerable she had ever been on a mission.

And just as unexpectedly and quickly as he'd begun the kiss, Mick broke it off. He drew back and tried to act unaffected, but Kylee saw the flush in his cheeks, heard his slightly ragged breathing.

He stood, and more of his reaction to her was visible. "Go home, sheila," he growled angrily. "Go home before you get us both killed." Then he walked away, never looking back.

Kylee watched him and didn't know what she was supposed to do. Half a block away, he turned a corner and was gone, and the kiss was still burning on her lips.

The sat-phone in her handbag rang. She answered. "Hello."

"Well," Barbara said, "that was interesting."

Feeling guilty and confused, Kylee glared at the sky,

imagining the satellite 23,000 miles out in space that stared down at her. "I don't want to talk about it."

"Meeting him there doesn't seem like such a good idea."

"I don't think he's a bad guy."

"Oh, and you definitely have the emotional distance you need to make that decision."

"Yes. I'm calm. I'm alert. I was just feeling him out about the possibility of recruiting him to our side. Having someone inside Creepstof's castle, so to speak, would be a definite plus." Surely Barbara couldn't argue with that.

"I see. Well, while you sit there feeling so calm and alert, you might want to take our bug off the back of your collar."

Feeling like an idiot, Kylee reached to the back of her blouse and found the miniature audio receiver with her fingertips. There was no doubt that it was the same device she'd placed on him earlier when she'd kissed him so unexpectedly.

Damn you, Mick Stone. But she had to smile. *So you're a game player, too.* That was something to know. She juggled the bug in her palm. "So what do we do?"

"You go back to the safe house," Barbara said. "Get some rest and lie low. In the meantime, I'll poke around the situation and see if we can leverage any more Intel. Whatever Egorov's scheme is, the clock is ticking."

Mick Stone couldn't get the memory of the woman's lips from his mind. Even during the long walk back to the Vltava River and *Guilty Pleasures,* even through the circular route he'd chosen to insure that he wasn't followed, his thoughts seemed consumed by her. He cursed himself. When he was on the job, he was always a professional.

The woman was taking the edge off his game and he resented her and his own weakness.

Still, he'd scared her today. When he'd found the tracking device on his shirt collar, he'd gone to the café and sat, hoping she would be drawn out of whatever hidey-hole she'd chosen for herself. He'd been about to give up when he'd noticed her in the shop across the street.

But now, surely now he'd put enough righteous fear in her that she would stay away. Her gadgets were impressive. The tracking device had been state-of-the-art, letting him know that whoever was paying her was wealthy and resourceful. Of course, Krystof Scherba wouldn't attract any other kind of enemies.

That was why Mick and Josef were getting paid so handsomely. That, and the fact that they probably had the cleanest record of all the security staff that Scherba employed.

Even before he stepped aboard the catamaran, Mick knew something was wrong. The noon sun burned down onto the river, raising silver highlights from the ripples left by boats and the river's natural currents. Scherba normally remained belowdecks during the heat of the day, either working on the computer or sleeping because he was a nocturnal predator.

"Stone," Scherba said, seated at a table in the stern. Radu stood at the man's side, arms folded across his chest and looking completely menacing.

"Mr. Scherba," Mick replied politely, centering himself. Josef wasn't in sight. If things went badly, Mick figured he could throw himself over the boat's side and swim for it.

"Did you enjoy lunch?" Scherba asked.

"What's this about, Mr. Scherba?"

Scherba looked displeased. "That's exactly what I

would like to know. I heard you had lunch with a woman a short time ago.''

Mick shrugged. "There are a lot of women in this city.''

"And you were at the movie set this morning.''

So he *had* been seen. Mick took a tense breath. There were a dozen men on the boat's deck, and all of them belonged to Scherba. "Sight-seeing.'' That sounded lame, but he wasn't exactly at his best. He couldn't help thinking that if he was in danger, Kylee Swain was as well.

"A woman,'' Scherba mused, "who vaguely resembles the description of the woman who invaded my boat last night. A boat that you have been hired to protect.''

"I was hired to protect *you,*'' Mick countered. It was splitting hairs, but it was also the truth. "And the woman I had a coffee with was brunette. Not blond.''

"In any case, she eluded the men I had following her.''

A knot of tension released in Mick's gut. If she had eluded Scherba's men, maybe she'd have the sense to get herself clear of the situation.

"Even if this is not the same woman,'' Scherba went on, "I find it disturbing that you, who have shown no interest in any of the women I have brought aboard this boat, suddenly find yourself in the company of two. Or possibly only one. Especially after entry was gained on my boat.''

"I don't know what you're suggesting, Mr. Scherba. If you don't like the protection I'm giving you, we can terminate this contract immediately.''

"No,'' Scherba said. "That won't be necessary. I have you, Stone, and I'd rather see if I can smoke your partner or partners out of the woodwork.''

A man rose behind Mick. His instincts screamed a warning at him even as the catamaran rolled on a wave and revealed the man's short shadow on the deck in front of him. He turned to run, but something bit into the back of his neck. Putting a hand up, he felt the feathered dart there.

Tranquilizer, Mick realized as the drug whirled through his head and distanced the world from him. He tried to reach the boat's railing and dive over, but Radu was there like a stone wall. The big man lifted his fist and swung toward Mick's face. With the drug in his system, Mick couldn't escape the blow.

Darkness shut him down immediately.

Chapter 6

Half an hour after ditching the tails she'd picked up after the conversation with Mick Stone, Kylee returned to her safe house. Losing the tails hadn't been hard, and hadn't even worked off the frustration she felt after talking with Mick. She'd come to the conclusion that he was insufferable, and she looked forward to breaking into Scherba's computer files under Mick Stone's nose.

In over her head. Ha! Well, they'd see about that.

The safe house came equipped with a satellite phone, television, a notebook computer and a fully stocked kitchen. It was a small third-floor walk-up apartment that was larger on the inside than it looked. The walls were reinforced and could take a direct hit from a tank. The safe house also had three exit routes.

Kylee raided the refrigerator and found a tin of cinnamon rolls. Once the stove was heated, she popped the rolls in and the small apartment filled with the smell of baking bread and cinnamon. Maybe it wasn't chocolate, but sugar would take the edge off her frustration with her situation and with the man. She just hoped it would also remove all those memories of his kiss.

As the rolls baked, she paced the small living room and watched the television coverage of the attack at the film location. No one knew why the attack had taken place or who was behind it. Everyone was aware that one of the stunt crew was missing, and the picture that was circulated to the viewing audience was several years out of date. The film company didn't have a good photo because Kylee wasn't featured in the movie.

The Czech police didn't identify the two men Mick Stone had killed, but the Stony Man intelligence teams had. Both men were part of Kapoch Egorov's terrorist regime, and they were connected to the team that had confronted Bethany Riggs in Cape Town.

There was no doubt that Egorov had sent them to Prague. He obviously knew that Bethany had gotten something important from Lyeta Denisov before the woman had been killed.

Barbara had arranged to get a message to Kylee's parents and to the film company that she was all right. Actual phone conversation would come later when the proper cutouts were made. Scherba and Egorov had people in their employ capable of putting a phone tap on her parents' phones and tracing the call back within a minute. One phone call would have possibly put Kylee back into the crosshairs of Egorov's henchmen.

When the rolls were ready, Kylee slathered them generously with white icing that was nearly pure sugar. The rolls were hot and soft and sticky, and she knew the sugar would slow her system down.

She ate half of the rolls and would have finished the

other half but Barbara called. Kylee knew it was the mission controller immediately: no one else had the number.

"We've got a problem," Barbara said.

"Fine," Kylee said. "And how are you doing now that you've been cooped up in a safe house, cut off from the outside world for almost two hours, not allowed to call home to let your mom know that you're okay—knowing full well that she's going to hold it against you and that you're going to get interminable lectures about calling home after you're shot at, which, by the way is going to be a new lecture because your mom never had a clue you were in the spy business, and—"

"What have you eaten?"

Kylee eyed a dollop of white icing on her thumb. "Nothing," she answered, feeling a little guilty. She licked the icing from her thumb. She wasn't so guilty that it would ruin her appetite.

"I thought you were supposed to go to the safe house and relax till I called," Barbara said.

"This *is* relaxed." Kylee eyed the remaining cinnamon rolls. And she could have relaxed, too. If Mick Stone hadn't stayed on her mind so much. "I've got more relaxing to do. Unless you have something else in mind."

"Scherba evidently doesn't trust Mick Stone anymore. When Stone got back to the boat, Scherba confronted him, then had one of his men shoot Mick with a tranquilizer dart."

The announcement slammed into Kylee's gut with the force of a wrecking ball. Part of the reason she had been driven crazy during the past two hours had been Mick Stone. She'd kept thinking about the kiss and the way he had held her so tight in the alley, about the way his hard, muscled body had fit so comfortably next to hers last night.

"You saw them do that?" Kylee asked, knowing Barbara had, through the sat-recon, or the mission controller wouldn't ever have said anything.

"Yes. After this morning, Scherba probably suspects Stone helped you get away last night."

Kylee cursed and started pacing. "I did that on my own."

"I know. We're pretty sure Mick is still alive."

Kylee vented a sigh of relief. She'd take one of Barbara's guesses over most mission controllers' facts any time. "Mick is still aboard the boat?"

"No. He's in a panel truck headed south out of town. The audio receiver you put on him this morning was coated with radioactive dust that we can track for seven to ten days. Even if he'd showered, the dust would have stayed in his skin for that time."

Kylee covered the cinnamon rolls and shoved them in the refrigerator. "I need transportation."

"Going after Stone might not be a good idea."

Taking a deep breath, Kylee said, "He saved my life today. Twice. He took a bullet for me."

"He was wearing a vest."

"And still could have gotten shot in the face. That's not just something you walk away from."

"No, it's not."

"If you want more of a reason," Kylee said, "let's consider this. Mick was hired as Creepstof's chief of security. Want to bet that Mick knows how to get into Creepstof's castle? Whatever information we're looking for that wasn't on Creepstof's notebook computer, it's at the castle."

Leaning forward to present a low wind profile, Kylee dropped her knee to within an inch or two of the highway surface to keep the BMW R1150 GS Enduro motorcycle laid over into the tight turn.

As it turned out, in addition to the safe house, Barbara Price also kept a garage hidden away that had over a dozen vehicles. The inventory had included Skodas, the most prevalent Czech-made vehicle, as well as Mercedes, BMWs, and Russian-made Trabant sedans.

When she'd seen the motorcycle, Kylee had opted immediately for the off-road muscle and lightning-fast maneuverability. The motorcycle would have come up short in a demolition derby, but she didn't intend for the action to get that serious. Stunt work and spy craft were all about control.

The terrain outside Prague was harsh and bleak. Snow-capped mountains towered in the distance. The Vltava River gleamed, a silver ribbon that wove through the landscape as the highway drew closer, then drew farther away.

Kylee clung to the motorcycle, becoming a piece of the powerful machinery as it hurtled in pursuit of the dark green, thirty-year-old Moskvich 2140 pickup that the Stony Man satellite recon teams had tracked Mick Stone to. The motorcycle's engine shrilled and growled as Kylee alternately backed off and twisted the throttle.

She wore riding leathers with a thermal liner to protect against the chill, gloves, motorcycle boots and a full-face helmet for the most protection possible. Deftly, just keeping the motorcycle under control, she closed the distance between herself and the target vehicle. She tried not to think about how injured Mick Stone might be. Scherba was the kind of guy who killed and crippled with no hesitation.

The Moskvich pickup was awkward and underpowered. In another life, the vehicle might have been a small family sedan, but the passenger compartment had been truncated to one seat to make room for the cargo area. Two men sat up front and the rear section looked like a huge metal square that had been welded behind the driver's compartment.

All Kylee could remember was the way Mick Stone had moved when the gunman came around the corner, how he had placed himself between her and the bullet that might have killed her. The men had been after her, not him. She knew that.

He had protected her.

Yet, he'd looked so deadly, so dangerous behind the .45 the night before aboard *Guilty Pleasures*. Even then, she knew, he wouldn't have shot her without serious provocation. The pistol had been there to scare her, and it had.

She reached inside her jacket pocket and took out the tear gas grenade she'd chosen from the cache of weapons that had also been in the garage. She pulled the pin and held the grenade in her left hand, trapping the spoon in place so the device wouldn't go off.

The Moskvich pickup pulled to the far right side of the highway and geared down for the long ascent up the steep climb. Other, faster cars, chose their moments and sped up around the pickup, not wanting to be held up.

Using the cargo cube to shield her from the driver's sight, Kylee accelerated, moving the bike up on the pickup's right.

Matching speed with the vehicle, Kylee released the spoon holding the tear gas grenade's detonator in check. She started counting down from three. When she reached two, she tossed the grenade through the open window.

The grenade bounced against the windshield, then rebounded into the seat between the two men. For a single comical second, the two men stared at the grenade in disbelief as it rolled from the seat and dropped onto the floorboard. Then both of them scrambled for the grenade as the Moskvich swerved out of control.

Kylee tapped the motorcycle's rear brake with her foot and zipped in neatly behind the Moskvich. Inside the pickup cab, the tear gas canister detonated with a *bamf!* loud enough to be heard over the motorcycle's engine. Bilious white smoke filled the cab and spewed from the open windows.

Swerving erratically, the driver managed to keep the pickup more or less on the shoulder of the road and brought the vehicle to a shuddering halt. Horns blared as motorists passed.

Kylee geared down and followed the pickup as closely as a fighter jet stalking prey. She dropped her right boot and waited for the two men to make their moves.

Both doors opened at the same time.

Kylee twisted the throttle and the motorcycle lunged forward. The front wheel came up off the ground and slammed into the driver as he tried to hold off a coughing and crying fit long enough to get a shotgun from the pickup cab. The man flew backward and fell in an unconscious heap.

Dropping her left foot to the ground, Kylee brought the motorcycle around in a tight turn. The spinning rear wheel spewed rock and dirt, then caught as she put weight back onto the bike. She roared back at the second man, but he dodged behind the pickup door.

Not wanting to chance losing the motorcycle, and her only means of escape, Kylee laid the BMW down on its side. Coming up from a crouch, she slipped a twenty-two-inch wooden dowel from her right boot. The hardened wood slipped smoothly through her fingers.

The gunman cursed at her and aimed his pistol. Before he could squeeze the trigger, Kylee whipped the short stick forward and rapped the man's exposed knuckles. She moved smoothly into an attack kata.

Well-versed in kung fu with some training in a half-dozen other disciplines, Kylee loved the fatal flute form she'd learned from her Wah Lum *sifu,* the teacher she had studied with the longest. The flute was one of the oldest musical instruments as well as being one of the oldest weapons used by the Chinese.

She flipped the stick over in her hand, rolling it back into her palm so that she grasped the weapon at the midway point. Turning her right side to the gunman, she rammed the end of the stick into the man's solar plexus, taking his breath away. He reached for her, but she remained in motion, stepping away again and whirling the baton around again.

The man's fingers snapped like twigs. Before he could howl in pain, Kylee slid her grip to the end of the stick again, then slapped the weapon into the man's temple. The man's eyes glazed and became unfocused, and he fell forward, landing on his face without even trying to stop the fall.

Kylee reached for her helmet and pushed the face shield up and out of the way. Cool air swept into the helmet and she drew in deep drafts. Then she noticed the two-way radio mounted under the dash.

"Oz," she called over the Stony Man earpiece.

"I'm here," Barbara said.

"They were carrying a radio." Kylee flipped the seat forward. Some of the tear gas still hung in the air despite the open windows and the wind, burning her eyes and throat and nose.

A red toolbox, two coats, a jack and a spare tire occupied the open space behind the seat. Beneath it all, she spotted the curved length of a crowbar.

"We're sweeping the area," Barbara responded. "We've tagged two possible chase vehicles." She hesitated. "We didn't catch them the first time around."

Kylee grabbed the crowbar and headed to the back of the pickup.

"Chase vehicles mean this was a setup," Barbara said. "I should have expected that. Scherba believed your rescue was involved with you. Scherba used a hostage situation to lure you out into the open."

"They still have to close the show." Kylee paused at the back of the pickup. "Where's Mick?" *Please let him be alive.* She didn't know what she would do if he was dead.

"On the other side of the door."

"Is he up and around?"

"Yes." The thermographic properties of the satellites saw through the metal box.

"Mick," Kylee called. She heard movement and tried again. *"Mick!"*

"What the hell are you doing here? Sheila, don't you know a trap when you see one?"

He's alive! The realization spun through Kylee, but his harsh tone and accusation brought her up a little short. Criticizing a rescue wasn't exactly the way things should go.

"They haven't caught me yet," Kylee reminded him. "And if I don't hear something more along the lines of 'thank you' in the next minute or so, I'm going to leave you in that box."

"Hurry," Mick growled. "And thank you."

Kylee rammed the crowbar behind the lock that secured the cargo door. Metal screeched as the locking mechanism ripped away. She opened the door and stared at the bloody and battered man who stood before her. Pain wrenched through her heart at the sight of him, and guilt spewed broken glass that cut deeply.

He wouldn't be in this situation if it hadn't been for me.

Mick raised his hands to protect his eyes from the sun. A short chain glinted between his wrists, revealing handcuffs. Another set of cuffs secured his ankles.

Kylee groaned at the sight of all the damage he'd endured.

Mick showed her a lopsided grin. "I figured I wasn't exactly a sight for sore eyes, sheila, but I have to admit, I've never gotten that kind of reaction before."

"Creepstof had you beaten because he thought you were with me." Guilt filled Kylee. She viewed her job as rescuing people, manufacturing get-aways.

"Aye, darlin'."

"And if you hang around there, the target is going to get the chance to kill you both," Barbara said.

"Can you walk?" Kylee asked. "Because I don't think I can carry you."

"I can walk."

"Step out and stand with your feet apart."

Mick did, but he swayed slightly as he moved. When he had his feet apart, leaving the chain between his ankle cuffs lying on the street's edge, Kylee held the crowbar in both hands and brought the sharp end down on the chain. The links parted with a snap.

"Give me your hands." Kylee repeated the process on the handcuff chain just as a car screeched into position behind the Moskvich.

"Down!" Mick shouted, shoving a shoulder into her and knocking her away from the rear of the pickup.

Instead of being bowled from her feet, Kylee rolled, the motorcycle helmet grinding across the small rocks for an instant, and automatically came up in a crouching position. She raced for the motorcycle.

Bullets slammed into the pickup's rear as Mick took cover on the vehicle's passenger side. He spotted the pistol lying on the ground and grabbed the weapon. Remaining in a crouch, he wheeled around with the pistol in his right hand, his left hand open and supporting his right wrist as he fired.

Four men occupied the black Trabant fifty feet behind the pickup. The man on the passenger side pirouetted and went down. The windshield broke across the driver's face in a spray of crimson. Evidently he'd had his foot on the brake, and when he died his foot slipped away. The Russian-made sedan rolled forward. A third man bolted from the car's rear, but he didn't go far before the pistol in Mick's hands blasted him down.

Kylee righted the motorcycle, threw a leg over and used the electric starter to fire up the engine. She slapped the face shield down into place, then dropped the gearshift lever into first with her foot.

"Car Two is in front of the pickup," Barbara said over the ear bud.

Kylee glanced toward the highway and saw the second Trabant skid to a stop seventy or eighty feet in front of the pickup. Three men boiled out of the vehicle as the reverse lights came on and the driver floored the accelerator.

"Mick!" Kylee yelled.

He rose, blood-covered with a new layer of dust over him. Despite his wounds and his battered condition, he looked inexorable, a man held together by his own strength of will. Bending down over the man Kylee had knocked out, he took two extra magazines from the man's coat. Still in motion, eyes narrowed against the afternoon sun, Mick ejected the spent clip and shoved a new one home.

He raised the pistol as he walked, focused on the targets in the other car. The pistol jumped in his hands.

Kylee's heart thudded inside her chest as she watched Mick coolly shoot one of the men, then turn his sights on a second. No emotion showed in those blue eyes: no anger, no remorse, no fear. He fired at the approaching car, but the driver ducked down and came on.

Watching him was horrible. She felt certain bullets were going to beat him down at any second and she could do nothing to prevent it.

"Mick!" Kylee yelled again.

Then he was at her side, throwing a leg painfully over the back of the motorcycle.

"Can you drive one of these, sheila?" he growled as he wrapped an arm around her midsection.

She felt the heated strength of his arm around her and was surprised at the sense of security that came with it. Despite the danger of the situation, she felt safe and protected. She'd seen him stand up to bullets twice now and never falter. Releasing the clutch and twisting the throttle, she guided the motorcycle forward, front wheel coming up as the Trabant collided with the Moskvich pickup.

"You've got a spotter in the air," Barbara warned over the headset.

Speeding out onto the highway, Kylee glanced up and saw a small transport helicopter in the air above them.

"We tracked the helicopter from the airport only minutes ago," Barbara said. "It came straight here. The hangar it came from is registered to one of Scherba's shell companies."

The helicopter closed the distance rapidly. A man leaned out onto the landing skid with a machine pistol.

Nine-millimeter bullets cracked against the worn tarmac of the highway only a few feet from Kylee and Mick.

Mick fired at the helicopter, missing nearly every time but scoring enough hits on the Plexiglas bubble to make the pilot back off. He swapped magazines, putting his last full one in.

"I don't think this was the ideal transportation for a rescue," he growled.

"Not if we were going to stick with the highway," Kylee agreed. She geared down, watching as the cars approaching her pulled into the ditch to avoid the yammering fire of the guy with the machine pistol.

Then she cut the wheel, powering the motorcycle off-road. She had to muscle the BMW across the rugged terrain, but in seconds she found a game trail that threaded through the trees over the mountainous country. The thick foliage protected them from the helicopter's spying eyes.

"Not bad, sheila," Mick said approvingly. "Not bad at all."

A glow of pride filled Kylee. She felt him lean more heavily into her, instinctively letting his body meld with hers until they almost felt like one. If it hadn't been for the possibility of bad guys popping out at any moment, Kylee thought she could have enjoyed riding like that for hours.

"So you're not a thief. You're a spy."

Burdened by the packages she carried, Kylee stood in the doorway and gazed across the darkened interior of the safe house. The hideout contained some amenities, but lacked clothing they both needed.

After getting Mick Stone cleaned up and bandaged, which had included far too much exposure to handsome naked male flesh, which had more of an effect on her than she would have liked, Kylee had gone shopping. That hadn't truly helped take her mind off the man and his body, though, because she'd thought constantly of the naked male the clothes would soon be covering.

Kylee felt irritated with herself. She'd never thought about a man so much in her life. And the circumstances couldn't have been any worse. And to top matters off, not only was she off her game, but Mick Stone was definitely not the kind of guy that should have put her there. He was way too serious.

"Maybe you want to speak up a little," Kylee said. "I think a couple of the neighbors didn't hear you." She closed the door with a bang. Wasn't he used to doing covert work? Didn't he have a clue what secrecy was all about? She felt irritated at him for that, too. Maybe her thinking about him all the time wasn't his fault, but possibly blowing their cover and exposing the safe house was definitely his fault.

Mick Stone sat in a chair by the window overlooking the Vltava River. Since his clothing had been ruined, he'd been forced to wear a towel to make some attempt at modesty.

Modesty, however, seemed to be something Mick Stone wasn't overly enamored of. He'd only put up token resistance to her offer of examining and treating his wounds, and he'd seemed comfortable with his nudity.

Two of the wounds, one at the back of his head and another along his left jaw had required stitches. Versed in medical care from working with her father and her brothers and taking care of herself, Kylee had used the safe house's ER-grade medkit to stitch the wounds closed.

"My voice didn't carry that far," Mick argued.

Kylee dropped the clothing on the couch near the door.

Mick eyed the packages doubtfully. "You bought all that for me?"

"Not all," Kylee said defensively. "Some. Some of that is for you." She hadn't been able to bring any clothes from the hotel with her. "There's outerwear down in the car. I just couldn't bring it all up."

A frown creased Mick's face. "The clothes I usually buy, sheila, they don't come in ribboned boxes and packages. I hope you have something in there fit for a man to wear."

"They were all out of leather and lizard hide," Kylee replied. "But there was a nice Roman toga I found that will upgrade your Tarzan attire."

Levering himself up from the chair, Mick grinned. "Oh, and you're a cold one, aren't you?" He crossed the room and trailed a forefinger along the line of her jaw. "I love it when a woman puts on that holier-than-thou attitude."

Kylee whipped her head to the side and tried to bite his finger.

Mick laughed and pulled his finger back. "A croc that moved that slowly back where I came from would starve to death."

Before he could move, Kylee shot her hand out and flicked his nose with a forefinger. He drew back too late.

"You're trouble, Kylee," he growled, putting his hand to his nose. "I knew that from the minute I put eyes on you."

"Then maybe you'll stay away." Although Kylee said that, she kept remembering how his lips had felt against hers. He'd just look at her and she'd feel the burn all over again.

"Trust me, Kylee. If we didn't need each other right

now, I'd be long gone." His voice sounded rough enough to almost qualify as rude.

"Trust me," Kylee said sharply, willing herself to put distance from the disturbing and unaccustomed feelings she was having about him, "we don't need each other."

"Sure we do. I don't intend to let Krystof Scherba get away with what he did to me."

"This isn't about you." Kylee felt a little irritated.

Mick regarded her and nodded. "No, darlin', it's not. But getting back a little for what he did to me is a starting point. I knew that Scherba wasn't a good bloke."

"Then what were you doing with him?" That bothered Kylee. After seeing Mick in action, watching him take the bullet that could have killed her, watching him kill their attackers without showing any fear, she couldn't think of him as a bad guy.

He looked away from her, appearing pained and chastened, very much like the young boy Kylee could imagine he had been. "It was a job. That's all. Just a bloody job." He paused. "And maybe it was a mistake, too. But it was money and it filled in some dead time for me, and I figured I'd probably be protecting Scherba more from other bad guys than from the good guys."

"Bad guys? Like a thief?"

He looked at her and smiled a little. "Yeah. Like a thief." His eyes narrowed forcefully. "And you need me too. I know how to get us into Scherba's little fortress, and I noticed that you don't like killing."

"No," Kylee replied. "I don't. I don't think killing is an answer." That was one big difference she saw between them.

"Sometimes, darlin'," Mick said in a soft voice, "it's the *only* answer. And if you beard Scherba in his den, then that's going to have to be one of the answers you're ready to give. Since you're not, I am.''

A wintry chill passed between them, and Kylee got the feeling they were standing on opposite sides of an impossible gulf.

Mick broke the uncomfortable eye contact first and started digging through the packages.

Kylee brushed him aside, feeling irritated that she wasn't getting through to him and wasn't taking notice of her the way she thought she wanted him to. After all, they were in a somewhat romantic get-away in Prague. The least he could do was pay a little more attention, but he acted as if she was merely a roommate. ''Don't just rummage through those things and manhandle them. Some of them are mine.''

''Thank God.'' Mick wore a look of mock horror as he held up a pair of pink bikini panties.

Kylee snatched the panties away and felt her cheeks burn. ''Underwear,'' she growled. ''Not a new concept. Everybody wears it.''

He looked at her blankly. ''I don't.''

Caught off guard, Kylee stared at him.

''Sometimes,'' Mick said, straight-faced. ''Sometimes I don't.'' He paused and grinned wickedly. ''Tonight I will. So you'll know and not have to wonder, you see.''

''I wouldn't wonder.''

''You might.''

''Not a chance, mister.''

Mick turned his attention back to the bags. ''So what did you think? That I'm a boxers or briefs man?''

''It never crossed my mind,'' Kylee lied. ''I bought both kinds. Maybe you can wear one of each.'' Then she noticed the smell of herbs and tomato sauce filling the room. ''What's that smell?''

"Dinner, I hope," Mick answered.

Abandoning her purchases for the moment, Kylee walked over to the small stove. Spaghetti sauce simmered in a pan on one of the burners. She raked the ladle through the thick contents.

"I didn't know we had fresh vegetables," she said.

"We didn't."

"These are fresh."

"So you're a thief, a spy *and* a detective. That's some résumé you're carrying there." Mick walked through the room with a pair of black jeans, a midnight blue turtleneck, socks, underwear and hiking boots.

"Where did you get fresh vegetables?"

"I asked the little old lady next door if she would mind stepping down to the market and getting them for me."

"You asked her?" Kylee had noticed the old woman earlier. The woman looked as though she could barely get around. And she hadn't appeared to care for Kylee at all.

Mick grabbed his towel. "Couldn't go down to the market myself dressed like this, now could I?"

"But you went next door dressed like that?"

"*Undressed* like this, you mean?" Mick grinned and wriggled his eyebrows suggestively. Then a pained look shot across his face because the movement must have pulled at the stitches in the back of his head. "Yes I did. She didn't seem to mind. Me being undressed like this even seemed to put a certain spring in her step."

I'll bet, Kylee thought, looking at the expanse of muscled leg and thigh that were revealed. Not to mention the sculpted chest and shoulders. Then she saw that he had caught her looking. She quickly turned her attention to the simmering saucepan and realized to her chagrin that the saucepan wasn't the only thing simmering.

"Maybe you could find your way clear to stirring the pasta while you're there," Mick suggested.

Kylee stirred, feeling the heat on her face and knowing it wasn't all from the stove. She had to resist looking over her shoulder.

"Unlike you," Mick said as he retreated down the hallway, "I don't fancy going skulking around Scherba's castle tonight after a hearty TV dinner, sheila. I want more substantial sustenance." He paused. "If that meets your approval, of course. You can always whip up one of those little freeze-dried concoctions for yourself."

"Fine." Kylee tasted the sauce from the ladle, surprised at how good it tasted.

"I'm a good cook," he called from the back room.

Remembering the way he had nearly captured her and the way he had stood up to Scherba's goons, Kylee couldn't help but be even more impressed. Then, wanting to keep her mind from thinking about him getting dressed in the next room, about the towel dropping from his waist, she crossed to the refrigerator and peered inside.

Then she knew he wasn't as perfect as she'd imagined. The cinnamon rolls she'd saved from earlier in the day were gone.

The pipes in the safe house worked better than the ones in the hotel where Kylee had been staying earlier. She stood in the hot spray cascading over her and thought about her situation.

Getting Scherba's notebook concerned her greatly. So did figuring out what she was going to do about talking to her mom about the spy career. *I only did it the one time* didn't sound like a good defense.

Kylee sighed and blew water out of her face. She'd reveled in the shower, but part of her mind had been on the fact that Mick Stone was on the other side of the door. She'd locked it, but she felt certain he could get through the lock in a heartbeat if he wanted to.

The door remained locked.

And Kylee had no clue what she'd do if he did enter the bathroom. Against her better judgment, she'd built fantasies about what would happen if Mick came through that door. Hot and delicious fantasies that were alien to her. No man had ever had that effect on her. She resented the fact that this one did now.

Giving up on relaxing, figuring that Mick would get suspicious if she continued to stay in the shower, Kylee turned off the water, got out and toweled off. She dressed in low-cut hip-hugger jeans and a bright turquoise turtle-neck pullover, which she felt certain emphasized her figure.

She examined the look in the mirror. *You're not going to be able to ignore me now, Mick Stone.*

Taking a deep breath, Kylee stepped out into the apartment.

Everything was too quiet.

''Mick?'' she called.

No answer.

''Mick?''

A quick search of the apartment let her know that he wasn't there. She found the note on the table.

Be back in a short while. Got something needs taking care of. Leave the dishes. I'll do them when I get back. Mick.

Kylee cursed and wadded the note up. She was stupid for having trusted him. Even if he didn't run straight to Creepstof and betray her—which she truly didn't think he would—there was every possibility that he was going to screw up whatever chance she had of completing the mission and figuring out whatever Kapoch Egorov was up to.

And why hadn't Barbara called her to alert her that he was on the move?

Retreating to the bathroom, she discovered that the satphone she'd taken in with her was turned off. Mick *had* been in the room, and he'd switched off the phone while she wasn't looking.

Or while you were indulging in one of those little fantasies of yours, Kylee chided, feeling mortified.

She pushed the emotion aside for the moment, knowing there was one person she could call who would know where Mick was. Smart and clever as he was, he still didn't know about the radioactive dust that had stained his skin. Even repeated showers wouldn't remove the dust, according to Barbara. It was time to find out how true that was.

Chapter 7

Mick Stone knew something was wrong even before the wide-eyed cat at the end of the narrow alley bounded from behind an overflowing trash can. He wore a Kevlar vest under the midnight-blue turtleneck Kylee had purchased for him, as well as a thigh-length leather coat, and he carried a .45 semiautomatic pistol. Both the body armor and the pistol had come from the weapons stores kept in the safe house where he'd left Kylee Swain.

He'd switched off her sat-phone, and had almost gotten caught while he'd thought of the lithe, rounded body on the other side of the bathroom door. It had taken all of his willpower not to step on into the room and go to her. The attraction he felt for her was so strong that he felt certain it had to be mutual.

But he was also equally convinced that the attraction wouldn't be lasting. That would be the curse of finding someone like Kylee, someone who flipped every switch in every nerve that he had. Finding someone like that had to mean that he was cursed with bad luck and that she wouldn't care for him. He'd seen other guys go through that and he was determined it wouldn't happen to him.

And that was a problem only if he lived that long.

The gunmen stepped from the shadows.

Two men on the right and one on the left were at ground level. A fourth slid into view on the second-story fire escape landing on the left. All of the men regarded him with flat-eyed gazes. They were also Radu Galca's men, trained murderers and worse. Two of them were men who had helped beat him at Krystof Scherba's orders.

Mick cursed and dodged back as he pulled the .45 from the paddle holster at his back. Turning sideways to present a smaller target, he pointed the pistol and fired two shots, aiming for the center of the nearest man thirty feet away.

The bullets caught the man in the chest and drove him backward into the man behind him. Gunfire raked the alley floor and the building walls around Mick. One of the bullets tore through the side of the jacket. His body protested the quick movements after the beating he'd taken earlier. Even though he kept himself in shape in his line of work, there was no quick bouncing back from the physical damage he had taken earlier.

The man on the second-floor fire escape landing opened fire with an assault rifle. A line of bullets tore across the building just in front of Mick, driving him back. He turned and ran, staying low.

A door opened along the wall in front of him. Industrial metal music thumped out into the alley. A young woman started to step out into the alley, obviously too deafened from the music to hear the gunfire.

Mick caught the young woman in the crook of his arm, getting a flash of the club inside filled with dancers and a long bar near the door. "Get back inside!" Mick roared, shoving the young woman back into the club. She and two young men sprawled to the floor in shocked surprise.

Before Mick had a chance to say anything, another round of bullets hammered the door. He ducked behind the open door, feeling it shiver against his hand. Dents formed along the back of the door, mute testimony that the bullets couldn't penetrate the thick steel.

Shifting hands with the .45, Mick peered around the side and saw the man he'd shot getting back to his feet. *Wearing a vest,* Mick realized. He brought his pistol up and aimed at the man nearest him, not letting the .45s barrel slide past the door's edge. He mapped the targets in his mind, deciding on a course of action in a split second.

He squeezed the trigger, placing the first round into the approaching gunman's face, knocking him down in a spray of blood. Riding the natural recoil of the .45, Mick trained his sights on the second-story man's head in line with the assault rifle.

Mick fired two rounds and saw the man stagger back from the second-floor landing, toppling over the railing and starting the fall to the alley floor. Screams sounded behind him in the club. Knowing that many of the clubs in the area had armed security against holdup men, Mick cursed and stepped away from the door, letting it close behind him.

He ran for the other end of the alley, dumping the empty magazine and shoving a fresh one home. Shots rang out behind him, letting him know the two men who had survived the return fire hadn't given up the chase.

Ten feet from the alley's mouth, Mick saw the headlights of a vehicle parked in the opposing alley across the streets suddenly flare to life. Rubber shrilled and the car fishtailed from the alley, streaking straight for him.

Mick stopped, knowing he would never make it clear of the alley before the heavy Trabant sedan reached him. He raised the pistol and took aim at the windshield over the driver's side. Light flashed from the cracks and fissure that took form as the bullets struck home.

The car was relentless, bearing down on him.

Mick kept firing. He didn't have enough time to reach the door behind him now, and the alley didn't offer any cover.

Then another vehicle, this one zooming in from the right, slammed into the Trabant sedan. Metal screamed as the second car hammered the first into the side of the building. Cracked brick and mortar rained from the wall, but the sound was lost in the noise of the crash.

"Mick!" Kylee Swain sat in the driver's seat of the second car. Her blond hair hung in disarray over her beautiful face.

The man in the rear passenger seat of the Trabant got out. He snarled curses and lifted the assault rifle in his arms, aiming at Kylee.

Mick brought the .45 up. He didn't know if he had one or two rounds left, but he knew only a heartbeat remained of Kylee's life if he didn't act quickly. He let out half a breath as he took aim, then squeezed the trigger.

The bullet hit the gunman squarely in the chest, knocking him down. Gunfire sprayed into the sky.

Running now, Mick changed magazines, then vaulted the Trabant's hood and raced to the back of the sedan. The metal gave way under his steps. The gunman was trying to get up when Mick landed on him with both feet, driving him back to the ground. Mick cracked the man across the jaw with his pistol, knocking him out, then scooped up the AK-47 assault rifle.

No one in the car moved.

Shifting his sights to the two men in the alley, Mick sent them on their way with a couple of well-placed shots.

"Mick!"

He turned his attention to Kylee, feeling relieved and angry all at the same time to see that she was out of the car. "What the hell are you doing here?"

Her jaw set stubbornly. "You left."

Across the street, a crowd started to gather.

"You're damn right I left," Mick growled. "I had things to do."

"What things?" Kylee lithely leaped onto the wrecked car's hood and walked over to join him at the back of the smashed Trabant.

"I wanted to make sure my partner got out of the line of fire. Scherba didn't say anything about him when I got back to the boat."

"Your partner?" Kylee looked confused.

"Yes." Mick's patience with her was wearing thin, but he knew it wasn't her fault. It was his. He shouldn't have gone off after her. He should have told Josef there might be trouble. He should have never left his friend. God, the guilt that ate at him was terrible.

Kylee glanced at the gawkers. "We've got to get out of here."

"In a minute." Mick turned back to the man he'd knocked out. He shouldered the assault rifle, then fisted the man's shirt and lifted the man from the alley. He slapped the man's face with his open hand till he groaned and came awake.

"Mick, you can't just—"

"Back off, sheila. This is my business, not yours." Mick knew that had to have offended her, but at the moment he didn't care.

The man gazed up at him fearfully, blood flowing freely from the corner of his mouth.

"Josef Szekeres," Mick grated. "Where is he?"

The man replied, mumbling in Czech.

"Josef Szekeres," Mick repeated, shaking the man fiercely.

The man pointed to the back of the Trabant.

Aching with fear, Mick pushed the man back against the pavement and stepped to the Trabant's rear. The wreck had sprung the lock, but lifting the trunk was still hard work.

When Mick had the trunk open, he stared at the body of his old friend. A crimson line showed where his throat had been cut.

A choked cry tore free of Mick's throat.

"Mick," Kylee called gently at his side. She pulled on his arm. "Mick."

He looked at her, not quite comprehending. "He's dead."

"I know," she said softly. "I'm sorry. But we've got to get going."

Sirens shrilled in the distance.

"It's not safe for us here," Kylee said. "We have to get back to the safe house, *now.*"

Mick nodded. She was thinking more clearly than he was. He got in the passenger side of the car and stared at the crumpled body of his friend as long as he could, until Kylee wrenched her car free of the wrecked Trabant and sped away.

Krystof Scherba was going to pay, Mick knew, and the man was going to pay in blood.

Kylee found Mick standing in the living room of the safe house, staring out at the catamaran tied up on the

Vltava River. Knowing that the object of his agony and hatred was so near and yet so far away filled Kylee with pain.

"I just got off the phone with my mission controller," Kylee said.

Mick nodded but didn't look at her.

"She's talking to some people in the State Department," Kylee said. "They're going to make sure the…the body gets shipped back to his wife. International favors, I guess."

"Always pays to know somebody who knows somebody," Mick stated flatly.

Kylee crossed the room and sat on the floor with her back to the wall near the window Mick stared through. She sat with her knees against her chest, her arms around her legs.

He acted as though she wasn't there.

"I'm sorry," she whispered.

"Josef was a good man," Mick said hoarsely. "He was…was a good father." He paused. "And he was the best friend I ever had. He stuck by me even after the CIA decided to pass on my services after the Hong Kong incident."

"What happened?"

"You mean that wasn't in my file?"

"No."

Mick waited a moment. "The CIA hired me to look after a special witness they had in New Jersey. Guy was going to testify against Chinese Triads that went all the way back to mainland China. If they were successful, a deal was going to be cut that would give them better Intel on Triad activities Stateside or something. I don't know."

Kylee understood. She didn't always know the overall

ramifications of her own assignments. Even the Egorov mission was something of a mystery.

"Anyway, I hired Josef in," Mick continued. "Took him away from his family again. His wife always hated me for that." He was silent for a moment. "We were watching the family when a Triad hit team tried to kill them. The assassins nearly killed their eight-year-old son."

Kylee listened intently, feeling even more guilt.

"The CIA wouldn't do anything about it," Mick said. "The boy was in the hospital. They didn't know if he was going to live or die. I went to Hong Kong, went after the Triad leader that had sent the hit team as a message. And I sent a message of my own. I killed him, and I killed eight of his people."

"And that's why the CIA put you on the black list?"

"Yeah. Turns out, the only guy their witness could testify against was the man I killed." Mick cleared his throat. "Josef stood by me, but it didn't do any good. We both had good records with the CIA. In the end, they pushed me out. Josef followed because he chose to. We've been putting together jobs we normally wouldn't have touched. Mainly just to keep his family financially afloat."

"And that's why you were working for Scherba?"

"Yeah. Until I got him killed."

"You didn't get him killed," Kylee said. "That was my fault."

He looked at her then. "Not your fault, Kylee."

"You were trying to protect me."

"Maybe. But my duty was to my principal, even though I thought he was the worst kind of slime. But even more than that, my duty was to my partner." His voice was ghost-thin, a shadow of anything she'd heard from him.

Feeling his pain so much, Kylee got up from the floor and walked over to him. She wrapped her arms around him, pulling him close.

He went stiff at first, then tried to push away from her. Kylee started to step back, then his arms swept around her with crushing intensity. She held on to him, and their mutual pain and guilt at surviving, the knowledge that they were going to risk their lives again in only a matter of hours, pulled them together.

Mick reached for her, cupping the back of her head in his big broad hands. She felt the calluses along his palms against her jaw, then she looked up at him and her breath caught in her throat as he leaned down to kiss her. That kiss transformed all those mixed feelings she'd been having into something totally different, into something so strong she couldn't ignore the pull.

She kissed him back, wrapping her arms around his neck and molding her body to his. She felt his hard chest against her breasts, felt her own reaction and desire building by the heartbeat.

His hands slid down her neck, across her shoulders and down her back. He cupped her bottom and pulled her to him, letting her feel the strength of his desire. Kylee pressed against him, feeling her body come alive with a rhythm of its own.

Mick broke the kiss and gathered her up in his arms. In three long strides, he carried her to the couch and gently placed her there.

Passion consumed Kylee's mind, pushing away any doubts she might have had. Her hands fumbled with her clothing and his, just as his did, both of them trying to undress each other as well as themselves. They never did quite get all of their clothing removed, but they got enough of it out of the way.

Kylee lay on her back, looking up at him as he drew back. He breathed in, rasping loudly. There didn't seem to be enough air in the room for both of them. Kylee knew she was breathing in gasps as well.

His shirt still on, but the buttons ripped away while her own turtleneck was pushed up so her naked breasts pressed against his chest, he looked down at her. "Are you sure?" he asked. His hard length lay against her tender flesh, so tantalizingly close that the sensation and the pulses of his own desire that shook him were nearly driving her crazy.

"Yes," she said hoarsely. "Yes, I'm sure." She reached down and took him into her hand, squeezing reassuringly to let him know what he was asking.

His fingers dipped into her, awakening her fully, arousing the molten core of her, feeling her own hunger trying to clasp and hold him. Then he removed his hand and grabbed a condom from his jeans, quickly sheathing himself before sliding his hips forward.

She matched his movement, felt his hardness push gently into her, penetrating her and stretching her. He went slow, trying not to hurt her, but her own wants drove her upward to spear herself on him.

He settled his hands on her hips, holding her tightly while he thrust into her fiercely. She met him, welding her own desires to his. Even when they fell off the couch, the hunger wouldn't be denied. Kylee rose above him, rising off him, then crashing back down, taking control of both their pleasures.

He reached up, taking her breasts in his rough hands, touching her nipples till they were hard points, then leaning up to kiss each one in turn. Without warning, Kylee hit her release, shuddering through it while he held her. He waited, raining kisses over her breasts and face. Then, when she could go on, she started the rhythm again and felt him surge against her till he filled her with his passion.

When he was spent, he turned her into his arms and cuddled her against him, letting her feel the hammerlike explosions of his heart inside his chest. To Kylee at that moment, it was the most comfortable and safest place in the world.

She kissed his face, and he rolled her over onto her back as he raised himself above her.

"Yes," she said, looking up into those cerulean-blue eyes.

"Yes," he agreed, and pressed into her again, finding the center of her even more deeply.

South of Prague, Krystof Scherba's castle stood on a promontory nearly two thousand feet up from the craggy rocks of the abbreviated bank fronting the Vltava River. The high stone wall, part of it hundreds of years old and part of it only dozens of years old, was topped by state-of-the-art sensors and alarms. A single road, covered in shale, wound up to the castle.

Impenetrable had come immediately to Kylee's mind when she'd first seen the structure.

That had been before Mick had told her about the old supply tunnel that led from the castle to the river. The tunnel had been built shortly after the castle had been constructed. According to Mick, a small docking area had once existed inside the mountain of rock. Boats traversed the river bringing supplies to and ferrying trade goods from the castle.

Now the supply tunnel was largely forgotten. Disuse and neglect had turned it into a warren for rats, bats, owls and slippery green slime that evidently got enough moisture from the nearby river to continue growing.

Also, despite the security improvements, the tunnel was largely unguarded. Nearly two hundred years ago, a group of pirates had penetrated the castle through the tunnel and took hostages that were later ransomed at great expense. As a result, the lord of the castle had ordered the tunnel mortared over.

During the short amount of time he had spent there, Mick had discovered that the tunnel led up to the wine cellar. Mick was certain the ancient mortar blocking the supply tunnel would give way easily. Once Scherba had returned to the castle, Mick had intended to rebuild a stronger wall over the tunnel. That hadn't happened, and the knowledge and Scherba's laxity now worked in their favor.

No one, to Mick's knowledge or the research available to Stony Man, had ever attacked Castle Creepstof. The cracker's wealth was all stored in Swiss and Cayman Island banks, or hidden between the cracks of cyberspace. Anyone breaking into the castle wouldn't have been able to get through Scherba's firewalls and encryption codes. Only the CD that Bethany Riggs had uncovered in Cape Town gave them the chance now.

Dressed in black jeans, a black turtleneck, and carrying a black backpack with everything Kylee hoped they would need, she followed Mick through the darkness. She and Mick both wore night-vision goggles from the cache of supplies at the safe house.

They had arrived outside the castle only a short time ago. Scherba remained on his boat, out of Mick's reach. He had been reluctant to let the man out of his sight, but Kylee had convinced Mick that getting into the computer system was the best revenge he could get for Josef.

They hadn't talked about what had passed between them, about the physical turn their relationship had taken.

It had been wonderful, but now Kylee felt somewhat guilty. She had taken advantage of Mick while he was vulnerable. Maybe they had taken advantage of each other.

Or maybe they had simply both been in the wrong place at the wrong time. Affairs happened like that, Kylee knew. She'd seen stars on movie sets through situations like that, and later regret it.

She didn't want to regret what they had shared. It had been wonderful. Even if, in the end, nothing came of it.

It was almost one in the morning. The day's exertions wore on her, and the last hours in the safe house hadn't exactly been restful. If it hadn't been for the adrenaline spiking her nervous system, she felt certain she'd be ready to collapse. Nine minutes after they'd begun their journey at the mouth of the cave that let out onto the Vltava River, they arrived at the plug of mortar and stone that blocked their way.

Mick, also dressed in a black turtleneck and jeans, looked like an alien insect in the night-vision goggles. The single monocular of the NVGs thrust out like a mosquito's proboscis. He wore a silenced Colt .45 in a shoulder rig and carried an H&K MP5 machine pistol favored by several special forces in armies around the world.

"Ready?" he asked, taking a short-hafted rockhound's pick and sledge from his backpack.

"Yes." Kylee took a sledge from her pack and stood on the other side of the mortared plug.

He swung the sledge.

The hollow boom of the sledge meeting the wall filled the tunnel, followed by echoing explosions that faded down the empty space below.

Kylee joined in, getting the timing immediately. Broken mortar dropped from the wall. The work was surprisingly easy, but the humidity trapped in the enclosed space was murder. In minutes, she was covered with perspiration and her breath began to drag through her lungs.

Mick Stone worked like a machine. Despite the damage he had taken at the hands of Creepstof Scherba's goons earlier, he seemed tireless and unyielding.

"Can your friend—" Mick asked as he swung "—still see inside the castle grounds okay?"

"Yes," Kylee answered, certain that was all she had the breath for after the long climb, despite her good physical conditioning.

"No Scherba?"

"No. Just the guards keeping the perimeter and inside grounds under observation."

Those security people remained with the castle at all times and were a risk, but if everything went right, they would never be encountered. Scherba's private quarters were off-limits to them.

A moment later, Mick waved her off. Kylee put her sledge down and rested as he inspected the damage they'd done. Her breath whistled against the back of her throat.

"We're through," he announced. "Let me have that crowbar."

Kylee passed him the crowbar from her pack.

Mick attacked the wall with renewed vigor. Chunks of mortar and rocks ranging from fist-sized to cantaloupe-sized dropped from the wall to their feet.

"We're leaving a mess," Kylee commented.

"Yeah, well they're going to know we were here anyway. As long as none of the guards decides to nip on down here for a bit of the grape with their tucker, we should be all right." Mick knelt and pulled stones out of the way.

Kylee joined him, shifting the rock and chunks of mortar back from the hole he had created.

Mick pulled his gloves on more tightly. "Not much head room, maybe, but I can get through all right." He squeezed through, duckwalking to avoid the low wall.

Kylee pushed his backpack after him, then passed the H&K MP5 to him. She shoved through her own backpack, then slipped through the opening. They took a moment to clean up the biggest part of the mess made by the forced entry, tossing the rocks and mortar through the hole in the wall.

"Good enough," Mick said. "As long as one of the guards doesn't come down here and walk around on this side of the shelves, he shouldn't notice anything."

Stray bits of broken mortar cracked under Kylee's feet as she followed Mick through the low, cavelike wine cellar, past the racks of bottles. He made no noise, moving as effortlessly as a big cat on ball bearings. He kept the silenced MP5 in one hand.

The castle was huge and drafty, and kept mostly in the dark except for a few security lights outside of rooms that weren't often used. Kylee was thankful for the flannels they both wore under their clothing. The trip along the river had been cold, but having to paddle in the dark for the last mile downriver to reach the castle had warmed them.

The wine cellar stairway let out into the spacious kitchen. Mick picked the lock and peered through, waving her up when he found the coast clear.

As they moved through the kitchen, Kylee planted a few of the F/X boxes from her backpack. Surprises for opponents always aided in get-aways. She also had some C-4 plastic explosive to add to the confusion if necessary. The plan was to come back through the tunnel quietly once Scherba's computer had been accessed with the encrypted disk.

From the kitchen, Mick led the way through a formal dining room that could have hosted a Shriners convention, then through the grand ballroom. Moonlight ignited at least a thousand points of light in the massive chandelier hanging from the tall ceiling nearly three stories up.

A curving staircase led up to the second story where Scherba's den-bedroom was supposed to be. Kylee followed Mick, aware of television noises farther down one of the main floor hallways.

Television noises meant some of the security personnel were nearby. But the thought only sent a thrill of electricity screaming through Kylee's senses.

Oh, Uncle Keiran, these throwback genes of ours are definitely going to get us killed one of these days. But the thought didn't even slow Kylee.

At the top of the stairs, Mick signaled Kylee back against the wall. In the next instant, she heard the scrape of shoe leather against stone that signaled the approach of a guard. The tinny sounds of a Walkman playing industrial music reached her ears as she flattened against the wall.

The man passed them, then some primitive sense seemed to call out a warning to him. He turned in their direction, his hand drifting down for the large pistol holstered on his hip.

Chapter 8

Mick moved out of the shadows like a wraith. The Y between the thumb and forefinger of his right arm caught the man in the throat and silenced the warning cry that had been about to erupt. Mick powered a left to the man's jaw and laid him out on the stone floor.

As the guard tried to get up, to get away, to draw the pistol from his holster and to breathe, Mick kicked him in the head. The guard fell. Before he could move again, Mick dropped a knee to the man's back and grabbed his head in both hands.

Kylee had seen the move in a number of action films and knew that Mick was about to break the man's neck and kill him. Nausea swirled through her stomach. Killing was a part of the spy business, but so far she had managed to stay away from most of it.

"No," she said.

Mick looked up at her. "Can't leave him behind."

"He's unconscious."

"No way of knowing how long he's gonna be unconscious, darlin'."

"Yes there is." Kylee took a tranquilizer pistol from her backpack and shot the man in the neck with a liquid hiss. "Six hours. We'll be in and out of here in that time."

Mick released the man's head and stood. The guard lolled, dead to the world. Grabbing the man around the chest, Mick hauled him to one of the bedrooms and shoved him inside.

"We're still operating on an unknown timetable," Mick reminded. "We don't know when this guy checks in with the standing post. He could have been on his way there now."

"Then we'll hurry," Kylee said.

Mick took the lead again.

"Oz," Kylee said.

"I'm here," Barbara replied. She was totally cool.

"Just checking."

"I've got your back," Barbara said. "As long as the communications are working, I'll be there for you."

Some of the tension in Kylee's stomach went away. Stony Man support had always been solid. Her adrenaline levels stayed peaked.

Creepstof Scherba's private chambers were covered in layered security locks and alarms. Thankfully none of the devices were time-coded, which would have provided an extra can of worms.

Still, penetrating that security took serious time and effort. Kylee worked calmly and quietly, focusing on the tools of the thieving trade, shifting from device to pliers to cutting torch as needed. The cutting torch stressed Mick the most because the concentrated flames and the cutting lit them up, making them easy to spot in the darkness.

"Mick," she said as she worked.

"Yeah."

"Where's the nearest smoke alarm?"

He was quiet for a moment. "Down the hall."

"Take it out before we trigger it." Kylee could have done the job herself in seconds, but she knew disabling the device would give Mick something to do instead of try to be patient.

Less than a minute later, he returned. "Done."

Nine minutes into the process, Barbara said, "Scherba is en route."

Kylee didn't pause. "Why?"

"I don't know."

"I didn't trip any alarms. You're tied in to the external warning lines, right?"

"You didn't trip any alarms."

"And if I had tripped something internally, the security on the premises would have been breathing down our necks by now." Kylee shifted back to the newest lock.

"Yes."

"It's a long drive from Prague," Kylee offered.

"He's not driving. He's flying. Remember the helicopter you encountered earlier?"

Kylee swore, drawing Mick's immediate attention. The castle had a helipad on top of one of the buildings. She brought Mick up to speed.

"Must be the computer," Mick said. "Maybe he doesn't trust the one you tampered with and he has a big deal coming up."

"How long before Scherba gets here?" Kylee asked.

"Twenty-two minutes. How long on the door?" Barbara asked.

"Fourteen. Fifteen. It's hard to say. Scherba didn't stint when it came to locking down his inner sanctum."

"Then you've got to use the disk and open a comm-link your friends can access."

"Yes." Kylee reached for the cutting torch again and saw Mick tense. "You did mention that this wasn't going to be easy."

"I did. But you're going to be cutting it close."

"Timing, Oz," Kylee said, feeling the adrenaline surge within her again. Now that the odds had stacked up against her, she felt even more excited by the op. "I've always told you timing was everything."

Fourteen minutes later, Kylee was through the final lock. She shoved her tools into the backpack and followed Mick inside.

The bedroom was opulent, furnished in expensive modern decor, including another round bed like the one on the catamaran. The computer station was to the right, filling the wall from floor to ceiling with peripherals. The ergonomic chair, wired for response to helicopter and fighter jet video games, listed for nearly ten thousand dollars.

"This guy takes his toys seriously, doesn't he?" Kylee asked.

"Yeah. Hold up." Mick crossed the room and disabled a laser light alarm that Kylee had already noted and that was on the Stony Man Intel Barbara had prepared. "Okay."

Moving quickly and confidently, Kylee sat in the chair at the computer, took out the encrypted disk, and brought the machine online. The monitor cleared while she was placing more F/X boxes.

"Scherba is three minutes out," Barbara stated.

"And the clock is ticking," Kylee said as she performed the keystrokes that brought the hidden OS online. "Got it."

Mick remained at her side, but she could feel the tension radiating off him and it jangled her nerves.

Kylee opened a phone line. "Okay, Oz, you should be in."

The monitor suddenly shifted to a database file-search screen. The cursor moved independently.

"If you're not in," Kylee said, "then we've got a ghost in the machine."

"We're in," Barbara said. "Let's see if it has what we're looking for."

A file lit up on-screen. The letters and numbers under the file shifted and changed, becoming "Egorov Last Rites."

"Is that it?" Kylee asked.

"Yes. You two should get clear."

"In a minute. Let's make sure you have what you need." Kylee looked up at Mick.

"We should be going," he said gruffly.

"We will." Kylee paused. "So which is it?"

"Which is what?"

"Boxers or briefs?"

For a second, just the barest hint of a second, tough guy Mick Stone looked embarrassed. Then he grinned. "Darlin', what if I told you I undressed to fit the occasion and went commando?"

"Then," Kylee said, feeling as though the room had warmed ten degrees, "I'd say you were probably really cold about now."

Before Mick could make a reply, the monitor cleared and a video presentation rolled. Kylee recognized Kapoch Egorov from the Stony Man files.

The Russian ex-spymaster turned international terrorist sat behind a large inlaid desk. Sunlight glowed against the windows behind him. He smoked a cigar, letting the blue-gray plume drift over his head.

"By now," he said in a gravelly voice, "reports of my impending death have doubtless circled the globe." He smiled without mirth. "Also doubtless, the majority of the world doesn't care."

"Oz," Kylee said, "are you doing this?"

"Negative. The program had a trigger on it we didn't catch. The second we opened the file, the presentation launched."

"Launched where?" A cold chill threaded down Kylee's back.

"Several places. We're trying to track them now."

On-screen, Egorov continued speaking. He leaned forward in his chair and his eyes took on a harsh hardness. "But the world will soon care. You will make them care, my friends and compatriots."

"Do you want me to shut it down?" Kylee asked. She checked the back of the computer and found the communications cable sheathed in steel coils.

"Too late," Barbara answered. "The transmission went out in a burst. What you're seeing is a playback. One of the bursts pinged Scherba's sat-phone e-mail. We were keeping his phone monitored for activity."

"So he knows we're here," Kylee said.

"He knows *someone* is there."

"Come on," Mick growled. "Time we were off, darlin'."

"During my years as a Soviet intelligence officer and those spent self-employed," Egorov said, "I have amassed a fortune. Now that I am dying, I sadly find that I can't take those riches with me." He smiled. "However, I have decided on a most unique memorial to me."

Hypnotized by the threat inherent in the man's words, Kylee watched.

"I have begun a money transfer from my hidden accounts around the world," Egorov went on. "During the next thirty days, there will be a contest. Every group or organization with an ax to grind against the United States or their European counterparts is encouraged to strike, to do their best to bring those countries to their knees. These people have hounded me for years. Now I will have my vengeance."

Kylee noticed that Mick was frozen at her side, his hand on her shoulder. But he was watching the screen as well.

"At the end of that thirty days," Egorov said, "an aide I have placed in charge of those monies will choose from among you a champion who has done the most to see that the so-called free world remembers me. The most destruction, the highest body count, the mass terror that is inflicted as a result of these attacks will be taken into account. The chosen champion will receive all those monies I have hidden away for so long. Use it to continue your own war against the United States and their allies. Use it with my blessing." He smiled. "And kill them all in the name of Kapoch Egorov."

The screen blanked.

"That son of a bitch is crazy!" Mick exploded. "Do you know what kind of mass murder this is going to cause?"

"Yes," Kylee said. "Exactly the kind that Egorov had in mind."

"*Move,*" Barbara said. "Scherba is landing *now.*"

Now that the computer speakers had quieted, Kylee heard the dulled throb of helicopter rotors through the thick castle walls. A heartbeat later, Klaxons shrilled throughout the structure. Emergency lights flared to life in the bedroom and the hallway outside.

"We're blown," Mick said. He brought the MP5 up in both hands. "Let's go."

"Oz?" Kylee said.

"We're downloading what we can get from Scherba's systems," Barbara said. "We'll do that till we're shut down. Go."

Hauling her backpack over one shoulder, Kylee stood and raced after Mick.

In the hallway, a man reached the top of the stairs and turned toward them with an AK-47 in his hands. A three-round burst from Mick's MP5 spilled the man back down the stairs.

"Guards have covered the lower floor," Barbara said.

At the same time, a hail of gunfire turned Mick back from the stairs.

"Crowded down there," he said. Blood shone on his left cheek where a bullet had narrowly missed splitting his skull.

Kylee relayed the message Barbara had sent.

"Looks like our back door is out," Mick stated grimly.

"The window." Kylee pointed at the window at the end of the hallway. "It overlooks the main grounds. We're only twenty, thirty feet up. We can jump."

"And then what?"

"There's a garage full of cars out there." Kylee raced to the window and yanked the drapes open, revealing the heavy steel bars.

"Well, that tears that," Mick growled.

Kylee reached into her backpack and took out some of the C-4. Expertly, she jammed the plastic explosives into place and inserted remote controlled detonators.

Mick kept the stairway clear with the MP5. Kylee

counted at least three men who had fallen to his skill with the machine pistol.

"Down," Kylee ordered, pressing herself against the wall with her back to the window. When Mick had hunkered down as well, she triggered the remote control.

The window blew out in a basso *Boom!* that ripped the bars from the mortar, shattered the glass, and shredded the drapes into flaming tatters.

Partially deafened from the explosion, Kylee rose and triggered the other F/X boxes she had throughout the castle. Maybe they wouldn't cut down on the number of people confronting them, but they would add to the confusion already in place in the castle, maybe split the security forces.

"Ready?" she asked Mick, yelling just to hear herself.

"As ever, darlin'," he replied, and he gave her a reassuring smile.

Burning drapes wreathed the window. Kylee ran forward, glanced down and found the grounds in front of the castle clear. With a lithe leap, she vaulted the window and dropped.

As soon as she touched the ground, she let herself roll. The backpack threw off her balance and she had to scramble to her feet instead of rolling up naturally. Mick landed beside her, reaching for her automatically, then seeing that she had managed on her own.

"The garage." Kylee pointed past the angel fountain that was the courtyard's centerpiece. Looking silver in the moonlight and golden where the high-intensity security lights hit it, water from an artesian well spewed from a cherub's mouth.

They ran.

Before they reached the freestanding garage that had housed horses and carriages in the past, the guards spotted them. Bullets chased them to the structure, then chopped into the stone as Kylee tried the door and found it locked.

She took a C-4 charge from her backpack, slapped it into place beside the lock and turned away to warn Mick. She touched the detonator and blew the lock to smithereens. When she looked back, the door stood ajar.

Trusting her gloves to hold for an instant against the superheated metal, Kylee grabbed the door and wrenched it open.

Emergency lights inside the garage illuminated a dozen expensive automobiles, SUVs and trucks. *Creepstof likes his automobiles, too.*

"See anything you like?" Mick asked as he reloaded the MP5 and the .45.

Kylee skipped the more expensive luxury cars like the BMWs and Mercedes coupe because they would have electronic keys. Those couldn't be hot-wired. Likewise for the upscale SUVs.

The blue-and-white 1965 mint-condition 427 S/C Cobra CSX3000 muscle car stood out like a mongrel at a poodle show. The sports car was a rugged two-seater that housed a 427 cubic-inch powerhouse of an engine. Low slung and equipped with a rear rollbar and side pipes, the Shelby Cobra looked like it was born to run, and it was.

"Yes," Kylee answered, smiling. Before she could move, a shadow shifted to her left.

The guard raised his Uzi.

"Gun!" Kylee yelled, and on the heels of that she heard another weapon open up behind her, letting her know the guard hadn't been the only one securing the cars.

She threw herself forward, hearing Mick's MP5 silenced stutter. The guard pointed his weapon at her as she kicked her feet out from under her like a baseball player stealing second.

Bullets cut the air over Kylee's head, then her feet cut the gunman's legs out from under him. He fell beside her, smacking face first against the stone floor. He shoved up and tried to bring his weapon up. Kylee met him with a right cross, putting all her weight and strength behind it.

His head turned and he dropped.

Pushing herself to her feet, she glanced up and saw that Mick was still standing, though he was bleeding profusely from a thigh wound. He'd never once moved, standing guard over her back.

"Let's go," he growled, staggering toward her.

Kylee slid out of the backpack, dropped it between the seats, then took out a Swiss Army knife. Reaching under the dash, she pulled out the ignition wires, bared them with the knife blade and touched them together.

Sparks jumped and the engine caught. The powerful V-8 rumbled like an impatient lion in the garage, filling the structure with its sound.

"Scoot over," Mick suggested, limping toward her.

Kylee looked at him. "Why don't you leave the driving to the professionals? That's where I'm leaving the shooting."

He grinned at her. "Okay then." He limped to the other side of the car and dropped into the seat.

Kylee pushed in the clutch, shoved the car into first and let the clutch out. The tires scalded the pavement as the Cobra leaped forward. She managed the tight turn and sped toward the garage door.

"Door's not open," Mick yelled above the engine roar.

"It will be," Kylee said.

Mick swore and took cover in the bucket seat.

Kylee reached to the sun visor and tripped the remote

control she'd spotted. The garage door opened smoothly just before they reached it. If the Cobra had been taller, the vehicle would never have cleared the door. She grinned as they slid through.

Two jeeps with armed men rocketed across the courtyard. Assault rifles spat muzzle flashes.

Foot heavy on the accelerator, Kylee sped toward both of them. Bullets screamed from the Cobra's rounded hood and trunk, punched a hole in the windshield.

Both jeep drivers pulled away from her, not wanting to follow through on the deadly game of chicken. Mick emptied the MP5 into one of the vehicles and it ran into the fountain only a short distance farther on, flipping over onto its side.

"The helicopter," Barbara warned over the earpiece.

From the corner of her eye, Kylee saw the helicopter lifting from the rooftop helipad. Everything in her screamed to get away.

The other jeep came around in a tight turn, staying in hot pursuit.

Kylee steered for the castle entrance, noticing at once that the big modern security gate was closed.

"I don't suppose the garage door widget works on that," Mick said as he reloaded the MP5.

Kylee tried. The gate remained in place. She brought the Cobra to a halt in front of the gate.

"I've got a garage door opener," she said. She shoved one of the remote detonators into a C-4 packet in the backpack, then threw the backpack at the bottom of the gate. Looking over her shoulder, she shoved the transmission into reverse and floored the accelerator.

The Cobra jumped backward, narrowly missing the oncoming jeep. The gunmen took cover, obviously fearing a collision. The jeep was at the gate when Kylee detonated the C-4 with the remote control

With the jeep parked nearly on top of it, the explosion lifted the jeep and the gunmen and threw them away, taking down the gate at the same time.

Kylee put the Cobra into forward gear and shot forward just as machine gunners in the helicopter opened fire into the ground where they'd been. She sped through the gate, but the helicopter pursued relentlessly.

The road twisted and turned like a broken-backed snake. Kylee pushed the envelope keeping the Cobra hurtling down the grade and clinging to the road without plunging over the side of the cliff. The mountain also provided partial cover at times.

"You can't outrun them," Mick shouted.

"I've got to," Kylee said.

He looked at her. "You can't get away from this one, Kylee."

"I can."

"Let me do this," he said. "I can do this."

"So can I."

"Maybe you can, darlin', but maybe you're going to be one turn shy before we reach bottom. I trusted you when I got into this car. Now I need you to trust me." Mick paused. "Stop the car."

Get away. Get away. Kylee heard the familiar voice chanting in the back of her mind.

The helicopter appeared over the mountain again, guns blazing. She turned quickly and it disappeared.

"Please, darlin'."

Reluctantly Kylee brought the Cobra to a stop, slewing around in a one-eighty that had brought them facing in the direction they had come.

Mick perched up on the seat, resting both arms over the windshield. The helicopter appeared an instant later.

Get away. Get away.

The helicopter gunners opened fire.

Coolly Mick waited.

Get away. Get away.

Kylee held steady as the helicopter closed on them. Twin rows of dust leaped up from the ground as the bullets slapped into the mountain.

Then Mick opened fire. Bullets tracked across the Plexiglas nose where the pilot was. Even at the distance, Kylee saw the man jerk back, saw Krystof Scherba scream in horror.

The helicopter fell over the side of the cliff and turned into a whirling orange and black ball of flame and smoke as it rushed like a fiery avalanche down the side of the mountain.

Mick sat back down in the seat. Pain racked his handsome face, but he smiled at her.

"Are you all right?" Barbara asked over the headset.

"We're fine," Kylee said, sitting in the moonlight as the castle streamed smoke above them. "Mission accomplished?"

"Mission accomplished," Barbara agreed. "Looks like you made one more get-away."

"I'll be in touch," Kylee promised.

Mick smiled at her. "You're a hero," he said.

She smiled again as if it was no big thing. "Again. If I can pull off the hang glider stunt they want for this movie, and chill my mom out about the whole spy business, I'm golden."

"You're already golden." Mick leaned in close and she knew he was going to kiss her.

Get away. Get away!

But she didn't move a muscle. The kiss was long and deep, satisfying in a way she had never felt before.

Mick pulled back after a time and looked surprised. "Not going to be the get-away girl?"

"We'll see," she replied, and ducked back in for another kiss. "We'll see."

*   *   *   *   *

END GAME

Virginia Kantra

* * *

For my daughter Jean, who has taught me so much
about kick-ass women with attitude.

Dear Reader,

One of the best parts of being a writer is the chance to immerse yourself in your characters, to get under their skins and into their hearts and minds. To be somebody else. To play pretend, with the certainty and enjoyment of a child.

While I was writing "End Game," I got to be beautiful, brainy, flamboyant agent Tory Grayson. It was quite a kick feeling like one of Charlie's Angels on a hot streak or a particularly intelligent Bond girl. And as if that wasn't reward enough, during the course of Tory's adventure, I also got to fall in love with Bishop Tyler, a man up to every challenge...including Tory.

I hope you have fun playing spies and lovers with me.

Virginia Kantra

Chapter 1

Of all the covert ops in all the towns in all the world, he had to walk into hers.

Victoria Grayson squinted across the sun-drenched courtyard. The pristine blue water was edged with exotic flowers and even more exotic guests. Light flashed from the men's watches and chains, gleamed from the oiled bodies of the women, sparkled on the waterfall—it was a fake, but it was a good fake—that anchored one end of the pool.

Her heartbeat quickened. She strolled to the lounge chair that held her sarong, trying to get a better look at the tall, lean man in the shadow of the palms.

DEA agent Bishop Tyler was the last man she'd expect to see as a guest at a drug lord's pool party.

The last man she wanted to see.

Which meant, the way her luck was running lately, that Mr. Shadow over there had to be him.

She knotted her orange sarong at her hip, her mind

racing. Maybe he wouldn't identify her? She had a different name, a different look, different hair color from the woman Bishop had known two years ago.

Yeah, and he hadn't missed a trick then, either, she thought gloomily.

Ducking her head, she watched him as she rubbed tanning oil on her chest, careful to avoid the heavy makeup under her jaw. She recognized the man's lean grace, his predatory profile, his utter stillness. It was definitely Bishop. She stroked oil on her upper arms, annoyed to notice her hands trembling.

Okay. This was not a disaster. She'd been undercover two years ago, too. Even if Bishop did connect spoiled socialite Tory Grayson with bad girl Angel Perez, her true identity, her real mission, weren't in danger.

Probably.

Yet.

But there was no denying Bishop's presence complicated a game that was hopelessly complicated already.

If he was a guest of Primo's, he was either dirty or he was undercover. She didn't think he was dirty. The man she remembered was as uncompromising as the desert and as solid as the mesas of his native New Mexico. He must be undercover.

This was her game, Tory reminded herself. Her move.

On the other side of the pool, Bishop slipped deeper into the cover of lush foliage. Her breath hissed in. If she didn't act quickly, she would lose him. Primo's Cayman Island estate was riddled with romantic, wandering paths designed for those guests who preferred to indulge their tastes for sex or drugs in semiprivacy.

She flipped the bottle of lotion onto the lounger and sauntered around the pool. *Queen to Bishop's four.*

"*Querida.*" A man's smooth, accented voice reproached her. "You are not running away so soon. The party is barely begun."

Check.

The voice, like everything else around her, belonged to Colombian financier Primo Valcazar.

Tory turned and flashed him her best gosh-I'm-glad-to-see-you-you-big-ol'-hunk-of-man smile. "I'll be right back," she said. She hoped. "I just have this one little thing to take care of first."

But Primo wasn't used to taking no for an answer. The man was confident. Maybe it was his looks and old-world charm. Maybe it was his money. Maybe it was the armed guards he'd posted around his estate.

"You could take care of me," he said.

"Oh, and I would love to," Tory cooed. Was she laying it on too thick? But no, Primo was nodding, apparently convinced that he was irresistible and she was dumb as a rock. "Only this is one of those things that really can't wait."

Primo looked blank.

"It's a girl thing." Tory couldn't quite manage a blush, but she lowered her eyes and her voice. "You know."

And Primo, bless his Latin American macho horror of feminine complaints, stepped back at once. "Of course," he said formally. "I will see you later, *querida*."

"Later," she promised, and bolted after Bishop in her three-inch, gold-tone pool sandals.

But the DEA agent had disappeared.

The graveled walk didn't even yield a footprint, she thought in disgust. That shot of color was only a hibiscus, trailing scarlet blooms across the path. That flash of movement was only a bird with a long brown tail and yellow eyes, darting from branch to branch. The tinkle of water and trickle of conversation floating from the pool behind her masked all sound.

Tory stopped, her three-inch spikes sinking into the gravel, and eyed the deep green foliage all around in frustration.

"Damn it," she muttered.

"I see your taste in boyfriends hasn't improved any," drawled a deep male voice behind her.

Her heart hurtled into her throat. She knew that voice. At one time, she thought she knew that man. Enough to give him her trust. Enough to give him her heart.

Now, of course, she knew better.

She turned slowly, cocked her hip, angled her chin and prayed he wouldn't notice the betraying beat of her pulse in her throat. Or the tightening of her nipples under her skimpy bronze bikini top. Or any of the other stupid physical reactions she couldn't control in his presence.

Bishop Tyler. He overwhelmed her. Still. Some of it was sheer size. He was six feet four—a disadvantage, he'd confessed to her once, when he was working undercover and trying to blend in. He was undercover now in a dark suit and a matching T-shirt, kind of a *Miami Vice* noire look. His hair was black. His skin was bronze, a legacy of his Native American grandmother. His eyes were black as anthracite. He stepped out of the green shadows by the side of the path like a Navajo warrior emerging from the mists of time or the pages of a romance novel and made her little heart go pitter-pat.

She smiled politely. "Excuse me. Do we know each other?"

His eyes glittered with black humor. "Nice try, Angel."

"The name's Victoria Grayson." That much, at least, was true. "Tory to my friends."

"I'm not a friend," he said flatly.

That hurt. She was surprised how much.

"No," she agreed coolly. "You're not."

"You remember, then."

"I remember some things."

"I remember." His dark gaze met hers. "Everything."

Oh, my. Her stomach jolted.

She tossed her head. "I suppose being left handcuffed to the flagpole in front of your department's regional headquarters would be memorable."

"Oh, yeah. And if I forget," he added wryly, "I have plenty of colleagues who still salute when they see me."

A bubble of laughter rose in her throat. She swallowed hastily. She could not afford to laugh. She could not afford to like him.

"Why did you do it, Angel?" Bishop asked.

All laughter died.

"You were going to arrest me for killing Guerrero." The heroin trafficker they had both been after when they'd met.

Bishop looked down his blade of a nose at her. "I hadn't decided yet what to do about Guerrero's murder."

"Oh, and I was supposed to stick around while you made up your mind?"

"You shouldn't have jumped into action without thinking things through."

She would have died before admitting his criticism hurt. "Funny, that wasn't an issue when Guerrero had his gun to your head."

"Which brings us back to your lousy taste in boyfriends."

She set one hand on her hip. "Are we talking about Guerrero now? Or you?"

"I'm talking about Valcazar. He's a dangerous man, Angel."

"It's Tory. And I can handle Primo."

"The way you handled Guerrero?"

She shivered. Despite her line of work, she was not a killer. She'd been recruited for her skills as a hacker, not her facility with guns.

"Yeah, that's what I thought," Bishop said. "Go home, Angel. Or Tory. Or whatever the hell your name is. You don't have any business messing with a man like Valcazar."

She did, actually. Because Valcazar's name had turned up recently in files recovered by Tory's fellow operative Kylee Swain. In addition to laundering money for the Colombian drug cartels, Primo Valcazar was now managing the fortune of dying arms smuggler and international terrorist Kopach Egorov. When Egorov croaked, his illegal millions could go to fund other terrorist groups. Unless Tory could access Valcazar's accounts and find and freeze Egorov's legacy.

None of which she was about to explain to Mr. Self-Righteous from the DEA.

She tilted her head. "What are you going to do about it? Arrest me?"

"I'd like to," Bishop growled. "But the Caymans belong to the U.K. I don't have jurisdiction here."

She knew that. It was one of the reasons her team had been called in. The agents for Stony Man Farm operated without respect for jurisdiction. It was a good thing, she sometimes thought, they were the good guys. But she wasn't sure Bishop would see it that way.

"So you can't make me leave."

He crossed his arms against his broad chest. "Maybe

I'll warn Valcazar your boyfriends have a tendency to wind up dead.''

"Or handcuffed."

But she'd underestimated her man.

"I'd be willing to try the handcuff thing again," Bishop said. "At a more appropriate time and in a less public place."

Oh, wowee.

The garden wheeled and righted itself like a spinning telescope with Bishop at its center. She was intensely, unbearably, focused on him. The details of his face were sharpened and magnified: the harsh cast of his cheekbones and the tiny white lines at the corners of his eyes, the suggestion of roughness at the edge of his jaw and the smooth brown skin of his throat. Her heart drummed. His eyes darkened.

He took a step toward her. "Angel—"

"You have to leave," they both said at the same time.

Her mouth dropped open.

Bishop glared. "I'm not going anywhere. I've got things to do here."

"So do I."

"What? Score a few lines? Notch a few bedposts? You can do better than that."

She couldn't blame him for supposing she was here to trade sex for drugs. She'd worked very hard to create that impression. The last time they'd met she'd been posing as Guerrero's girlfriend. Given her cover, she should be touched that Bishop even cared what happened to her. But his patronizing attitude pissed her off.

And his presence still compromised her mission. What if his activities aroused Primo's suspicions? What if his attempts to protect or reform her got her kicked out before she hacked her way into Primo's computers? Why hadn't

Barbara Price, Stony Man's mission controller, warned her the DEA was conducting an operation in the Caymans?

"You have no idea what I can do," Tory said, and pivoted on her three-inch heels and stalked away.

"Angel. Tory!" Bishop called softly after her.

She didn't look back. She quickened her stride until she was almost running, stumbling down the gravel path. Heart pounding, chest heaving—she glanced down to check the effect—face attractively flushed, she burst onto the sun-drenched patio around the pool.

"A man!" she cried. "In the bushes! Help!"

There were men around the pool: guests in silk shirts and gold chains who smelled like musk and money, and bodyguards with thick necks and thicker arms who wore jackets despite the heat. Her cry shattered the scene like a stone. The guests scattered like carp. The guards drew guns and sprinted up stairs, dashed down paths and muscled into the shrubbery.

Jeez. She didn't want Bishop shot. She just wanted him gone. She screamed again, to warn him.

One of the male guests, a big blonde with a square red face, patted her arm comfortingly. "Do not worry. Primo has excellent security. They will catch your man in the bushes."

Tory smiled wanly. She hoped not.

"Did you perhaps see his face?" persisted her comforter. He had a slight European accent. German, maybe, or Austrian. "Did you recognize him?"

Tory shook her head. If Bishop was identified as DEA, Primo's men wouldn't just rough him up and toss him out. They'd kill him.

The possibility froze her deep inside.

"You are distressed," the German said.

Well, yeah. She strained to hear shouts or gunshots, for some clue that Bishop had either been captured or had gotten away.

"Is there anything I can do? Anyone, perhaps, whom I can get for you? A special…friend staying with you?"

Oh, oops. His slight hesitation tripped her alarms. The friendly German wanted to know who she was sleeping with.

Adrenaline thawed her brain, warmed it into working again. It was like a game. A chess game, with the ending dependent on the opening moves. She had to find an opportunity, an in, a weakness in her opponents' position, to win.

She didn't trade sex for drugs. She didn't trade sex for anything. But she desperately needed access to Primo's computers and for that she needed an entrée to his house. Playing a beautiful, bored, rich young woman with a drug habit had gotten her invited to his party. But was it enough to let her stay?

"Miss Grayson is here as my guest," Primo interrupted. "And I am desolate that her visit has been disturbed."

Tory brightened. Desolate was good. She could work with guilt.

"Oh, Primo," she sighed, and turned to him in not-entirely-feigned relief. "I was so scared."

Primo put his arm around her, a possessive move that didn't escape the German. "Don't be, *querida*. This intruder will not trouble you again."

"You caught him?" She didn't have to fake the tremor in her voice.

Primo frowned. "No. But my men assure me he has left the grounds. One of them saw him go over the wall."

So Bishop was safe. Gone.

Good.

She tried to feel happy about that, but the truth was it was no easier now than it had been two years ago.

Get your head in the game.

"Thank you, Primo." She rested her forehead on his shoulder—a bit of a feat, since she was five feet eleven and wearing three-inch heels, but she managed it. "I feel so safe here. Not like at the hotel."

Way to be obvious, Tory.

He stroked her back. "You are not comfortable at the Meridian?"

The Meridian was a millionaires-only resort on prime island real estate. Barbara Price had booked Tory's room to support her pose as a wealthy good-time girl. It had been nice for the day or so it lasted. But now Tory waved all that luxury away with a flutter of her manicured nails.

"It's comfortable, I guess. But it's kind of lonely. And, like, boring, you know?"

She peeped at Primo through her lashes to see how he was taking this.

Pretty well, apparently. His face had the sleek, satisfied look of an overfed cat. His hand slid down to cup her bottom. Creep. She resisted the urge to stamp her heel into the arch of his foot.

"A beautiful woman should not be lonely," he said solemnly.

Oh, please. Who wrote his dialogue? Jerks-R-Us?

"Perhaps you would permit me to send one of my men to fetch your bags from the hotel," he continued. "Here you will be safe and entertained."

Entertained? Oh, yeah, absolutely. She always found it entertaining to break into the private office of a Colombian drug cartel financier so that she could use his personal computer to evade his system's security.

Safe? She wasn't so sure.

"You are so nice to me, Primo. But—" Tory raised her head from his shoulder. "You will understand if I'm not, uh, real good company for a day or two?"

Primo's handsome face clouded. "I do not understand."

She put her lips close to his ear. The German was still watching them, his smile indulgent, his eyes cold.

"My 'girl thing,'" she whispered. "Remember?"

Primo's arm dropped from around her waist. But Tory was betting now that he had invited her to stay, in front of another man, he would let it stand. Heck, he had enough bedrooms.

"You must still be my guest," he said politely. "We will find some other entertainment until you are...well."

She felt a flash of triumph. She was in.

She hadn't changed.

Spread-eagled against the red tile roof like a captive staked to an ant hill, Bishop watched as Angel—Victoria, she called herself now—flirted and fanned herself in the courtyard below. The sun beat down. The tiles scorched his skin. He burned from a combination of sun and need, of anger and admiration and lust.

She hadn't changed at all.

Oh, her hair was different, auburn and wavy instead of black and straight, and her name was different, and she'd done something mysterious to her face in the way that women did to change the emphasis of her eyes and lips.

But those eyes were the same, bright and sharp as a copper knife. The mouth was the same, lush and tasty. The take-me body, the screw-you attitude...oh, yeah, she was the same woman, all right.

She could still make him want her with a look. Hell,

she didn't even have to look. All she had to do was breathe. All she had to do was stand there, breathing, to make him want her so bad he ached.

He wasn't the only one, either. Valcazar had his hands all over her.

Bishop's gut knotted. He told himself it didn't matter. Tory didn't want his protection, and Valcazar was a dead man anyway.

But whatever his mind told him, his gut wanted her away from here. And his heart—his stubborn, stupid heart—just wanted her. She was a lying, amoral, opportunistic survivor who had saved his life and betrayed his trust, and he wanted her.

Bishop laid his face against the red clay tiles and burned.

Chapter 2

Apparently the slut suite came with its own bathroom. Thank God.

Tory kicked her sandals off by the door and padded barefoot over the thick white carpet. She passed her matched and monogrammed luggage, parked neatly at the foot of the all-white bed. Long white draperies stirred over open white shutters at the tall French windows. Even the furniture was painted white and gold. Yuck. All the white in the world couldn't disguise that the place was built with drug money. Blood money.

Her skin crawled. She wanted a shower. She tugged the bathroom door shut behind her and turned on the light. Her reflection sprang at her from the mirror over the sink.

She jumped. Jeez. She wasn't usually this edgy on a job. The encounter with Bishop had rattled her more than she wanted to admit.

Sliding two fingers beneath the edge of her bronze bikini top, she drew out her personalized cocaine pipe.

She'd told an amused and indulgent Primo that she didn't like to share. But the tiny pipe was more than a party girl's expensive affectation. Because, in addition to the pretty gold plate and the diamonds that winked on the side, her pipe had other special features: a hidden button that sucked in the fine white powder and an internal compartment that held the drug so it never entered her system.

She depressed another diamond on the side of the pipe, opening the secret compartment, and shook a single line of coke—with a twenty-five-dollar street value, courtesy of her friendly host—into the toilet.

"I've seen drugs dumped like that before," a deep voice observed behind her. "But in my line of work, they're usually wrapped in plastic."

Her heart jumped. Her hand tightened on the slender gold pipette. Slowly she straightened and met the dark, sardonic gaze of Bishop Tyler reflected in the mirror above the sink.

He was safe. Relief sang through her veins. That was good.

He was here. That was bad.

And he'd just watched her lose a thirty-minute high down the toilet, which was going to be very hard to explain.

"I thought you were gone," she said.

He pushed aside the white shower curtain and stepped out of the deep claw-foot tub. Too tall. Too close. "Obviously."

She backed into the sink. He followed. Her toes curled into the cool tile. She wished, now, she hadn't kicked off her heels at the door. She'd always needed every inch, every advantage, she could take against Bishop.

She straightened her spine. "What are you doing in my room?"

"Hiding."

"Bad idea. I called the guards on you once already, cowboy."

"But you didn't tell them who I am."

He loomed over her, tall and unfathomable, staring down at her with those hot, dark eyes.

"So?" she asked. Not a particularly clever reply but certainly smarter than *Take me,* which was the only other response that popped into her brain.

"So." His warm breath skated across her face. "I figured maybe you'd decided to feel sorry for me."

She'd never met a man who needed a woman's pity less. "Wrong. I thought you'd be out of here by now."

"I'm remarkably hard to get rid of."

"I remember," she said.

"Do you? What else do you remember, angel?"

Too much. Too well. Her breathing hitched. "I remember you think I'm a cokehead slut with homicidal tendencies."

"Maybe I was wrong."

She tossed her head. "If you were, you wouldn't admit it."

"A cop who ignores the evidence is a bad cop. Why did you ditch the coke down the toilet, angel?"

"I don't know what you're talking about."

She almost groaned. That was so lame. His nearness must be short-circuiting her brain cells.

"Your pipe." He plucked it from her fingers and turned it over in his hands. "It's clever. Where did you get it?"

The pipe had been developed for her in the Stony Man labs, but she couldn't tell him that. The problem with working for a supersecret government agency was that it was supposed to *stay* secret, even from other agencies of the same government.

She shrugged. "I picked it up a while ago. Does it matter where?"

"I haven't decided yet." He handed the pipe back to her. "Why didn't you tell Primo I'm DEA?"

She widened her eyes in fake surprise. "You mean he doesn't know?"

One corner of Bishop's mouth quirked. "If you keep answering all my questions with questions, this is going to be a real short conversation."

"Okay by me. You're the one who wants to talk."

"You don't want to talk?" His voice was husky. Low.

Her body hummed. Maybe their closeness got to him the way it got to her. Maybe he was remembering the way it had been between them.

Or maybe he was just making sure they weren't overheard by one of the brute squad in the hall.

Tory stuck out her chin. "Not unless you're going to tell me what you're doing here."

"Good," Bishop said. "Because I don't want to talk either."

She was staring him straight in the eye. So she couldn't pretend later, even to herself, that she didn't see the kiss coming.

She saw. His eyes darkened. His gaze dropped to her mouth.

He moved in on her slowly, leaning his weight on the sink behind her, trapping her between his lean, hard arms and his hot, hard body.

She had the time and the training to evade him. She wasn't an expert at hand-to-hand combat like her fellow operative Bethany Riggs or a stuntwoman like Kylee Swain, but she could shoot and gouge, kick and claw. After she'd been recruited by Stony Man, Barbara Price had seen to it that Tory had the skills she needed to survive in the field. She could protect herself.

Against any man but Bishop Tyler.

Bishop was prepared for her to resist. Whatever he knew of her past—*You think I'm a cokehead slut with homicidal tendencies*—he didn't really believe that after two years she'd let him break into her room, barge into her life and stick his tongue down her throat without some kind of protest.

She surprised him. She'd always been able to surprise him. It was one of the things that drew him to her, and one of the reasons he distrusted her.

He kissed her with his eyes open. He wanted to see her face. He wanted to gauge her reaction. Was she the woman he remembered? But up close, the details blurred. She smelled different, a combination of tanning oil and some musky scent Angel Perez could never in a million years afford.

But the feel of her was the same—sleek and lush. Her mouth was the same—full and soft. The taste of her was gloriously familiar, shockingly hot.

When he took her mouth the second time, she opened to him like she was welcoming him home.

Her strong, smooth arms slid around his shoulders. Her generous breasts pressed his chest. He skimmed his hands up her nearly naked back, her skin warming his palms like heated silk. Her fingers stroked his nape.

And then she reached into his hair and tugged, hard.

Frustration speared him. But it was loss that hollowed his chest; regret that roughened his voice.

He raised his head. He was breathing hard. "What?"

"I don't want this."

Yes, she did. She was breathing hard, too. He noticed and was glad.

"A cop who ignores the evidence is a bad cop," he reminded her. "Your face is flushed."

She glared at him. "Too much sun."

"Your pupils are dilated."

"Too much coke."

"I saw you dump your drugs down the toilet. You want this, angel. You want me."

"I don't have time for you," she said.

His temper lit. "In a hurry to get back to Valcazar?"

She didn't hit him, as he expected and perhaps deserved. She went rigid in his arms. "Actually, I am. He's expecting me to come down for dinner."

"Are you going to do everything he expects you to do?"

Her eyes glittered. With tears? Or fury. "I do what I have to. I do my job."

Realization seeped into him like water soaking into sand.

"What is your job, angel?" he asked quietly.

Her mouth tightened as she realized her slip. Too late. She pushed at his shoulders.

He let her go but repeated his question. "What is your job? You're not DEA. If you were local law enforcement, you wouldn't be outside the country. What are you? FBI? CIA?"

She thrust her tumbled hair behind her ears in a quick, defensive gesture. "Oh, please. Do I look like a spook in a suit to you?"

"No, you don't." She looked exotic. Angry. Apprehensive. "Interpol?"

"You're crazy. Or smoking something from your last bust." She pulled a thick white towel from its metal bar and wrapped it around her body. "I have to shower."

He crossed his arms and propped against the door. "Go ahead."

"Without an audience," she said through her teeth.

"How about someone to scrub your back?"

"I do fine on my own," she told him, and he was pretty sure she wasn't just talking about her shower. "Beat it, cowboy."

If he left her alone, he could search her luggage. He shrugged.

"Suit yourself," he said, and strolled out.

Tory sagged.

This was going amazingly badly. She had hours—at the most, days—to find Primo's office, install a port on his computer that would allow her access to his accounts, and establish a connection between the drug lord's fortune and Egorov's terrorist network.

Most cracking—breaking into a computer system—was not the result of programming genius or computer wizardry. Usually it was a simple matter of persistence and the plodding repetition of a number of tricks that exploited common system weaknesses. It took time and concentration. And Bishop Tyler was diverting her time and destroying her concentration.

Tory rattled the shower curtain closed and cranked the faucet. She needed to get in touch with Barbara Price. Maybe Stony Man's mission controller could pull some strings to get Bishop recalled to the States. At the very least, she could tell Tory what the DEA agent was doing in the Cayman Islands.

Tory dropped her towel and her clothes and stepped under the water. Unfortunately, the transmitter-receiver earplugs Barbara used to communicate with her operatives in the field were currently masquerading as a pair of big gold earrings at the bottom of Tory's suitcase. She hadn't dared risk wearing transceivers to a pool party. Besides, if Primo ever got close enough to stick his tongue in her ear, he would have noticed them. So until Tory dressed for dinner, she was flying blind and solo.

She wrapped herself again in the towel and squeezed her hair over the sink. Straightening, she scowled at her reflection, at her straggling hair and scrubbed face and the faint scarlet lines under her jaw. Despite several successful surgeries, the scars would never completely disappear. A makeup therapist at the burn center had taught her to mask them. But her makeup bag was in her suitcase, along with her hair dryer and clean underwear.

She didn't want Bishop to see her like this. She didn't want to display her scars any more than she wanted to reveal her identity.

Tory stuck out her tongue at the mirror and felt absurdly cheered.

"You're over it," she told her reflection. "You're over him."

Her reflection stared back at her with troubled eyes and didn't say a word.

Tory pulled her hair forward to hide her scars, secured her towel more tightly over her breasts and sauntered out to battle.

He wasn't there.

Tory scanned the empty white room. What a relief. What a…disappointment.

And then Bishop slid from behind the open wardrobe door and glided to the center of the thick carpet. Against the backdrop of the white, feminine room, he looked big and dark and dangerous. Her heart stuttered.

"You can knock off the silent Indian scout routine," she said crossly. "I'm not impressed."

Black laughter leaped in his eyes. "Tell me what would impress you."

She would have cut out her own tongue first. Because the truth was, he had always impressed her. In the shifting shadow lands of covert ops, Bishop stood like a mountain, strong and uncompromising. His integrity was one of the things that made him so attractive.

And so dangerous. Because what she was about to do violated numerous national laws and several international agreements.

She arched her brows. "You want to impress me? How about you turn your back while I put on some clothes?"

"I've seen you naked," he reminded her softly.

Yes. The memory shivered through her. She tucked her hands into her armpits so he wouldn't see them tremble.

"Two years ago," she said. "And it was dark."

His gaze remained fixed on her face, probing, burning. "Both times?"

"Yes!" she snapped, and then flushed, realizing what she had revealed. She remembered. Every detail. *Both times.*

He held her gaze until the blood drummed in her ears. Without a word, he turned his back and stared at the long windows on the opposite wall.

Tory drew a shaky breath. Clothes, she ordered herself. Now. Move.

Hurriedly she hauled a suitcase onto the white bedspread, unlocked and unzipped it. For a second she frowned at the contents, tissue-thin fabrics in violent colors. She'd chosen her underwear this time around to provide herself with cover, not coverage. But it couldn't be helped now. She grabbed a handful of flame-colored silk.

Half-crouched behind her open suitcase with one eye on the back of Bishop's black head—she wasn't leaving him to search through her scanties while she went into the bathroom to dress—she stepped into her panties, shed the towel and fastened her bra in front. It was like getting dressed in gym class. She'd always hated gym class.

She pulled her bra straps onto her shoulders and adjusted herself into the cups. At least in gym class she hadn't had to worry about exposing herself to a hard-headed, soft-spoken cowboy who'd once threatened to arrest her for murder.

She dropped her red dress over her head, wiggled it past her hips, patted and tugged it over her breasts.

With a sigh of relief, she unlocked the second suitcase to retrieve her makeup and jewelry bags. Turning back to the mirror, she applied cosmetics with a quick, practiced hand: first the green-tinted base that masked her scars and then a light foundation and then her party face. She pursed bright red lips at the mirror. Almost done. All she needed was...

She untied the pretty fabric bag that held a tangle of bright chains and shiny earrings. Watch, yes. Necklace, got it. All she needed was—

She frowned, poking through the glittering pile with her finger. They were here. They had to be here. Panic skittered under her skin. Silly. They were right— She patted another pocket, ran her fingers along a seam.

Where were they?

"Looking for these?" Bishop drawled.

Her stomach sank. She met his eyes in the mirror for a long, significant moment before she turned.

He held out his hand. Winking in the center of his palm were two big gold earrings.

She took a step forward.

He closed his hand. "Are they yours?"

Don't overreact. She moistened her lips. Flashed him

a smile. "Since you got them out of my bag, I'd be a fool to say no, wouldn't I? Besides, they match my dress. May I have them, please?"

He didn't withdraw his hand, but he didn't open his fingers, either. "Where did you get them?"

"They were a gift."

"Who gave them to you?"

She tilted her head. "Jealous, cowboy?"

"Suspicious."

"It's because of your job," she told him. "It makes you suspect everybody."

"Actually, it's because of yours. And this." He nudged one of the earrings with his thumb, flipping it to expose the back—the open back, with the transceiver inside.

Okay, this was bad, she thought, staring down at his palm. How bad? How did she make it better?

"I can see that brain of yours working from here," he said softly. "Why don't you make it easy for both of us and tell me the truth?"

She took a deep breath. "What do you want to know?"

"I want to know what you're doing here."

"You've already made up your mind about that. 'Score a few lines, notch a few bedposts.'" She bared her teeth in a smile. "Remember?"

"I was wrong about you," he said. "You're not what you seem."

His admission might possibly have made her feel better. If she'd thought for a minute that he believed it. Or if she believed it herself.

"Very nice," she said. "But it doesn't matter. I used to be."

He frowned, genuinely puzzled. "Used to be what?"

A cokehead slut.

She shook her head. "It doesn't matter," she said

again. "I have to go. Primo is expecting me. May I have my earrings, please?"

Silently he gave them to her.

She clicked her tongue over the broken back. "Didn't your mommy teach you to be careful when you played with other kids' toys?"

"I'll buy you a new one," he offered. "If you tell me where you got it."

"Nice try, cowboy." She bent the seal back in place with her fingernail. That should hold the transceiver. Now if only it worked...

She really needed to talk to Barbara.

"You're thinking again," Bishop observed.

Tory flipped back her hair and inserted an earring. "You have a problem with women who think?"

"Only when they let emotion cloud their judgment."

She tilted her head to fasten the other earring. "You still haven't forgiven me for that flagpole thing, have you?"

He leaned a shoulder against the wall, regarding her in the mirror. "Is that why you did it? You figured if I couldn't forgive you, I wouldn't follow you?"

Her hand jerked and she poked the back of her earlobe. "Ouch."

"The truth hurts, doesn't it, angel?"

"That wasn't the truth," she said coldly. "It was my earring."

Bishop met her eyes in the mirror and smiled, knowing and slow. As if he really saw her and liked what he saw. Tory's heart beat faster.

Stupid. All he saw was an image of her.

And that was all she was going to let him see.

She combed her still damp hair with her fingers and turned. "How do I look?"

Her challenge sizzled the air and fired Bishop's blood like lightning on a summer plain.

Her red dress was cut high and low, revealing too much leg, too much breast, too…much. She looked magnificent. Staggering. Like a barbarian queen who accepted blood sacrifices. Hell, if she asked him, he'd open a vein himself.

And she was going downstairs in that dress to let Primo Valcazar put his murdering hands all over that smooth, soft, golden skin….

Bishop's gut formed a quick, hard knot.

"Those your working clothes?" he asked.

If his reaction offended her, she didn't let it show.

"Yes," she said. "Don't wait up for me."

And she was gone.

Chapter 3

"**Y**ou didn't tell me when you recruited me for this job that I'd be spending all my time in the bathroom," Tory said wryly to mission controller Barbara Price. After dinner, she'd holed herself in Primo's elegant first-floor powder room to make her sit rep—situation report.

"Is your location a problem?" Price's calm voice was only slightly distorted by the loss of one transceiver. Bishop's tampering had apparently broken more than the back.

Tory cupped her hand over her remaining earring. "Not at the moment. Tell me where I'm going."

"Valcazar's private office is on the second floor of the east wing at the end of the corridor."

Tory sat on the edge of the closed toilet seat. "Access?"

"The French doors to the balcony on the courtyard side of the building are double-locked," Price said. "Much too time-consuming. And they're visible from the guard post in the garden. Your best chance is the door leading from the second-floor hallway. There's also a connecting door through his personal suite.''

''Bedroom?''

''Bathroom.''

''Well, that's something,'' Tory muttered.

''Is the bedroom a problem for you?'' Price inquired.

Tory fluffed the ends of her hair. ''Are you asking about my sex life, Barbara?''

''I'm asking if you can handle Valcazar.''

''I can handle him. I just don't want to wake him up when I break into his office.''

''Which you will do tonight.'' Price's statement was carefully balanced between order and question.

''I've got to, don't I?'' Tory said, and her question wasn't a question at all. ''Unless you've managed to access his accounts from your end.''

''Tokaido is working on it,'' Barbara Price said. ''He's doing a data search of all six major clearing banks in the Cayman Islands.''

''I thought Valcazar's accounts are legally protected in the Caymans.''

''They are. But if we can trace the money back to Egorov, a known terrorist, we have the go-ahead to seize or freeze it clandestinely. Assuming you can get behind the firewall Valcazar installed on his own system.''

Tory made a face at the gilded cherub floating at the top of the mirror frame. ''No pressure, though, right?''

''Not unless you consider that if you can't identify and isolate Egorov's millions before they're integrated into the world markets, the fallout of his financial empire could go to fund literally hundreds of terrorist cells and splinter groups.''

Tory's stomach hollowed. "Gee, I'll try to remember that."

"Is there anything I can do to help?"

"Now she asks," said Tory. "Yeah, can you get the DEA to suspend their operation here until I'm in and out?"

Her transceiver was silent. Tory tugged her earlobe. "Hello?"

"Stony Base here. Can you repeat, please?"

"The DEA. They have an agent on the inside. I want to close down the Colombians as much as anybody, but I don't want this guy to spook Primo. Or get in my way."

"The DEA is not conducting an operation in the Caymans."

"They're not after Primo?"

"I didn't say that," Price corrected her. "Valcazar was implicated in the death of one of their agents two weeks ago. Certainly they want him. But as long as Valcazar stays off American soil, any investigation has to be co-ordinated through international law enforcement and his host country."

"Well, maybe somebody forgot to tell them that, because they definitely have a man here. Bishop Tyler. Used to be in the El Paso field division."

"I remember Agent Tyler." There was a new note in Barbara Price's voice, aware, amused. "He was the agent in charge when you ran the Guerrero sting."

Tory squirmed. She sometimes thought Stony Man's mission controller was all-seeing and all-knowing. It was too much to hope that the handcuff incident had escaped her notice. Tory could only pray that Price hadn't also picked up on how swiftly and how hard one of her key female operatives had fallen for a cowboy from another agency. "Right. Anyway, could you find out what he's doing here, please? And tell Tokaido to be ready. I'll open the port tonight.''

She should be back by now.

Bishop's jaw clenched. The back of his neck throbbed with tension.

Don't wait up for me.

Hell. He was good at waiting. His job demanded it. He'd used the time to search her room for bugs and cameras, to search her luggage for false bottoms and high-tech toys. The room was clean. The larger suitcase had a slim-line computer, similar to a Toshiba mini laptop, sewn behind the lining of the side. He was impressed with both the gadgetry and the hiding place. He'd almost missed it, and he was a pro.

Which meant that she was...

Trouble.

He had enough doubts about what he was doing here. He didn't need a distraction, too.

Fists in his pockets, he stared through the slats in the white louvered windows at the darkened courtyard. The decorative torches around the perimeter had almost burned out. At three in the morning, Primo's party was finally winding down.

A solitary waiter, his shoulder holster spoiling the fit of his white jacket, lounged against the empty bar. A lone swimmer—male, blond, fiftyish—plowed doggedly through the pool, his body silhouetted by the underwater lights. A guard with a Russian-designed, Chinese-made semiautomatic SKS held casually at the ready smoked in the shadow of the palms. Most of Primo's guests were asleep or drunk or stoned, in their own or someone else's bed.

And Tory? Where was she?

Bishop had a sudden, burning vision of her, her hot, lush body licked by her flame-red dress, and pushed it away.

It was time to go. Valcazar was probably in bed, too, alone or with—

Hell. If Tory was with him it was just one more factor to deal with.

And he would, Bishop thought grimly. Deal with her. When the time came.

He was wearing black: black shirt, black pants, black jacket. The outfit had helped him blend in with the guests around the pool. Now it would help him blend in with the shadows. He had a Colt .38 Super in a holster at the small of his back and a set of lock picks in his pocket. He went out the way he came in, silently, through the windows and over the roof.

He knew the way. He'd had a long time to study the layout when he was lying on the roof tiles that afternoon.

The building was laid out in a rough U around the pool with the dining room, kitchen and staff all housed in the truncated west wing and Valcazar's private suite opposite. The second floor was dotted with tiny balconies like a hotel. Apparently Valcazar figured his security was good enough—or his reputation bad enough—to discourage housebreakers.

His mistake, Bishop thought as he flattened himself behind a gable to evade the cursory inspection of the guard below. Not the first mistake Valcazar had made, but maybe his last.

Swinging himself over the gutter, Bishop dropped quietly to the balcony outside Valcazar's office window.

And saw…her. Tory.

His jaw clenched and then relaxed. His breath expelled with a hiss.

She wasn't in the drug lord's bedroom.

In fact, she wasn't with him at all.

She was sitting at his desk, her back to the long windows, her bare shoulders gleaming silver in the light of his computer screen. Her long-fingered hands moved with elegant authority over the keyboard. Either she knew what she was doing or she'd been coached by someone who did.

Bishop slipped lock picks from his pocket.

Inside the dim room, the display vanished abruptly. Tory leaned back as numbers scrolled on the screen too fast to be read, almost too fast to be seen.

Bishop slid a diamond pick down the keyway and worked it out again gently. Four pins. No problem. He tapped them softly, rapidly, as he scooted the pick back in and out of the lock. The plug rotated, and he grinned a wolf's grin in the dark. One down.

Tory missed the faint click, her attention apparently focused on the computer monitor.

And one to go. He pressed with the tension wrench, raking the pins with the pick. Nothing. Gently, almost absently, he let his hands flow through the motions and combinations they knew, trying to finesse the lock. Still nothing. He set his teeth and tried again.

He glanced up as Tory tapped another series of commands and hit the enter key.

About a third of all locks simply couldn't be picked. What would he do if this was one of them? Knock on the glass and demand she let him in?

He eased the tension on the lock and felt for the pin stack with the most resistance. He pushed it up above the shear line—not too hard, not too far, *gently*—and let it fall. When all the pins were free, he exerted pressure on the latch until he felt it give.

He was in.

He waited until he saw the guard in the courtyard cup his hand to light another cigarette. And then he cracked the door and slid inside.

He didn't make a sound. But Tory's head lifted. Her shoulders stiffened. She swiveled slightly in her chair until he guessed she could just see him from the corner of her eye.

She spun all the way around. *"You,"* she said in soft disgust.

He stepped in front of the black leather couch that jutted from the wall so he was no longer visible from the window. "You were hoping maybe for Valcazar?"

"Valcazar is busy."

"You can't know that."

"I saw him go into a guest's bedroom. With the guest," she added, in case he missed the idea. "I figure even Primo can last for twenty minutes. Longer, if he's been drinking."

He refused to concede her point. "I still could have been a guard. Do you want to get into trouble?"

"I want you to stop sneaking up on me."

"And I want you to stop poking in where you don't belong."

She stuck out her chin. "Guess neither one of us is going to get what we want, then."

He looked her over in the silver glare coming from the computer: her reddish-brown hair haloed by the screen behind her, her gleaming bare shoulders, her smooth bare thighs disappearing into the curve of her skirt.

He'd come for revenge.

But he wanted *her.*

At the moment it seemed he could have one or the

other. But what if he could have both? What if he could have her and use her against Valcazar?

He met her eyes, letting her see the heat in his, and drawled, ''Don't bet on it.''

Her chin went up another notch. ''Stop trying to distract me. You don't belong here, either.''

''I have business with Valcazar.''

''Not official business.''

Bishop narrowed his eyes. ''How would you know?''

She hesitated. Rehearsing lies, he bet. But she surprised him.

''I'm not going to tell you,'' she said.

Okay. She wasn't lying. She just wasn't telling the truth.

He smiled grimly. ''Fine. Let's talk about what you're doing in Valcazar's office instead.''

''I don't have time for this.''

''We could help each other.''

''I don't need your help.''

''But you do need my cooperation.''

''And what are you going to do if I refuse? Yell for the guards?'' She shook her head so that the ends of her hair brushed her shoulders. He wanted to touch her. Her hair. Her skin. ''They'd shoot you on sight,'' she said.

Bishop regarded her thoughtfully. If she wasn't moved by bribes or threats...

''You could try trusting me,'' he suggested.

She snorted and turned her attention back to the computer screen. ''Oh, yeah. Like that ever worked.''

He scowled. ''You never gave it a—''

He stopped and lifted his head like a wolf scenting danger.

''Never gave it a what?'' Tory demanded.

And then she heard them, too. Footsteps, a long way down the hall.

She swiveled and reached for the keyboard. She'd already opened the port that would give her access to Primo's files. But if he became suspicious—if he shut down and restarted the firewall for any reason—she would lose it. She was still in the process of setting up her backup device, a WiFi connection between the firewall and the main computer on the backbone ethernet.

Bishop lunged and grabbed for her wrist.

"Wait," she said.

"Now," he grated.

She resisted his grip long enough to exit the program. Bishop dragged her from her chair.

Too soon.

She stumbled toward the tall dark windows.

The door handle turned.

Not soon enough.

He pushed her down behind the couch and fell on her like a ton of bricks. Heavy. Hard. Tory swallowed a grunt. She watched light spread across the floor as the door to the office opened. Who was it? A guard on his rounds, alerted by the dim glow of the computer or the murmur of voices? Or Primo, doing a little late-night money laundering?

Dark shoes crossed her field of vision. Go away, she thought at them.

Her heart thundered. Her cheek pressed the carpet. Primo really needed to talk to his housekeeping staff about the dust under his furniture.

Oh, God. What if she sneezed?

The guard paused by the window. Would he notice it was unlocked?

She squeezed her eyes shut and tried not to think about sneezing. Bishop lay on top of her, a deadweight.

Not dead.

She shivered. She did not want him dead. And anyway, he felt warm and alive as he crushed her to the carpet. His breath rasped in her ear. His scent—musky, male—enveloped her. With her eyes closed, all her other senses were working overtime. She could feel the edge of the computer disk sharp against her breasts and Bishop's belt buckle hard against her spine and the bulge of his arousal hot against her bottom.

She sucked in her breath. Was that really—? Oh, yes. It definitely was. He was physically aroused.

Oh, for heaven's sake. Any second now they could be discovered. Captured. Killed. This was hardly the time to be thinking about sex. She squirmed slightly and felt him twitch in response. She opened her eyes. Maybe it was a testosterone thing?

The dark shoes left the window and crossed the carpet to the desk.

Tory breathed through her mouth, trying not to inhale carpet fibers. Maybe it was adrenaline. Because as embarrassing as it was to admit, she was the teeniest bit turned on herself. Instead of distracting her from Bishop's hard, hot body, her sense of danger actually heightened her awareness. His solid weight pressed on top of her. His warm breath caressed the side of her face. His hard erection nestled against her soft bottom.

Response spread low in her belly, warm and liquid. She flushed.

This was ridiculous.

Dangerous.

Delicious.

Her eyes slid shut. She strained for the sound of their

intruder, but all she could hear was the heavy rhythm of Bishop's breath and the thud of her own heart. He nuzzled her ear. He kissed her neck, his lips lazy and warm, and she shuddered in delight.

She really should stop this. Stop him. But how? Her hands were trapped beneath her chest. She couldn't speak. She didn't dare struggle.

He rocked against her, higher, harder, nudging her legs apart, and she bit back a moan.

Okay. Enough was enough. She was not enjoying simulated sex on Primo's dusty office carpet with his guard standing four feet away. All right, she *was*, but she was going to stop. Right now.

Wiggling one hand from underneath their bodies, she reached back until she touched Bishop's muscular thigh. His warm, solid thigh. She pinched him, hard.

He grunted. "What did you do that for?"

She froze. He was going to get them killed. "Shh. He'll hear you."

"Who?"

"The guard."

"The guard left." Bishop brushed his lips against her temple. "About a minute ago."

She levered off the floor so fast she cracked her head on his jaw. She sat up, rubbing her scalp. Bishop eased back, nursing his chin.

She eyed him bitterly. She hoped he hurt like hell. "I knew I couldn't trust you," she said.

"Considering I just saved your ass from the guard—"

She stood, brushing carpet fuzzies from her skirt. "Did not. I could have handled the guard."

Somewhere down the hall, a door banged. Footsteps rushed.

Bishop went very still. "Good. Because he's coming

back, and it sounds like he brought reinforcements. Get behind the couch.''

She lifted her head to glare at him. ''I am not getting back behind that couch with you.''

Bishop swore. She ducked beneath the desk. He dived behind the couch.

And the door opened.

Tory's heart pounded as the lights sprang on. This time the shoes had been joined by combat boots. This was a different kind of search. This time Primo's guards weren't investigating. They were hunting.

She hugged her knees. Maybe hiding under the desk wasn't such a bright idea. Unless she could convince them she was waiting next to Primo's office wastebasket to have sex with him when he returned? If a White House intern could do it...

The combat boots kicked aside the chair.

She took a deep breath, prepared to lie and determined to fight.

The guard's knees bent as he stooped to look under the desk.

And Bishop jumped from behind the leather sofa and crashed through the window.

The other guard shouted in Spanish. Shoes and boots stomped broken glass on their way to the tall French doors. A machine gun rattled the night.

It was a chance.

It might be the only one she got.

Tory rolled from beneath the desk and scrambled across the carpet. Both guards had followed Bishop outside onto the balcony. She slipped through the open office door and sprinted down the dimly lit hall toward her bedroom.

Chapter 4

He'd saved her life. She could hardly stand it. She certainly couldn't let him get away with it.

"You left me," Tory said.

Bishop slid through her balcony door. Dirt streaked his forehead. Sweat sheened his harsh face. His black suit was ruined.

"I did not leave you," he said through his teeth. "I diverted the guards."

Yeah, by jumping through a window and nearly getting himself killed. She was furious at the risk he'd taken. Who did he think he was? James Bond?

She arched her eyebrows. "By leaving me?"

He shut the louvers carefully behind him. "After this afternoon, Valcazar's people were looking for a man in black." He shrugged. "It seemed like a good idea to give them what they were looking for."

"And if it hadn't worked?"

"It did."

He strolled forward into the light of her bedside lamp. His jacket wasn't just creased, she noticed. It was torn. In fact—

Concern clutched her chest. She shifted the laptop off her knees. "Did they *shoot* you?"

"No."

"But your jacket—"

He eased it off his shoulders. Winced. "They may have scored the suit."

"And your arm." She scrambled off the bed, horrified. He was hurt, and she was goading him. "You're wounded."

He smiled thinly. "Glass shards. I'm fine."

"You're bleeding. Let me see."

The streak on his forehead wasn't dirt. It was blood. Blood dotted his cuffs, smeared his beautiful hands. His strong, brown wrists were scored with thin slashes like defense wounds from breaking through the glass. Her heart cringed in helpless sympathy.

"Bathroom," she announced firmly. "These need to be washed."

His black eyes glinted. "Funny, I never figured you for the nurturing type."

She refused to let that sting. "I never thought of you as the self-sacrificing type, either, so we're even."

She paused to flip a corner of the duvet over her computer and then dragged him into the bathroom.

He stood very close as she cranked on both faucets.

"I can sacrifice," he told her quietly. "For the right cause."

Tory squeezed water from a washcloth over his cuts. He was asking her—nicely—if the cause had been worth it. Maybe now she owed him an explanation for what she'd been doing in Primo's room. His blood swirled in the white basin and flowed down the drain.

She gave the washcloth another twist. "It's a good cause. I was able to install a port in Primo's security system that gives me access to his accounts. Not to steal," she added hastily. Just because she wasn't Florence Nightingale didn't mean she was a thief. "I'm tracing illegal activity in his accounts."

His mouth twisted.

Hot blood prickled her face. "What?"

"Angel, I don't give a damn about Valcazar's accounts. Although if you did something that makes life difficult for him, I'm glad. I was talking about getting you out of there in one piece."

Oh. Oh, my. Did he mean that she was his "right cause"? That he cared about her?

She blotted his forearms. Several of the cuts still bled. At least there didn't seem to be any glass stuck in them.

"I guess I should thank you for coming to my rescue, then."

"I didn't go to Valcazar's office to rescue you."

Right. He despised her. She had to remember that.

"Oh, yeah? Then what were you doing there?"

"His bedroom doesn't have a balcony."

"So?"

"So his office provided the best access."

She arched her brows. "Access to what? It's not like he keeps a thousand kilos of cocaine in his sock drawer."

"I wasn't searching for drugs."

"What, then?"

"I was looking for Valcazar. I came here to kill him."

Tory's mouth dropped open. Her stomach lurched. "You can't."

Bishop smiled. Not a very nice smile, either.

She shivered. "Okay, maybe you could. But you shouldn't."

"Fond of him, are you?"

"No. God, no."

She didn't care about Primo. But she did care, too much, about Bishop. And acting outside the law he believed in to assassinate someone—even someone as slimy and deserving of death as the Colombian moneyman—would destroy him.

"It's not about Primo," she said. "It's about you. You're Mr. Law-and-Order. You don't kill people."

His black eyes were unreadable. "I don't carry a gun for show. I'm authorized to use force when circumstances require it."

"You're not authorized to use anything down here," Tory said frankly. "That's why my agency was called in."

"What is your agency?" He was wearing his impassive Indian face again. She couldn't tell if he was skeptical or downright suspicious.

"What are your circumstances?" she countered.

He stripped his shirt off. Things were definitely heating up. "Are you offering to trade information, angel?"

Her gaze skimmed his hard, lean muscle, his flat, brown nipples. She swallowed. "I'm thinking about it."

She escaped to the bedroom to dig antibiotic ointment out of her makeup bag.

Knowledge of Stony Man Farm, its existence and operations, was strictly on a "need to know" basis. Two years ago, Tory had been able to pull off her mission without Bishop learning a thing. But if he whacked Primo before she traced the flow of money from the terrorist Egorov, the drug lord's assets would be frozen and she'd have no way to access Egorov's millions. And she needed

that money. At least, she needed to make sure it didn't
fall into the wrong hands.

She uncapped the tube of antibiotic and began to smear
it over the angry red slashes on Bishop's arms.

"All right," she said. "Let's talk. You go first."

Bishop smiled. "Not a chance."

She attempted a pout. "Don't you trust me?"

"Not that much."

Smart man.

She dabbed on more ointment, trying not to notice how
warm his skin felt beneath her fingers. "You have to trust
me a little or there's no point in my even talking."

Bishop crossed his arms against his naked chest. "Try
me," he suggested softly.

Oh, boy.

Tory drew a deep breath.

"I work for a Special Operations Group that reports
directly to the President."

His dark brows drew together. "You're a spy."

"No. I track money. Drug money. Terrorists' money. I
find out where it came from and I take steps to keep it
from being spent in ways that could hurt the United
States. Kind of like a—" what would he find believable?
reliable? "—an accountant."

"You don't look like any accountant I ever met."

"You shouldn't judge by appearances."

"This from a woman who uses her looks to get what
she wants?"

Ouch.

"I use the way I look. I'm not defined by it."

His gaze clashed with hers, and then he nodded, ceding
the point. "So what did you do before you became an
accountant for Charlie's Angels? Police academy? CIA?"

Her heart pounded. "Nope. I was exactly what you thought I was."

"And what was that?"

"A cocaine-sniffing party girl with too much time on her hands and really bad judgment in boyfriends."

His black gaze never wavered from her face. "Last time I checked hiring guidelines, that wouldn't automatically qualify you for a government job."

"It didn't." She struggled not to fidget. "Can we talk about you and Primo now?"

"No. I still want to hear about the boyfriend."

Fine. She was over it. She could talk about it, if talking would get her what she wanted.

She needed Bishop's cooperation. She was sorry to lose his good opinion, but, hey, she'd never had that anyway, right?

"My boyfriend sold drugs. To me. To my best friend. Until one night she got high and wrecked the car we were in. The car burned. She died. The boyfriend walked. And I spent about a year in recovery. Satisfied?"

"Not by a long shot." Bishop's voice was grim. "So that explains your scars."

He'd noticed.

Her fingers fluttered to her throat. "Yes."

"But not what you're doing here."

"I got—"

Depressed. Frustrated. Angry.

"—really bored in the hospital," Tory said. "My best friend was dead. I didn't want to see the boyfriend again, ever. And my friends, the people I thought were my friends, didn't want to see me. I wasn't fun anymore. Burns make you cranky. And I wasn't pretty anymore. At least not for a long time. So—" She shrugged. "I made new friends. Online, where nobody could see me."

Her tone was wry. Her words were matter-of-fact. But Bishop felt himself responding to the things she did not say, to the memory of pain that deepened her eyes, to the defiant courage that lifted her chin.

"Online," he repeated. "You mean like in chat rooms?"

"Some. Sure. Why not? I had a lot of time on my hands."

A year in recovery, she'd said. He tried to imagine it and failed.

"You were in bed the whole time?"

"No. They were ruthless at the burn center about getting us up for PT—physical therapy. But I couldn't sleep at night." Her smile flickered. "Bad conscience, I guess."

Or pain. He'd read somewhere the pain from burn injuries was intense. Intolerable.

"So you surfed the Net."

She nodded. "At first, it was a distraction. Well, and company. Only then I started to really get into it. I wasn't just hanging out on bulletin boards with the crackers and freaks, I was taking classes in computer programming. I'd never done that well in school. But I was, like, *good* at this."

He nodded. He was good at his job, too. He understood her satisfaction. "So when you were released from the hospital you applied for a job working with computers?"

"No. While I was still in the hospital, I hacked into a really badass computer system, and some very scary guys in suits showed up to offer me the choice between a job and jail. I took the job."

Bishop scowled. "They threatened you?"

"They gave me an opportunity."

"For what? Penance?"

She winced. But she recovered quickly. "Payback,"

she said. "Every time I stick it to a drug dealer, it's pay-back for my friend. And for me."

Revenge.

He understood that, too.

"Besides," Tory added, "I like the rush."

She would. She was still a junkie seeking a high. The only difference was she was a danger junkie now, addicted to thrills, seeking an adrenaline rush.

She rummaged in her open suitcase for a T-shirt and tossed it at him.

He caught it one-handed. "What's this?"

"A shirt. Put it on. I sleep in it, so it should fit you."

She slept in this? The short hem would barely cover her, her nipples would be visible through the thin white cotton.

Don't think about her nipples. Think about what she's doing here. "Don't Valcazar's girlfriends have to wear red lace or black leather or something?"

She shrugged. "I like to be comfortable in bed."

She had to be kidding him. Or coming on to him. But nothing in her eyes or her voice suggested she was teasing in any way.

Under the flamboyance and the hair dye, could she really be that earthy? That unaffected?

Or was she just that good an actress?

He pulled the shirt over his head.

She watched, her hip cocked, her chin angled. "So now that I've bored you with my life story, why don't you explain to me why you want to kill Primo?"

She never gave up. He wasn't sure if that made her somebody he could respect or just a pain in the butt. Bishop adjusted the T-shirt over his holster in the back, trying to figure how little he could get away with telling her.

"You're doing that silent Indian thing again," she said. "Stop it."

He nearly grinned, which surprised him. He hadn't felt much like laughing for the past couple of weeks. "I'm after Valcazar for the same reason you are."

She blinked. "You want the rush?"

"I want payback."

"For what?"

"Valcazar killed somebody I used to know. Tortured and then killed him."

"Who did he—" Her eyes widened. "The other agent. Two weeks ago."

"You know about that?"

She tapped her gaudy earring, the one that held the tiny transceiver, with one red fingernail. "I hear things," she explained. "But this isn't the first time an agent has been killed in the line of duty. What makes it personal?"

"He made it personal," Bishop said harshly. "Valcazar. He knew Benny and I worked together when I first joined the agency. Hell, I was best man at his wedding. Valcazar mailed me his hands." Anger and grief rolled through him like a storm. "Tied. Benny's wrists were tied. He was still wearing his wedding ring."

She made a soft sound of shock and distress. "That's terrible."

He could not meet the sympathy shining in those wide, copper-brown eyes. Better to hold on to his rage.

And his resolve.

"Yeah," he said tightly. "It was. Benny was a real by-the-book kind of guy. He taught me to follow procedure, to respect the law. And then this son of a bitch Valcazar throws in my face that within the law there's nothing I can do to avenge Benny's murder. My hands are tied, too."

"I can help you to build a case against him. I can help you ruin him."

"I don't want him ruined," Bishop said flatly. "I want him dead."

She frowned. "I can't help you there."

"I don't need your help."

"No, I mean, I can't let you do it."

He let his gaze travel over her with insulting familiarity. She was a tall, stacked woman, curves and muscles packed on a five-eleven frame. But she was no match for him physically.

"You can't stop me."

She didn't back down. "I did once."

"You caught me off guard. It won't happen again."

"How can you be so sure?"

"I searched your bags, angel. No handcuffs this time."

She stuck out her tongue at him.

He almost grinned. "Feel better?"

"No," she said frankly. "I have a job to do. You're making it harder."

"I could make it easier. Why go after the bastard's money when he's going to be dead soon?"

"Because *this* bastard isn't my primary target."

"Who is? The cartel?"

"No. Look, I'd tell you, but—" She bit her lip.

"Then you'd have to kill me?" he suggested with heavy sarcasm.

She glared. "Not funny."

"You want me to play by your rules, you have to explain the game."

"Right."

He waited. And maybe she wasn't as immune to the silent Indian routine as she liked to pretend, because eventually she said, "Ky—one of my associates recently recovered information linking Primo Valcazar to Kopach Egorov. Heard of him?''

The name was familiar. ''Isn't he into drug trafficking?''

''Drug trafficking and arms sales. Also extortion, kidnapping, murder, espionage. If it's bad, Egorov has probably done it. He used to be a spymaster for the KGB. Now he works—worked—for anyone who can pay him.''

''And you think Valcazar hired him.''

''I don't think Primo could afford him. Egorov isn't cheap.''

''So what's the connection?''

''That's what I'm here to find out. Egorov has disappeared. Word is he's dying from a new strain of virus he was financing for sale as a biological weapon. Which would be good news, except he's leaving a fortune in dirty money, and nobody knows where that is, either.''

He remembered the numbers scrolling in the dark and Tory's pale, intent face. ''And you think Valcazar might be the key to getting the money.''

She nodded.

''You're the big computer expert. Why not just hack into his system?''

''Believe me, I tried. But Primo's security was designed by a real genius—a cracker named Scherba, who also worked for Egorov. The only way I could access Primo's files was to get on-site and open a private port in his firewall.''

Bishop had only the dimmest idea what she was talking about. Except for the ''on-site'' part. He got that.

''That's what you were doing in Valcazar's office tonight?''

''Yes. Only we were interrupted before I finished installing my backup connector. So I'm stuck here until the job is done.''

"How long will that take?"

He could wait a few more days to kill Valcazar. He had two weeks' leave before he was due back on the job.

Assuming, when this was all over, if he survived and Valcazar was dead, he had a job to go back to.

"I don't have long," Tory said. "Electronic communications and financial transfers happen incredibly fast. If my agency can't access Primo's accounts for even a few days, he could move enough of Egorov's money that we'd never find it.''

"Move it where?"

"To whatever groups Egorov designated. Groups considered enemies of the United States.''

He tried to understand what she was saying and what she was plainly, carefully, not telling him. "Terrorists, you mean.''

Another nod.

Hell. Bishop had been a DEA agent for ten years. He knew all about the unholy triangle of drugs and guns and terror. He couldn't act in any way that furthered the causes of terrorism or put innocent lives at risk.

Even if it cost him, well, everything. His revenge. His honor. His heart.

"Then you'd better get to work," he said. "I'll watch."

Just for a moment, she looked at him the way he'd once dreamed she would, like he was Eliot Ness and Cochise rolled into one.

And then she shrugged and moved toward the bed. "Do what you want. There's not much to see. Unless you get off watching megabyte money transfers.''

He bit back his disappointment.

"Not me. I don't even do my checking online.''

He got a glimpse of inner knee, a flash of upper thigh, as she climbed onto the bed. His mouth watered. He hoped to God his tongue wasn't hanging out.

She balanced her computer on her thighs and then twisted to punch the pillows behind her. "Why don't you come lie down? There's room on this bed for both of us."

Another poor schlub might have been fooled by her warm-voiced invitation and think she had something other than a nap in mind. But Bishop knew better.

You shouldn't judge on appearances.

Victoria Grayson was a talented operative. She might dress like a high-priced hooker, she might call herself an accountant, but the United States government didn't send out party girls or number crunchers to catch a guy like Egorov.

She had a job to do.

The least he could do was get out of her way.

He shoved his hands in his pockets. "I'll pass, thanks. Last time I went to sleep with you, I woke up handcuffed to a flagpole."

She laughed. It was a good sound. So good it even made him feel better for a while.

She turned her attention to her laptop and got to work.

Chapter 5

"You don't look happy," Bishop observed several hours later. "Got a problem?"

Tory pressed her fingers to her eye sockets, trying to push back her headache and rub moisture to her eyes at the same time. Too bad she couldn't massage her brain while she was at it.

Did she have a problem?

Oh, yeah. She had several. In fact, right now her second-biggest problem was unfolding himself from the chair by the window and strolling toward her, looking big and dark and disgustingly sexy for someone who had been up all night. His eyes were hooded, he needed a shave, and she wanted to drag him down beside her and—

Right. Like that would help solve anything. Lack of sleep was clearly affecting her brain. And her hormones.

"Maybe. A small one," she said.

"Want to talk about it?" His voice was amazingly gentle. She didn't want to talk at all. She wanted him to touch her. And that was such a really bad idea, it made even talking seem okay.

"How much do you know about money laundering?" she asked.

"I know it has three stages," he said, surprising her. "Placement—that's when the dirty money, usually cash, enters the system. Layering. And—what's the third one?"

"Integration. That's when the money has been moved around electronically until people like me can't tell where it came from. Once that happens, the money can be used without fear of seizure."

"And that's your problem?"

"No, that's the pattern. The problem is the things that don't fit the pattern. I've traced infusions of cash to Egorov, but the money is only transiting through Primo's accounts. If it were going to fund terrorist groups, which is what I was told to look for, then the money would go through almost a reverse process. That is, I should be able to track transactions where the money is leaving legitimate financial investments and going back into the black market."

"Dirty to clean to dirty," Bishop said.

She sighed in satisfaction. "Finally, a man who understands."

His black eyes glinted. "I understand you better than you think. So where is the money going?"

She sat up against her sagging pillows. "That's the part I don't get. The money's being moved by a computer virus in the banking system. The virus is yanking the bulk of Egorov's criminal fortune, funneling it through Primo's accounts and then depositing the money into a bunch of different accounts. But when I trace those accounts, they all belong to Shane Dellamer."

Bishop raised his brows. "Shane Dellamer who owns

Dellamer Enterprises? Shane Dellamer who's running for the senate?''

"Congress. Yes. But why would a rich guy politician from New York be laundering billions of dollars for a known terrorist and arms smuggler?''

"Put it another way," Bishop suggested. "Why would a dying terrorist and arms smuggler be leaving billions of dollars to a legitimate businessman?''

Tory shook her head, too tired to think clearly. Pearl-gray light was beginning to streak the louvered doors. "The connection has to be the virus. There's something familiar about its encryption style. But—''

"Either way, now that you know Dellamer's crooked, can't you take the money?''

"Not without setting off widespread panic in the stock market." Tory rubbed her temples again. "I need to talk with Barbara.''

"Who?''

"Barbara Price." She touched one earring. "My mission controller.''

Oops. Maybe she shouldn't have told him that.

I'd tell you, but—

Then you'd have to kill me.

But Bishop simply shrugged. "Fine. Go ahead.''

Tory opened her mouth. Closed it. It was ridiculous. She'd bared her soul to this man, but she couldn't call her boss with him listening.

Bishop held her gaze a moment. His mouth tightened as he recognized the reasons for her silence. "I'll go in the bathroom while you call. But when I get out, angel, we talk.''

He should have known she'd find some way to frustrate him.

By the time Bishop finished his shower, Tory was

asleep, huddled in the big white bed like a little girl. Her knees were drawn up. Her arm bent beneath her pillow, cradling her head.

Tenderness punched his chest. And yet there was nothing childlike in the curve of her hip rounding the covers or the swell of her breast beneath the red strip of silk.

Contradiction flowed into contradiction, each teasing his curiosity, feeding his hunger. He let himself study her, exposed in sleep: the faint scars under her strong jawline, the lines of strain around her lush, full-lipped mouth, the purple shadows beneath her heavily mascaraed eyes. The long red nails of her outstretched hand caressed the computer keyboard.

He wanted her. He always had. The puzzle of her called to the cop in him. But her appeal ran deeper than that. He wanted to understand her, take her, have her, keep her.

Keep her? Where had that sprung from?

Once, maybe…

But he couldn't think about a future with Angel Perez or Victoria Grayson. He didn't have a future. Going after Valcazar would pretty much kill his career.

Hell, it might kill him.

He started to cross to his chair by the window. Tory turned and sighed, displacing the computer. He caught it before it slid to the floor and then stood there, like an idiot, looking down at her.

There's room on this bed, she'd told him.

There was.

And the chair was damn uncomfortable.

With a shrug, he shucked his pants and shirt and crawled into bed beside her. Only for the night. One night. To sleep. That's all he wanted.

He lay beside her, listening to soft whisper of her

breath, smelling the wild perfume of her hair and the deeper notes of her skin.

God, he was such a liar.

His mouth was hot and unexpectedly gentle.

Tory parted her lips and arched against the mattress, mindlessly seeking more of his heat. Her body throbbed. Her breasts tingled.

Bishop was in bed with her, kissing her, and it was wonderful, but she wanted more. More heat. More weight. More pressure. Restlessly she slid her legs against the wrinkled sheets. She lifted her hips in invitation.

His warm mouth glided down her throat to her breast and found her nipple. He suckled her hard, and she moaned.

"It's all right," he said, his voice husky. Concerned. "It's only a dream."

Only a dream.

Tory opened her eyes. Her body was tight. Swollen. Achy. Her red dress was up around her waist.

Bishop was in bed with her, leaning over her, hard and hot and close, his weight depressing the mattress. He smelled wonderful, like soap and something musky, male, that suggested sleep and sex. But his mouth wasn't anywhere near her breast.

Only a dream.

"Darn," she said.

His black eyes narrowed. "You were having a nightmare."

"No, I wasn't. I was dreaming about you." She blinked. "You and me."

She felt his sudden tension. "Was it a good dream?"

She moistened her lips. His gaze followed the movement of her tongue. "It was...pretty good."

Not enough. Not nearly enough.

"What was I doing?"

"Well, you—" Her heart hammered in her chest. "You kissed me."

He raised one dark eyebrow. "That's it?"

She squirmed, embarrassed. Defensive. Turned on. "My breast," she said. "You kissed—"

Her hand lifted to brush her right breast, the one closest to him. The nipple poked against the fabric, unmistakable, insistent.

"Like this?" He lowered his head and suckled her through the silk. His mouth dampened the fabric, drew on her breast. She felt the pull all the way to her womb.

She gasped. "No."

She pulled at her neckline, pulled the scarlet strip of silk aside, exposing herself to him, her darkened areola, her tightly beaded nipple.

"Like that," she begged him.

His eyes flamed. He lowered his head and tasted her in one slow lick. She moaned. He took her in his mouth, teasing her with his teeth and tongue, feeding greedily on her breast. His knuckles brushed the soft side. His hand, she realized vaguely, was clenched.

His head jerked up. A flush stained his harsh cheekbones. He was breathing hard. "Was that all?"

She touched him with her fingertips, relearning his face. His skin was firm and warm. His lips were soft. "I'm afraid so." She rubbed his jaw experimentally. His light beard prickled the pads of her fingers. "It was pretty disappointing, actually."

"Disappointing." His tone was flat. Dangerous.

She grinned. He was so easy to tease. "Yes. And then I woke up."

His expression turned predatory. His hand left her breast and slid over her stomach.

She sucked in her breath. This wasn't teasing. "Bishop?"

He pressed his hand between her thighs, parting them. "I can't leave you disappointed."

This wasn't play. The desire in his eyes, the clamor of her senses, the hunger in her heart were all real.

"Bishop, no. Really. Bishop—"

He tugged the elastic of her panties, stretching them out of his way. She was already wet, swollen and soft with desire. They both shuddered as he found her with his fingers. He touched her, stroked her with undeniable skill and devastating intent, real and rough and urgent.

Her head fell back against the pillows. He moved over her, his weight pinning her to the mattress, and pressed his mouth to her scars. She trembled. She could feel him blunt and hot against her hip, heavily aroused. He wanted her. Knowing what she was, knowing what she had done, he still wanted her.

The knowledge seared her heart. Her blood drummed in her ears. His breath labored. And then…and then…

And then she heard it. A soft knock on the door.

"Señorita?" A woman's voice. "Are you awake?"

Bishop froze like warm, hard marble above her.

"Don't say anything," Tory whispered, her fingers tightening on his shoulders. "And she'll go away."

Maybe.

Another discreet knock. *"Señorita?"*

Tory held her breath, straining for the sound of footsteps. Keys jingled in the hall.

Bishop swore and rolled away from her, grabbing for his clothes.

"Just a minute!" Tory called, sitting up. She looked wildly around the room. Where the hell was her computer?

Bishop shoved something at her. Her fingers registered the hard, smooth shape of her laptop. She shoved it under the duvet as he loped barefoot toward the bathroom, carrying his pants, and shut the door.

Just in time.

A stout woman in a plain black dress pushed her way into the room, a big chrome tray in her arms. "Good morning, *señorita.* I have brought your breakfast."

"That's great," Tory said weakly, maneuvering the laptop to the foot of the bed with her toes. "Thank you. Just put it on the—"

The maid deposited the tray with a thump. "And fresh towels for your bath," she said, making briskly for the bathroom door.

"No!" Tory cried, lurching half out of bed.

The woman stopped, her square, plain face radiating disapproval. "No towels?"

Tory yanked hastily at the top of her dress. Last night's dress. She could just imagine what the woman was thinking. *Dirty slut.*

"No, I meant—" She sidled toward the breakfast tray. "Is that fresh orange juice?"

"*Sí.*"

"Wow." Tory took a sip. Tried a smile. "Terrific. Thanks."

The woman's face relaxed slightly. "You are welcome. Now I will just put these towels—"

"You know, a shower's probably a good idea," said Tory. "Thank you so much."

She plucked the towels from the astonished maid, bolted past her into the bathroom and shut the door in her face.

Bishop stood in the claw-footed tub behind the shower curtain, zipping up his pants. She held up the towels like a trophy.

He leaned closer, his warm breath tickling her ear. "Get back out there."

His soft words raised goose bumps up and down her arms.

"Why?"

"Do you want her to make your bed? Search your room?"

She sucked in a breath. *No.* Dropping the towels, she burst back into the bedroom.

The maid looked up, startled, from fluffing the pillows at the head of the bed.

"I changed my mind about the shower," Tory announced sunnily, helping herself to a roll from the tray. "I decided to have breakfast first. Uh, in bed," she added, since the woman showed no signs of moving away.

The woman's mouth snapped shut like a change purse, with a disapproving snap. "You wish me to come back later?"

"Oh, no. I've been trouble enough." Tory smiled determinedly until the other woman smiled back. "I'll put the tray in the hall when I'm done."

The maid's reply was blurred by a faint vibration in Tory's ear.

The transceiver. Barbara.

"Thank you so much," Tory said. She took a pillow from the maid and tossed it on the bed. The unmade bed. Did that bulge at the bottom hide her laptop?

"I just love the orange juice." She shepherded the stout woman to the door. "And I won't forget that tray!" she promised, nudging her out into the hall.

She closed the door and leaned against it, listening for footsteps. One, two, three...

"You're good at getting rid of people," remarked Bishop.

She should be getting used to the way her heart bumped

whenever he appeared. Of course, it would help if he didn't sneak up on her all the time.

She shot him an annoyed glance over her shoulder. "Some people."

He came up behind her, resting one arm on the wall beside her head, trapping her between his hard, lean body and the door.

"You want to get rid of me, angel?"

Her knees weakened. Yes. *No.*

"Would it make any difference?" she asked.

His amusement was a puff of warm air on the back of her neck. "Not this time."

He ought to go. She ought to make him go. For the sake of his career, for the sake of her mission. For the sake of his soul. And yet...

The transceiver vibrated again, a reminder and a warning.

There were agents in the field who swore Barbara Price saw everything. Kind of like God, or that annoying second-grade teacher who always caught you with gum in your mouth or notes in your desk. It was true Stony Man's mission controller had access to satellite video relays with thermographic overlays that allowed her to see through most buildings.

Even into bedrooms? Just whose heat patterns had Price been observing this morning?

Tory ducked under Bishop's arm, fiddling with the back of her earring. "Good morning, Barbara," she said. "What can you give me on Shane Dellamer?"

Chapter 6

At least she hadn't made him leave the room this time, Bishop thought, listening to Tory's one-sided conversation with the mystery mission controller. Maybe she was beginning to trust him.

Or maybe she'd forgotten he was there.

"Dellamer hired Scherba to set up his company's security?" she asked sharply. "Are you sure?" She ran her red-tipped fingers through her mane of hair. "Well, you've got Scherba in custody, don't you? You could ask him."

She paced to the window, cupping her ear with one hand. "Ask harder," she suggested.

Bishop grinned. Apparently when the stakes were high, Tory-the-spy was a lot more bloodthirsty than Tory-the-party-girl.

His smile faded. But then, he knew that. He'd watched her take down Guerrero.

"So you think Dellamer's ripping off Egorov? Kind of

risky pissing off an international terrorist, isn't it? Or does he figure he's safe since Egorov is out of the picture?''

Bishop helped himself to a roll from the breakfast tray. He hadn't eaten in twenty-four hours.

''What do you mean, Egorov's not out of the picture?'' Tory's voice rose. ''How do you know?''

Bishop stopped buttering his roll.

''Yes, I knew Beth was investigating—*Egorov* ordered the hit on Lyeta? Why?'' She was still listening, still pacing, still scowling. ''But Lyeta didn't betray him. Not until he did his vanishing act, anyway. Okay, yes. Yes, I'll be careful. Jeez. Any other bad guys you want me to be on the lookout for while I'm down here?''

Bishop put the roll down, his appetite fading.

''Thanks, but I can't leave yet. If Primo restarts his system's firewall, we won't have any way to access those accounts. Ask Tokaido if he can use the port to pinpoint who's behind the Dellamer buy-up. Tell him I'll get the WiFi connector installed and report back to you tonight.''

At that point, the conversation meant very little to Bishop. He wasn't sure what it meant for Tory, either. But he could see how it had scoured away her hard, bright veneer, letting her fear, her frustration, her confusion shine through.

''Want to tell me what that was about?'' he asked quietly when it was clear Price had terminated the connection.

Tory's knees sagged. She sat on the edge of the bed. ''I'm not sure I can.''

Bitter disappointment speared him.

Well, what did he expect? She didn't trust him. Didn't trust him to keep her safe. Didn't want him to help in any way.

And maybe she was right. God knew he hadn't been any damn use to Benny.

Bishop didn't say anything. He made sure he kept any trace of what he was feeling from his face. But his silence or his stillness must have given him away, because Tory shook her head wearily.

"I'm not sure what to tell you because I don't know myself what's going on. At least I was right about the encryption style—Scherba wrote the virus that's hijacking Egorov's millions from Primo's accounts. And Dellamer hired Scherba."

She was simply sharing information. It was hardly a declaration of love. Or even of trust. But it was a declaration of truce, of sorts, and he did his best to respond to it.

"So can you arrest Dellamer? Or seize his accounts?"

She sighed. "I don't know. On the surface, everything points to Dellamer. But the money isn't being deposited to him directly. It's all going into the company."

"It's his company."

"Yes, but a huge stock buy-up like this could take control of it away from him. Particularly if his connection to Egorov became known."

"So Dellamer doesn't benefit. Who does? Egorov?"

"Egorov is dying. Even if he's still alive, he might as well be dead. All his money is gone." She scowled at him. "What?"

She was animated again. Arguing again.

"You sound pretty sure of yourself," he said.

"So?"

So a moment ago, she hadn't. If she had to argue with him to feel better, then he would argue. If she wanted to talk, he would talk.

Whatever she needed.

''So, I'm no computer genius. I'm sure as hell no accountant. But I do know you don't have a crime without a motive. Somebody's benefiting from all these high-tech money transfers. The key is to figure out who.''

''And how do you suggest I do that?''

''Valcazar.''

''I told you, the money is only transiting his accounts.''

''You think he doesn't know that? If I had millions of dollars switching columns on my computer, it would sure get my attention.''

''It doesn't work like that.'' But she looked thoughtful. ''You think he knows who benefits?''

''Knows or suspects.''

''And you don't have a problem with me conning him for this information?''

Conning him, no. Sleeping with him, yeah. He had a very big problem with that. But he wouldn't insult her by telling her so.

''I could ask him for you,'' he suggested with grim humor.

''No, thanks. I think he'll talk more without a gun to his head.''

''Your call. I trust you.''

Her big brown eyes focused on his face with painful intensity. ''Do you?''

Did he?

She was a resourceful, clever, opportunistic liar involved in heavy, dangerous covert ops. But would she prostitute herself for her mission?

''Trust you to get information from a guy like Valcazar?'' He shrugged, trying not to make a big deal of it. Trying not to betray how much it mattered to him. How much she mattered to him. ''Sure.''

Her eyes narrowed. "I'm not sleeping with him," she announced abruptly.

He held her gaze. "I know."

"How do you know?"

"Because I know you. And you don't do anything the easy way."

She closed her eyes. When she opened them, they were soft and brilliant as the night sky over White Sands.

"Thank you for that."

He took a step closer. "I don't like things easy myself."

Her throat moved as she swallowed. "No?"

"No."

Her smile slid into him like a knife, unexpected, devastating.

What the hell was he doing? A little trust was fine. A little affirmation seemed called for. But no promises. Until Valcazar was dead, he had nothing to offer her. And after...

"Besides," Bishop said, "if the son of a bitch does step out of line—"

"—I'll handle it," Tory said.

"—I'll kill him," he said at the same time.

"I am glad to see you are recovered," Primo said smoothly behind her.

Tory nearly dropped her plate down the front of her white caftan.

Oh, crap. She was standing in front of Primo Valcazar in a teeny-weeny white bikini and a totally see-through white caftan that covered everything but hid nothing. Including the fact that it was highly unlikely she was suffering from any "feminine indisposition."

Her fault, for wearing white.

Her fault for letting herself be distracted into forgetting her cover.

She turned, smiling hard enough to sell toothpaste. "Thank you, darling. I do feel a little better."

Primo's hard gaze dropped to the plate she'd prepared for Bishop. "Your appetite is improved."

Since she'd loaded up with coconut shrimp, lobster salad, two rolls and three pineapple kabobs, she couldn't argue with him there.

"Everything looks so good," she explained. "I should probably eat it before it gets—"

He took her elbow, preventing her escape. "I trust your other appetites are similarly recovered?"

Oh, yuck. "Actually, darling—"

His grip tightened. "Because my hospitality is not without price. You have eaten my food. You sleep beneath my roof. You have used all the facilities of my house."

He meant he'd watched her put a couple hundred dollars up her nose over the past two days. Couldn't blame the guy for wanting a return on his money.

Tory tossed him another smile and threw in an eye flutter for good measure. "You're very generous."

He dragged her closer. "I can be more generous, I promise you."

She forced herself not to stiffen as he rubbed his face against hers, marking her with his jaw like a cat. His beard rasped and stung. His breath was hot, his hair oily.

He nuzzled her neck. She clenched her teeth, her mind making calculations with the speed of a computer chip. She could dump her lobster salad on his eight hundred dollar loafers. She could kick his family jewels up to his tonsils. Probably.

Or she could go to his room and ply him with booze

and compliments until he whispered sweet nothings in her ear about Dellamer Enterprises. Hey, it could happen.

And if it didn't, she could always hit him over the head with a lamp and sneak into his office to install the WiFi connector. It would ruin her cover, but once Stony Man had uninterrupted access to Primo's computer, her usefulness here was limited anyway.

"Primo. I have been looking for you."

It was the big fair German, Klauen. She didn't remember seeing him by the pool. He must have come down the stairs.

Primo lifted his mouth from her shoulder. "Later, Eric." He sounded impatient.

"I think now," Klauen said mildly.

For one second, Primo's mask slipped and his heavily handsome face looked ugly. Brutal. His hand moved up her thigh and thrust between her legs. Before she could react, he groped her, casually, shockingly, intimately.

Tory jerked.

Klauen looked away.

Primo laughed and then, satisfied he had reestablished his control, released her. "Run along, *querida*. We will find ways for you to thank me another time."

Tory burned. She watched him strut away, arm in arm with the square, fair German, and tried not to throw up in her plate of lobster salad.

The bedroom door closed with a snap.

She was back.

The knot of tension in Bishop's gut eased. But he kept his face impassive, kept his attention on the screen in front of him. She wouldn't thank him for worrying about her.

"Shouldn't you be hiding in the closet or something?" Tory's tone was sharp.

She was upset. Pissed off because he'd appropriated her laptop without permission?

"There is no closet," he pointed out calmly.

He had an answer to an e-mail he'd sent to Joe Epstein, an IRS analyst he'd met through the Justice department. He clicked on it, feeling the rising edge of excitement that told him this was it, the piece of the puzzle he'd been searching for.

"The bathroom, then," Tory snapped. "You didn't know who I was. I could have been anybody bursting in here. The maid. A guard."

"I knew."

Distracted, he scanned the note from Epstein.

"How?" she demanded.

"The sound of your walk. The smell of your perfume..."

"Don't you pull that Indian tracker garbage with me. You can't smell my perfume from the other side of the door."

At the bottom of the second paragraph, he found it. He had it! A match. A name.

Grinning, he looked up at her. "Okay, maybe I was watching out the window and saw you leave the pool. What took you so long to get up here, anyway?"

She froze, just for a second, before she smiled and held up the plate. "I stopped to get you something to eat from the kitchen. You wouldn't believe the spread they had in there. If Primo ever gets out of the money-laundering business, he could make a fortune as a caterer."

Her voice was amused, her face relaxed. But he'd already caught it, that moment of stillness, that instant of hesitation that told him she was lying.

"What happened?"

"Nothing."

He was out of his chair and across the room before she could move. He trapped her chin in his hand. Close up, he could see the faint red welts on her cheek and neck and shoulder. Not scars. Not sunburn. Whisker burn, the unmistakable mark of a man's beard dragged carelessly across tender skin.

"What happened?" Bishop repeated through his teeth.

"Nothing I couldn't handle," she amended quickly.

"Was it Valcazar? Did he touch you? Force himself on you?"

"I told you I would handle it." But her voice was shrill. Tears sprang to her eyes. "I handled it. *Damn it.*" The words burst out of her. She touched the pads of her fingers to her lower lashes, glaring at him. "I'm crying. I never cry."

"I'll kill the son of a bitch," Bishop growled.

"No," Tory insisted. "It's okay. I'm okay. It sort of comes with the job, you know?"

"And that's all right with you?" he asked savagely.

Tory raised her chin. "Do I like being groped for the good of my country, do you mean? No. But I'm not ashamed. I refuse to be ashamed. I'm smart and I'm strong and I'm good at what I do. I can use my brains and my body to get the job done when going in with guns blazing would be a disaster. I don't have a problem with it. And if you do, screw you."

Bishop stared at her, his gut churning, his heart torn, his mind in turmoil.

She *was* smart.

She *was* strong.

And she was crying.

"I don't know what you want me to do," he told her, his voice rasping. "I don't know what to say. You're right. I know you can handle things. I trust you to handle things. But then I see that bastard's mark on you, I see that he's hurt you, and I want to hunt him down and break his neck. Maybe that makes me the worst kind of chauvinist pig, but that's how it is.

"I hate it that I can't protect you. Can't help you. All I'm doing is hiding in your room while you face this thing alone."

She was shaking, hugging herself as if she was cold. In that getup, she probably was. But she still lifted her head proudly, still looked him squarely in the eye.

"Maybe I don't feel so alone," she said. "Not when I know you're here. Not if I can trust you to understand."

He'd called her a liar once.

But she was being as honest with him now as any person could be. She'd laid her heart out there for him.

This is who I am. This is what I want. Take it or leave it.

He owed her equal honesty at least.

So he met her gaze, letting her see his hunger, his frustration and his need.

"I'm here," he said. "I'm not going anywhere."

"Then *be* here," she whispered. "Be here for me."

She took one step forward, uncharacteristically awkward in her white platform sandals, and fell into his arms.

It was going to be all right, Tory thought as Bishop caught and held her. His chest was hard. His hands were impossibly gentle as they gathered her to him, as he stroked the hair back from her forehead and cupped her face. She trembled with reaction and relief, with lust and gratitude.

Everything was going to be all right.

"Do you have something else you need to do right now?" he asked. "Because this time I'm not stopping."

Primo was probably talking to Klauen in his office. She

couldn't install the backup connector until they were gone.

"So, don't stop," she told Bishop.

Don't ever stop.

But he did.

She was clinging to him, to the strength and reassurance of his big body, when he pulled her arms from around his neck and turned away.

She stared after his broad back, confusion and loss swirling inside her. "What are you—"

He picked up a chair, the strong, solid muscle under his T-shirt shifting, and wedged it under the door handle.

"I'm getting ready to make love to you." He turned, his face hard with desire, his eyes dark with purpose. "Now."

Tory shivered.

They'd had sex before, she reminded herself. Twice, in one amazing night two years ago. There was no reason to be nervous. He wasn't Primo.

Bishop stalked toward her. He moved so gracefully she sometimes forgot how big he was. Not just tall. His shoulders were broad and sleek, his chest heavy with muscle.

He stopped in front of her, not touching her, close enough that she could feel the heat rising from his skin. His expression was primitive.

Now.

Her insides clenched.

Damn it, she wasn't going to stand here waiting for him to take her like some ancient god helping himself to the latest virgin sacrifice.

She grabbed his shoulders and kissed him with everything she had.

And he liked it. She felt the hard edge of his hunger, felt the wild surge of his blood as his body thickened and pulsed against hers. And then his fingers speared into her hair, cradling her skull, pulling her head back.

He dropped a warm kiss on her forehead. He brushed a soft kiss on her nose. He closed her eyes and teased her mouth with kisses, rubbing his lips lazily over hers until her breasts were full and aching. Until her heart beat high and wildly as a bird's. Until she shook with want.

She struggled to keep her head, scrambled for footing in the warm, dark tide of sensation. "Are you trying to prove something here, cowboy?" she murmured.

"Yes," he said flatly.

Startled, she met his eyes. The fierce male possessiveness of his gaze stopped her breath.

He kissed her again, longer, wetter, deeper. Her body recognized and responded to the suggestiveness of his kiss, to his blatant possession of her mouth. Still kissing her, he walked her backward until the back of her thighs bumped the mattress.

"Wait," she gasped.

His arms tensed. He let her go.

She dashed across the room. Dumping the contents of her makeup bag on the dresser, she searched frantically through the tubes and compacts and brushes until her fingers closed on a small, square packet.

She held it up triumphantly. A condom.

Bishop's smile broke over her like the sun cresting a mountain, warming her to her bones. He shucked his shirt. He dropped his pants. He was gorgeous, hard and dark and heavily male.

She stumbled toward him in her ridiculous high-heeled sandals, struggling to yank the gauzy white caftan over her head. "I feel like an idiot in this thing."

"You don't look like an idiot." He smoothed the silk

from her shoulders, untangled it from her hair. "You look beautiful. Like an angel."

Her heart shook. So did her knees. "Don't let the white fool you, pal. I'm no angel."

"I know what you are," he said quietly. "I know what I want."

And it seemed, impossibly, that he wanted her.

He kissed her, he touched her, he eased her back on the soft white bed. He filled his hands with her breasts and made love to her with his mouth.

She was prepared for his strength. She understood his hunger. His tenderness destroyed her.

He rocked her, rode her gently until she was soft and wet, until she was clawing at his shoulders and crying out. And then, only then, he plunged to the heart of her, again and again, taking her with slow, powerful, penetrating strokes.

Be here for me.

I'm here.

She wound her arms around his neck, her legs around his waist, claiming him with her body as he claimed her with his thrusts. He pushed into her, all the way in, stretching her, filling her, until sensation swamped all her nerve endings, until emotion flooded her heart. She was overcome. Swept away.

Bishop felt the crest take her, sucking the last of his control, roaring through his body like floodwaters through a dry riverbed. He groaned and pounded inside her, shuddered and came.

Be here for me.

I'm not going anywhere.

But when he woke an hour later, wanting her again, Tory was gone.

Chapter 7

Tory slunk through the bushes in her little black catsuit. She was Jinx. She was Catwoman. She was Emma ''in times of stress keep your bowler on'' Peel.

Bishop's lovemaking—because that's what it had been, making *love,* not simply sex—had left her feeling sexy and powerful. And almost believing in happily-ever-afters.

The installation of the WiFi connector in Primo's office had gone without a hitch. She'd scaled a tree at the far end of the garden—not so easy, even in the catsuit—to secure a second wireless access point to its trunk. The point in the tree would pick up the signal from Primo's office and relay it outside the limestone walls where it would be easily read by the Stony Man network. Now all she had to do was slip undetected into the house, convince Bishop to give up his plans for vengeance and devise an exit strategy.

She grinned in the darkness. Piece of cake.

Her boots squelched in the mulch that bordered the path. Up ahead, it widened into one of the garden's trysting spots. Orchids glowed in the moonlight. The air was fragrant with the jumbled scents of flowers and the sea. As settings went, this one was pretty darn romantic. Except, of course, for the goons with guns still making their rounds.

And the man waiting for her on a bench in the moonlight was definitely the wrong man.

Primo.

Her stomach dropped. She took a quick step back.

Too late. He'd seen her.

He stood. And maybe he wasn't waiting for her, after all, because his heavy brows lifted in surprise. Although that could have been because of the catsuit. He was either going to think she was into very kinky sex or know she was up to something.

"I knew you were eager, *querida*. But not so eager you would follow me."

Oh, please. She wouldn't follow Primo Valcazar if he were driving the hearse in a funeral procession. On the other hand, she really wanted to know why he was out here. Alone. In the middle of the night.

So she fluffed her hair with her fingers and stepped out into the moonlight. "It got late. I got lonely. I wondered what you were doing."

"I am meeting someone."

"Should I be jealous?" she asked archly.

He couldn't possibly be buying this. But the man's ego was amazing. Apparently he could.

"No. This is business, *querida*."

She pouted. "You don't do business in the garden, silly."

Primo's gaze flicked toward the house. He didn't reply.

Tory moistened her lips and tried again. "This some-one…can she offer you more than I can?"

"This someone has a great deal to offer. If he can be persuaded to pay."

Unbelievable. She was actually getting somewhere. "Pay what?"

"The price of silence."

Jeez. It was like trying to make sense of B movie dialogue. The guy really needed a new scriptwriter. Was he talking extortion? Blackmail?

Bishop was convinced Primo knew or suspected something. *Somebody's benefiting from all these high-tech transfers… If I had millions of dollars switching columns on my computer, it would sure get my attention.*

Now who had Primo been spending enough time with to—

"Are you meeting this person alone?" she asked.

Primo's eyes narrowed. "Why do you ask?"

"Well…I'd hate to think you were putting yourself in danger."

Come on, she thought. Brag to me. Tell me about the hold you have on your mysterious big moneyman.

But Primo scowled. "Are you threatening me, *querida?*"

"No, of course not. I'm just worried about you, darling."

Primo stepped closer. His hand came up to cup her cheek. She forced herself not to recoil.

"You are worried," he repeated.

Her heart drummed in her chest. "A little."

"About me."

She widened her eyes. "Of course."

His hand slid from her face to her throat. He caressed

her neck before his eyes changed, hardened. Before his fingers flexed and dug in.

"Prove it," he said, and tightened his grip on her throat.

You could die from lack of air in about three minutes. Of course, you'd lose consciousness much faster. Constricting the carotid artery to cut off the supply of fresh blood to the brain was a danger. And a crushed windpipe was no joke, either.

Tory windmilled her left hand and chopped Primo's forearm below the wrist, clobbering his pressure point and forcing down his arm.

Her right hand came up hard, the heel of her palm smashing into the base of his nose with enough force to break it.

Not to kill. She didn't intend to kill him. But she definitely heard the crunch. The pain sent him stumbling back, both hands clapped to his face. He drew his palms away. Stared at his blood, black in the moonlight. Stared at her, his eyes dazed. Disoriented. And pitched forward on his face to the turf.

Damn. She didn't think she hit him that hard. Maybe he fainted at the sight of blood?

Dropping to her knees, she grabbed his shoulder to roll him over. She should check for a pulse. But when she flopped him onto his back, she didn't even bother to reach for his jaw. The large, gaping exit wound in his chest kind of made measuring his heartbeat unnecessary.

Primo was dead. Shot in the back from under cover.

And Tory was terribly afraid she knew who did it.

"Bishop," she whispered.

No reply.

My God, she was lucky the guards hadn't heard the gunshot and come running. He must have used a silencer.

''Bishop!'' she hissed.

Nothing. Her heart quailed. This was going to require one hell of an exit strategy.

Hooking Primo's body under the arms, she dragged it deeper into the shadows. The longer it took the guards to find him, the longer she had to find Bishop.

He wasn't in her room.

Tory stopped just inside the door, her gaze panning from the balcony to the bed where she'd left Bishop sleeping. He wasn't there. No, he was still out on the grounds somewhere, having successfully blown away Primo, her hopes and his future with a single shot.

So much for happily-ever-after.

It was time to get the hell out of Dodge. Now that she'd completed the wireless connection to Primo's computer, her job was done. The longer she stuck around, the greater the risk of discovery.

But for the first time in years she was more worried about someone else's safety than her own. For the first time, she had someone she didn't want to leave behind.

You're good at getting rid of people.

She sniffed. She didn't even know if he was coming back. Self-important cowboy jerk. The only evidence he'd ever been in her room was the laptop he'd left running by her chair.

The laptop. What was he doing with her laptop?

She crossed the room. It was a simple matter for her to scan the computer's memory and retrace Bishop's steps. There were e-mails, several e-mails, to colleagues he'd met through the Special Operations Division, a joint law enforcement unit comprised of attorneys, analysts and agents from the Justice department and an alphabet soup of other agencies: DEA, FBI, IRS and Customs. In his e-mails, Bishop made no secret of the fact that he was in the Caymans investigating his mentor's death. He'd even included a list of Primo's houseguests.

Tory's stomach sank. She wanted to believe Bishop's e-mails proved he was resuming an official role in an authorized operation. Except now everyone and his kid brother knew Bishop was gunning for Primo. When Primo turned up dead, Bishop was going to look very, very guilty.

She opened the final e-mail, a two-paragraph report on Dellamer Enterprises from an IRS analyst named Epstein.

You've got several investors on that list you sent me, Epstein had typed. *No surprises there. Dellamer stock is in every mutual fund portfolio I know, including yours and mine. But the big stockholder is Eric Klauen. Word on Wall Street is he's positioning himself for a move to take over the company.*

Whoa. Tory blinked. Klauen and Dellamer? There was a connection she hadn't looked for. But Bishop had.

Primo had to have known that Egorov's illegal fortune was being used to buy up shares in Dellamer Enterprises.

Klauen was Primo's houseguest and a player in Dellamer stock.

Which meant...well, she didn't know what it meant. But it was a pretty fishy coincidence. She read on.

Shane Dellamer's a tough son of a bitch, Epstein had written. *I don't see him giving up control of his company that easily. But if there were another scandal and stock prices fell, your boy Klauen could probably pick up enough shares to swing it.*

A scandal. Okay. Tory's teeth worried her lower lip. Like Enron. Or Microsoft. Shane Dellamer's giant financial empire was already under investigation for anticompetitive practices and antitrust violations. If word hit Wall

Street that its CEO was also accepting large infusions of cash from a known arms smuggler and international terrorist, well, that would certainly be a blow to the company's reputation. Dellamer might even face criminal charges. Investor confidence would go down. Stock prices would plunge.

And Eric Klauen would swoop in and make a killing.

Bishop's voice echoed at the back of her mind. *Somebody's benefiting from all these high-tech money transfers. The key is to figure out who.*

And he had. At least, he'd known what rocks to go poking under to find a snake.

She was impressed. And pissed off.

This was her case. Her assignment. If Klauen was a bad guy, then he was her bad guy, damn it. Why hadn't Bishop leveled with her?

The thought that he'd hardly had time crossed her mind, but she squelched it.

The fact that she'd pretty much cut him out of the action while she played computer whiz in Primo's office was irrelevant.

And the idea that he could be putting himself in danger right this minute and she didn't know where he was made her crazy with worry.

She glanced again at the e-mail, but it didn't offer a clue. *Let me know if you're thinking of making adjustments to your 401K. Best, Joe.*

If Bishop was planning for retirement, maybe he didn't intend to deep-six his career. Tory frowned and shut down her computer.

He could still die before he collected his pension.

Eric Klauen's room was clean. Either he was innocent, or he was a professional.

No guns. No drugs. No knives. No explosives. No communication devices beyond a cell phone.

Disgusted, Tory went through his shaving kit one more time. Nothing there that would hold up the search line at an airport: pain reliever and cold remedies—she checked them both out—razor with replacement blades, toothbrush and dental floss, some high-end guy's cologne, nail clippers and a bottle of bronzer. She unscrewed the top of the bronzer and squeezed a dab onto her finger.

It was green. Well, greenish. And very thick. In fact, it looked just like the makeup she used to cover the scars under her jaw.

Tory's teeth clicked together. Interesting. But nothing else suggested Eric Klauen was anything but what he represented himself to be, a middle-aged German businessman with neat habits and expensive tastes. His shirts were silk, his shoes Italian leather, his money clip platinum with his monogram.

She rubbed it with one of his handkerchiefs to take her prints off. KE. Now that was odd. Shouldn't it be EK? Unless—

"Do you like it?" the German asked in his soft, almost unaccented voice.

Tory froze with her hands poised above his open dresser drawer. Boy, it was really too bad he didn't keep a gun in there. "Very nice." She squinted over her shoulder to see if he happened to have one pointed at her. He did. A Beretta 9mm, it looked like. Her pulse speeded up. "Where did you get it?"

"It was a gift."

"From your wife? Girlfriend?"

"Mistress. You can turn around, Miss Grayson. I have no intention of shooting you. Yet."

The nail clippers made a lousy weapon. So did the ra-

zor. Tory turned, a pleasant expression pasted on her face.
"Right. Thanks. Why isn't your mistress traveling with
you?"

"She is dead."

Tory hoped he hadn't shot her for snooping through his
drawers. "Gee, I'm sorry."

"Don't be. It was fitting." He smiled without humor.
"You might say I am dead, too."

Tory stiffened. "I don't understand."

But she was afraid she did.

"I am Kapoch Egorov."

Tory took a deep breath and looked him straight in the
eye. "Who?"

Klauen/Egorov shook his head. "Unconvincing, Miss
Grayson. You know very well who I am. In fact, you and
your colleagues almost forced me to make a change in
my plans."

"I don't really—" Oh, the heck with it. "What plans?"

"Retirement."

She nodded toward the Beretta in his hand. "That
doesn't look like you're retiring to me."

"It is a problem. Kapoch Egorov, who made his fortune
in the ruins of the Soviet state, has too many enemies to
retire. However, Eric Klauen, an honest investor, could
live out his life quite comfortably. Assuming he could get
his hands on Egorov's money."

"And that's what all this was about?" She was disgusted. Incredulous. "Lyeta's death, the terrorist threat,
the secret bank accounts, the financial transfers were all
about protecting you and your money?"

"Yes. It was a good plan," he insisted. "The only two
to suspect me were you and Primo. And Primo is not alive
to talk about it."

Her heart started to thud. "*You* killed Primo?"

Egorov shrugged. "Who else?"

Hope tingled through her like circulation returning to a numb limb.

He didn't know about Bishop.

Bishop had not killed Primo.

Maybe some kind of sappy happy ending was possible after all—if she could stay alive.

Tory stuck out her chin. "Why are you telling me this? Are you going to kill me, too?"

The gun never wavered in Egorov's hand. The black hole at the end of the barrel focused on her forehead like a third eye. "I could. It would be a good idea. Or I could find another use for you."

Something moved at the corner of Tory's vision. She blinked, trying to see without turning her head, but it was gone.

"Do I get a vote?" she asked.

"You get a choice. I miss Lyeta. Even in my new life, I could use a woman of your…talents."

That sounded creepy. She took a step forward anyway. "You don't know me."

"But I understand you better than you think. I investigated you, Miss Grayson. You only accepted the job with Stony Man to avoid jail. I can offer you much more. You can be rich and useful, even appreciated. Or you can be dead."

Dead was looking more and more likely.

She fluffed her hair with her fingers, moving closer. "Which of my talents are you particularly interested in? Because—"

"Stop there," Egorov interrupted. "Or I'll shoot."

"Drop your weapon," Bishop ordered grimly from the doorway. "Or I shoot."

Egorov's gaze shifted. Just a fraction. Just for a second.

It was enough.

Tory crouched and went in low, hooking the back of his legs with her ankle. Her sweep caught him at the back of the calf. He went down, backward, hard. The Beretta choked. A bullet smacked the ceiling. Plaster rained down on them.

Tory rolled frantically across the carpet, trying to give Bishop a clear shot. But the bed was in the way, and Egorov was no novice. He reversed, grabbing her ankle in one hand, and raised the gun in the other. His cold blue eyes were murderous.

Tory's heart stopped. Not good.

Before Egorov could steady his gun, another shot cracked through the room. Egorov jerked. His hand tightened convulsively on her ankle. His gun wavered. Blood dribbled from his mouth. And then his grip relaxed, and he collapsed facedown on the carpet.

Tory sagged in relief.

"Nice shot," she said to Bishop.

"Body shot," he said dismissively. His black gaze met hers, and something inside her melted. "I didn't want to miss. Come on."

She scrambled to her feet. "Where are we going?"

"I don't know. But my gun doesn't have a silencer, and Valcazar's body is in the garden, so we better get wherever it is fast."

She stooped for Egorov's gun, shuddering as her fingers brushed his. "You didn't kill him."

Bishop raised his brows. "Sure I did."

"Primo," she clarified. She could feel herself grinning foolishly, but she didn't seem able to stop. "You didn't shoot Primo."

"I didn't have time. I was too busy looking for you."

Bishop swore and ducked back into the room. "Guards. We'll have to go out the window."

She could hear them in the hall: doors opening and closing, boots muffled by the carpet, voices raised in confusion. She hurried to unlatch the window.

Egorov's room was on the north side, away from the courtyard. She looked down at the stone face of the building.

"Oh, cripes."

"It's not that bad," Bishop said, close to her ear.

"Right." Tory took a deep breath. "You go first."

And it wasn't that bad, really, not with his hands guiding her feet, not with his low, sure voice directing her movements. At least she was standing on the ground a few minutes later, heart pounding, fingers scraped, manicure ruined, but whole.

Lights blazed in all the windows. Shouts echoed from the courtyard. A car engine started in front of the house.

She touched Bishop's forearm. "This way."

He followed instantly. "Where are we going?"

"We can't get through the gate. But there's a place where the trees grow close to the wall. We could go over."

Bishop nodded. "Let's do it."

They blundered through the grounds, heading for the far end of the garden.

"How did you know where to find me?" Tory gasped.

"Process of elimination."

Flashlights danced on the path in front of them. They both froze. When the guards moved on, Bishop continued. "When I didn't find you in Valcazar's room, I checked the gardens. His body was there, but you weren't. So I figured maybe you'd put two and two together and come up with Klauen."

The limestone walls glimmered through the trees to their left. Tory angled toward them. "I only suspected Klauen because I read the e-mail from your IRS buddy. How did you know Klauen was involved?"

"I didn't. But I'd put together Primo's guest list when I was casing the house. I sent it around and asked if any of the names on the list were connected with Dellamer."

"This is it." Tory patted a familiar tree trunk. The smell of almonds drifted down to them in the dark. "We can get over the wall here."

Bishop looked up. "I'll give you a boost."

They scrambled and clambered over the high stone wall, bruising knees and scraping elbows; dropped to the other side. Shells and gravel crunched underfoot. An empty ribbon of road gleamed at the bottom of the grass-covered hill.

"A car would be good," Tory said.

Bishop started downhill. "We're only a mile from town."

"I hate walking."

He slanted an amused look down at her. "What are you going to do? Call a cab?"

"Well, actually..." She dug into the pocket of her cat-suit. Her fingers closed on something hard. She drew out her hand and showed him the transceiver, winking in the dark. "I thought I'd call a cleanup crew."

Tory settled into the corner of the cab. Privacy glass separated the front and back seats. Bishop's shoulder was propped against the opposite window. His arms were crossed. His hooded gaze was focused on her face. If the driver glanced in his rearview mirror, she would appear to be talking to him.

"The port number is 828," she told Barbara Price

through the transceiver. Bishop's left ankle rested on his right leg. He moved his foot so that the sole of his shoe almost brushed her knee. "If it shuts down, tell Tokaido he can still access the accounts through the wireless network."

"It's done," Price assured her. "In fact, he's already frozen Valcazar's accounts."

"Oh. Great." Tory shifted her knees, but Bishop moved again, subtly crowding her. She glared at him. "Well, as soon as I get back, we can get to work extracting Egorov's investments from the Dellamer business."

"Tokaido's doing that," Price said. "You're not scheduled to come back yet."

Tory sat up. "We're not headed for the airport?"

"No, your cab is taking you back to the Meridian resort, where you have a seaside cottage reserved for the next several days. What you do with that time is, of course, up to you."

Tory could barely bring herself to look at Bishop, listening intently beside her. "This is no time for a vacation."

"On the contrary, it's the perfect time. You've accomplished your mission. Egorov's fortune is being turned over to our government, and Egorov himself has been eliminated as a threat. You're overdue for a break. Enjoy it."

"Did you hear that?" Tory demanded, affronted. "She's taking me off assignment. She said I'm overdue for a vacation."

Bishop smiled. "You are. We are." He took her hand, lacing his long, strong fingers with hers. "About two years overdue."

The gleam in his eyes made her heart pound harder than it had all night. It was one thing to give herself to him in the heat of action. This was something else. Something new.

Something she wanted very much.

She glanced pointedly at their clasped hands. "What is this?"

Bishop lifted her hand in his and brushed a kiss across her knuckles. "This," he told her, his smile spreading from his eyes to his voice, "is the beginning of a beautiful friendship."

* * * * *

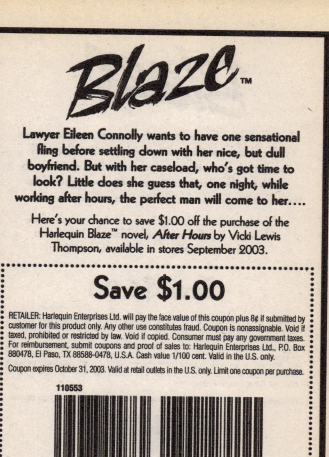

Blaze™

Lawyer Eileen Connolly wants to have one sensational fling before settling down with her nice, but dull boyfriend. But with her caseload, who's got time to look? Little does she guess that, one night, while working after hours, the perfect man will come to her....

Here's your chance to save $1.00 off the purchase of the Harlequin Blaze™ novel, *After Hours* by Vicki Lewis Thompson, available in stores September 2003.

Save $1.00

110553

5 65373 00076 2   (8100)0 11055

© 2003 Harlequin Enterprises Limited   HBCOUPITSUS

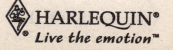

HARLEQUIN®
® *Live the emotion*™

Visit us at www.eHarlequin.com

Blaze™

Lawyer Eileen Connolly wants to have one sensational fling before settling down with her nice, but dull boyfriend. But with her caseload, who's got time to look? Little does she guess that, one night, while working after hours, the perfect man will come to her....

Here's your chance to save $1.00 off the purchase of the Harlequin Blaze™ novel, *After Hours* by Vicki Lewis Thompson, available in stores September 2003.

Save $1.00

RETAILER: Harlequin Enterprises Ltd. will pay the face value of this coupon plus 10.25¢ if submitted by customer for this product only. Any other use constitutes fraud. Coupon is nonassignable. Void if taxed, prohibited or restricted by law. Void if copied. Consumer must pay any government taxes. Nielson Clearing House customers submit coupons and proof of sales to: Harlequin Enterprises Ltd., 661 Millidge Avenue, P.O. Box 639, Saint John, N.B. E2L 4A5. Non NCH retailer—for reimbursement submit coupons and proof of sales directly to: Harlequin Enterprises Ltd., Retail Marketing Department, 225 Duncan Mill Road, Don Mills, Ontario, M3B 3K9, Canada. Valid in Canada only.

Coupon expires October 31, 2003. Valid at retail outlets in Canada only. Limit one coupon per purchase.

52604717

HBCOUPITSCAN

HARLEQUIN®
Live the emotion™

Visit us at www.eHarlequin.com

If you enjoyed what you just read,
then we've got an offer you can't resist!

Take 2
bestselling novels FREE!
Plus get a FREE surprise gift!

Clip this page and mail it to The Best of the Best™

IN U.S.A.
3010 Walden Ave.
P.O. Box 1867
Buffalo, N.Y. 14240-1867

IN CANADA
P.O. Box 609
Fort Erie, Ontario
L2A 5X3

YES! Please send me 2 free Best of the Best™ novels and my free surprise gift. After receiving them, if I don't wish to receive anymore, I can return the shipping statement marked cancel. If I don't cancel, I will receive 4 brand-new novels every month, before they're available in stores! In the U.S.A., bill me at the bargain price of $4.74 plus 25¢ shipping and handling per book and applicable sales tax, if any*. In Canada, bill me at the bargain price of $5.24 plus 25¢ shipping and handling per book and applicable taxes**. That's the complete price and a savings of over 20% off the cover prices—what a great deal! I understand that accepting the 2 free books and gift places me under no obligation ever to buy any books. I can always return a shipment and cancel at any time. Even if I never buy another The Best of the Best™ book, the 2 free books and gift are mine to keep forever.

185 MDN DNWF
385 MDN DNWG

Name	(PLEASE PRINT)	
Address	Apt.#	
City	State/Prov.	Zip/Postal Code

* Terms and prices subject to change without notice. Sales tax applicable in N.Y.
** Canadian residents will be charged applicable provincial taxes and GST.
All orders subject to approval. Offer limited to one per household and not valid to current The Best of the Best™ subscribers.
® are registered trademarks of Harlequin Enterprises Limited.

BOB02-R   ©1998 Harlequin Enterprises Limited

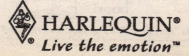